D0529342

# The Inverted Jenny: Mystery, Money, Mania

Incredible stories of intrigue surround the world's best-known stamp error—the United States 24¢ airmail stamp of 1918, the legendary upside-down Jenny. From the discovery of the sheet of 100 at a Washington, D.C., post office, the story of the inverted Jenny stamps unfolds in bizarre twists. The stamps have been sold, resold, lost, found, stolen, recovered, sued over and cared for by some of history's most unusual characters.

**by**
**George Amick**

Published by Amos Press, Inc., 911 Vandemark Road, Sidney, Ohio 45365. Amos Press also publishes *Linn's Stamp News*, the world's largest and most informative stamp newspaper, and the Scott line of stamp catalogs, albums and publications.



400081

ISBN 0-89487-089-0

*To George E. Amick Sr.*

# Introduction

The Jenny invert is not just another postage stamp.

Which is a little like saying Caruso was not just another tenor.

Only 100 of the inverts were produced, in a single sheet, by a still-unexplained printer's error.

They emerged from (and in an odd way, symbolized) the haste, improvisation and adventure of the world's first airmail service — that leap of faith by pilots who went up never knowing just where, or how, they would come down.

To William T. Robey, the broker's clerk who bought the stamps at a post office window, they were 100 winning lottery tickets, and a fulfillment of his own premonition of good fortune.

To the next man who owned them — one of the century's great eccentrics — they were briefly captivating, but in time became objects of almost monumental unconcern. He was Colonel Edward H.R. Green, an enormous man with a cork leg and unlimited wealth for indulging his hobbies, which included, at various times, stamps, coins, orchids, yachts, jigsaw puzzles, diamond-studded chastity belts, female teenage wards and Texas politics.

The colonel broke up the sheet of inverts, kept some of the choicest specimens and sold the rest. And over the years since then, the singles and blocks have traveled far and wide.

They have associated with unusual characters. They have had strange things befall them. They have been sold and resold, lost and found, stolen and recovered and sued over, lovingly cared for and grossly mishandled and subjected to hairsbreadth escapes.

From the beginning, because stamp collectors have lusted after the Jenny inverts, the prices have been bid up to levels that have astonished non-collectors, starting with the *New York Times* editorial writer who said of Colonel Green's original purchase:

"Even for a set of stamps as 'hard' as that — to use the word of boy collectors — $20,000 does seem too much."

As the price of a single Jenny has climbed, from three digits to four, to five, to six, laymen have continued to watch in wonderment.

Consequently, it is the Jenny invert which the layman thinks of when he thinks of a stamp rarity.

And so it turns up in his fiction. Richard Forrest, for instance, in the thriller "Death Under the Lilacs," has a kidnapper demand a block of inverts as part of the ransom. Actor Richard Pryor, casting about in the film "Brewster's Millions" for ways to quickly unload large amounts of cash, hits on the idea of buying an invert and using it to mail a postcard.

And it hovers on a giant wall mural high above visitors to the Smithsonian Institution, painted there with the Fort McHenry flag as examples of the best-known treasures of the museum's collections. (The Smithsonian also sells neckties and coasters and other souvenirs emblazoned with the invert.)

It is the philatelist, of course, who is most susceptible to the lure of the inverted Jenny. Ownership of a C3a (its Scott catalog number, used by the cognoscenti) puts a collector into a highly exclusive club; many a great modern accumulation of U.S. or airmail stamps has never included one.

The basis for this passion is as hard to analyze as the collecting instinct itself. Harder, in a way. A Jenny is not a possession a stamp collector can haul out on a whim, like a set of National Parks or Famous Americans, and look at and gloat over.

Robert S. Fisher, a Keokuk, Iowa, corn products manufacturer who owned an invert for a couple of years in the 1950s, told me: "I finally felt it was so fragile that I worried that something might happen to it," and he sold it. Former U.S. Solicitor General Erwin Griswold said of his Jenny invert: "I was glad to have it, and enjoyed the ownership of it. However, it was an almost completely psychic satisfaction. I almost never saw it, as I felt that I had to keep it in a safe-deposit box in a bank. Indeed, from October 1967, when I came to Washington, until the spring of 1979, when I turned it over to Harmers (for auctioning), I did not see it a single time." Other owners have carefully guarded their anonymity, thus forgoing the bragging rights which one would think would constitute much of the lure of possession.

Beyond the many strange things that have really happened to the Jenny inverts, there has been developed an apocrypha of stories about bizarre things which didn't happen. Sorting out fact from fiction has been one of the challenges, and provided much of the enjoyment, of researching this book. Along the way, however, I encountered a few anecdotes which I could neither prove nor disprove. They came second-hand or third-hand, with key details missing, and the principals themselves now dead.

One was about a collector who almost took his Jenny invert with him to the grave — until at the last minute frantic searchers thought to look inside the casket, in the deceased's coat pocket. Alfred Hitchcock would have loved it.

Another centered on the sad experience of a proud owner who lent his copy to a Chicago department store to be exhibited, only to get it back much the worse for the scotch tape which a lunkhead of a store employee had used to fasten it down. (This copy could have been position 40, which has sustained some otherwise-unexplained damage during its travels.)

Then there was the tale of the widow who remembered — after she had given away her late husband's books — that he sometimes hid valuables between the pages, and perhaps that explained what he had done with the Jenny invert she had been unable to find. (Some day, someone, leafing through some obscure old volume somewhere . . .)

These were "the stories that got away." Fortunately, many others didn't. They are told in the pages that follow.

— George Amick

# Contents

1. The Purchase ........ 1
2. The Experiment ........ 9
3. The Rush ........ 15
4. The Mistake ........ 31
5. The Pursuit ........ 39
6. The Takeoff ........ 45
7. The Sale ........ 61
8. The Resale ........ 71
9. The Eccentric ........ 81
10. The Dispersal ........ 91
11. The Forty-One ........ 103
12. The Memories ........ 109
13. The Climb ........ 117
14. The Peak ........ 127
15. The McCoy Heist ........ 141
16. The Miller Heist ........ 155
17. The Proofs ........ 169
18. The Next Invert ........ 173
19. Jenny Miscellany ........ 185
Appendix ........ 201
Notes ........ 225
Index ........ 245

Chapter One

# The Purchase

*"My heart stood still."*
— **William T. Robey**

William Thomas Robey lived before the days of state lotteries or of casinos in Atlantic City, where he vacationed, or he might have retired rich. He had a lucky streak, his wife Caroline claimed, and it showed up in modest ways. "If he took a chance at a wheel," she said, "he always won the candy."

In the one truly spectacular moment of Robey's life, however, his luck brought him a great deal more than that.

On the morning of Tuesday, May 14, 1918, as Robey left their one-bedroom apartment at 1420 Harvard Street in Washington, D.C., he

**A 24¢ stamp picturing a Curtiss Jenny mail biplane was prepared by the Post Office for the new airmail service.**

was feeling at least a few vibrations of impending good fortune. He was on his way to his job as a cashier at W.B. Hibbs and Company, stockbrokers and bankers. But first he intended to stop at the post office. A new 24¢ stamp was to be sold that morning, made for use in the airmail service that would begin the next day between Washington, Philadelphia and New York. William Robey was a stamp collector, and he had arranged to exchange covers — stamped and postmarked envelopes — with fellow collectors at the other two points on the route. Each person would address his covers to himself in care of the others, then apply the new stamps, which would be canceled with special "first trip" postmarks and carried through the air to their destinations.

But the 29-year-old Robey, father of an infant daughter, had something else in mind, something that could mean a lot of money to a man who was alert — and lucky.

The new stamp was a bicolor, with a red frame containing a blue Curtiss Jenny biplane, the kind that would carry the airmail. Bicolored stamps in those days required two passes through the printing presses. In the past, on rare occasions, sheets emerged from the process with the second impression upside down, escaped inspectors' eyes and reached the outside, where they commanded big premiums. Stamp collectors love errors because of their scarcity; color inverts, the most striking of errors, are the most prized of all.

The chance such a thing would happen with the new stamp seemed reasonably good. The country was in the midst of the World War, and the Bureau of Engraving and Printing was working night and day to print currency, Liberty bonds, postage and revenue stamps and other wartime necessities. On top of that, the Bureau was pinched by a shortage of skilled workers and had to recruit engravers and printers from other trades.

On May 10 Robey had written to one of his friends, Malcolm H. Ganser of Norristown, Pennsylvania, near Philadelphia:

"It might interest you to know that there are two parts to the design, one an insert into the other, like the Pan-American issues. I think it would pay to be on the lookout for inverts on account of this."

And it would become part of family tradition that when Robey left Apartment 3 on the morning of May 14, he told Caroline that he wanted to get to the post office early because "I have a very strange feeling there's going to be a mistake." It was, as events proved, not unlike Babe Ruth pointing to the bleachers just before digging in at the plate.

As Mal Ganser would write later: "Of course hosts of other collectors no doubt had the same thought, but few would have the opportunity of buying the stamps when first put on sale, and even those with that chance figured that the lightning wouldn't strike them anyway."

The official notice had said the "aeroplane mail stamps" would be available at five places in Washington that day: The main post office on Massachusetts Avenue next to Union Station and the branch offices on New York Avenue, F Street, 11th Street and Pennsylvania Avenue. The stamps also had been placed on sale the afternoon before, unannounced, at the main post office, but Robey probably didn't know that. The station at 1319 New York Avenue was only six blocks from

**The post office at 1319 New York Avenue in Washington, D.C., where Robey bought the sheet of airmail inverts.**

his job, and it was here that the hopeful stamp customer chose to make his purchase.

At this point the sequence becomes a little hazy, and so does Robey's precise motivation for his post office visit, because he later gave three accounts of his experience that differ in some of their details.

In a letter to Ganser the next day, he wrote that he looked at a few of the 100-stamp sheets, "but everything was OK. At 12:30 something told me to go back to the same office at another window and look at some more." That suggests that his search for inverts was at least as high a priority for him as his need to buy stamps for covers.

In an article written for the *Collectors' Journal* 12 days later, however, he said he "secured a sheet as soon as same were placed on sale" at 9 a.m. — meaning a normal sheet — "and later, at 12:30 p.m. returned to the post office for a second sheet."

Finally, in a much longer narrative he wrote in 1938 for *Weekly Philatelic Gossip*, Robey explained that on his first visit, only a few poorly centered sheets were available, with more stamps expected at noon. So he decided to wait, came back "promptly at noon" with $30 he had withdrawn from the bank, found the same clerk on duty, and asked him if he had received any more airmail stamps.

The earlier versions are doubtless more reliable than the one written two decades later. Whatever the preliminary details may have been, however, what came next was an electrifying moment. No collector, hearing the story, can fail to imagine himself there, his own feet where Robey stood, his own elbows on the post office counter, his own eyes seeing what Robey saw and hardly comprehending it.

The clerk "reached down under the counter," Robey wrote in the 1938 account, "and brought forth a full sheet and my heart stood still. It was the sheet of inverts. It was what you might call 'a thrill that comes once in a lifetime.'

**Robey's "heart stood still" at the sight of 100 stamps like this one. (Stamp is position 57 on the sheet.)**

"Without any comment, I paid for the sheet and then asked the clerk if he had any more sheets. He again reached under the counter and brought up three additional sheets which he said were all he had. An examination showed these sheets to be normal. Had they been otherwise, I wonder how I would have paid for them with only six dollars in my pocket?"

At this point, according to his letter to Ganser, Robey — possibly giddy from his good fortune — blurted out: "Give me another one like the one I just bought." Robey went on: "He asked to look at it, but I held onto same firmly, and when he saw what it was he slammed the window down and I presume he at once got into communication with officials regarding same."

In his 1938 version, he added: "Needless to say, I left that office in a hurry with my sheet of inverts tucked safely under my arm."

One of the enduring myths of the Jenny invert story is that a man ahead of Robey at the post office window was given the first chance at the freak sheet and turned it down. The Post Office Department itself repeated this anecdote in a 1954 press release noting the 36th anniversary of the permanent airmail service. However, Robey himself labeled the story "absolutely false."

"At the time I made my purchase there was no line and no one was ahead of me at the window," he wrote in 1938. "Can you imagine the post office trying to resell a sheet of stamps that had once been refused for being imperfect by having the airplane upside down?"

In hope of finding more inverts, Robey turned left off New York Avenue onto 11th Street and went straight to the branch post office at 514 11th, four blocks away, still with only $6 in his pocket. The stamps there were all normal.

"Highly elated," he then returned to Hibbs and Company, located on 15th Street half a block from the U.S. Treasury, and showed his find to a fellow worker, also a collector. The associate immediately left to search other branch post offices.

* * *

Elsewhere in the city, in the towered Post Office Department headquarters on Pennsylvania Avenue, Captain Benjamin B. Lipsner was feeling the pressure of a job in which many things were poised to go wrong.

Ben Lipsner was a dapper, mustachioed young Army officer with a generous allotment of self-esteem. Though not a pilot — he was a lubrication specialist, with a special aptitude for developing and maintaining records — he had a deep interest in aviation and had worked his way into a prominent, if somewhat ill-defined, role in setting up the new airmail service. Army planes and pilots would do the actual flying for the Post Office, but Lipsner, still in the Army himself, was technically on loan to postal authorities, who had instructed him to coordinate the work of the two departments at the three landing fields. However ambiguous his status, Lipsner clearly felt that he carried a

**Though not a pilot, Captain Benjamin B. Lipsner had a prominent role in the launching of the airmail service.**

heavy personal responsibility for the airmail's success or failure.

He had a lot, in fact, to worry about. The new service that would begin the next day would be the world's first regularly scheduled transportation of mail by air, and it would go off under the personal observation of President Woodrow Wilson and other high officials. The mail planes, however, still hadn't arrived at their departure points. Two of the pilots, thanks to Post Office politics, were fresh out of flying school. Some members of Congress thought the whole project was impractical; others were indignant over its diversion of men and equipment in the middle of a war.

It was while he was pondering all this, Lipsner recalled, that he learned that some of the stamps for the new service had been sold with their airplanes flying upside down.

He did not take it well. "My cup was full to overflowing," he said. "Reacting like an eruption of Vesuvius at what seemed to be a deliberate plan to upset my dreams, I forgot all my other worries for a while and set out to trace down the error. In the face of the strain I had been under, this comparatively small problem expanded into a huge monster that threatened the very existence of an airmail service."

For all Lipsner knew, the printing blunder had been repeated thousands of times, with the results streaming across post office counters, into the hands of the public, onto envelopes and into the mailstream, a ludicrous fleet of airplanes flying wheels up, underscoring the absurdity of the whole program.

But he was relieved to learn that only one sheet of the errors was known to have been sold, and that apparently the buyer was a stamp collector, who would be most unlikely to use the stamps for mailing letters.

As Lipsner told it later, he personally confronted the offending stamp clerk — whose name is lost to history — and got this plaintive response:

"A fellow asked for a sheet of airmails and I handed him one without looking at it. And anyway, how was I to know the thing was upside down? I never saw a plane before."

Lipsner turned his attention to other matters. He had no way of knowing that of the many things that would go awry with the new airmail service that week, the only one that would matter to history would be that little sheet of postage stamps.

Chapter Two

# The Experiment

*"Visionary, utopian and absurd."*
**— Senator William H. King**

The launching of "aeroplane mail service" May 15, 1918, was a milestone in postal history, but it was even more than that. As the world's first system of scheduled flights, at prescribed times over prescribed routes, it marked the beginning of all commercial aviation.

It was also a project put together in great haste.

Planes, pilots, postage stamps, even the act of Congress necessary to get the service off the ground, were all procured at virtually the last minute. Pushing everyone to produce were two oddly matched Texans: Albert S. Burleson, the tall and aristocratic ex-senator who had been Woodrow Wilson's postmaster general since Wilson took office in March 1913, and Otto Praeger, second assistant postmaster general (whose responsibilities included mail transportation), an ex-newsman from San Antonio, short, energetic, opinionated, cigar-smoking and perpetually rumpled.

To Burleson, Praeger and others, airmail was an inevitable step on the road of progress, and the sooner taken the better. Back in 1909 Thomas Alva Edison, with remarkable prescience, had told a reporter: "In ten years flying machines will be used to carry the mails. They'll carry passengers, too. They will go at a speed of 100 miles an hour."* In 1910 Representative Morris Sheppard — yet another Texan — introduced a bill directing the Post Office to study whether "aeroplane or airship mail" was a practical idea. The prevailing skepticism was expressed by *The New York Telegraph*, which wondered whether airmail would require apartment mail chutes that went up instead of down, and suggested that "love letters will be carried in a rose-pink aeroplane,

* — Edison should have stopped while he was ahead, but he went on to say: "The flying machine . . . will never be a great weight carrier. It will be used for the mails, but not freight."

steered by Cupid's wings and operated by perfumed gasoline."

In the next six years Sheppard and others in Congress tried without success to win approval for such a program. For most of that time the idea was ahead of the technology; airplanes were too frail, too slow, too limited in range and too unreliable to offer a credible alternative to the mail train.

The Post Office itself was extremely interested, however. It gave full cooperation to a number of small demonstration projects — essentially stunts — in which pilots at air meets and exhibitions carried sacks of mail a short distance through the air. The first of these took place September 23, 1911, when pilot Earle L. Ovington, sworn as a temporary mail carrier, flew some 15 miles from Nassau Boulevard to Mineola, Long Island, with a mailbag containing 1,900 pieces on his lap.

In 1912, in a kind of glimpse into the future, the Post Office issued a parcel post stamp showing a Wright-type airplane of that day carrying mail — the world's first stamp to picture a plane. Four years later, the department advertised for bids from private operators to fly regular routes in Alaska and Massachusetts on an experimental basis, but got only one offer, and that one failed to include the required bond.

Outside the department, the fledgling aviation establishment, made up of manufacturers, pilots and assorted visionaries, was anxious to prove that airplanes did indeed have a practical value. Beginning with the firing of the "guns of August" in 1914 and increasingly thereafter, planes showed their usefulness as tools of war. Congress finally was brought on board when the National Advisory Committee for Aeronautics, a newly formed interdepartmental agency, recommended that the Post Office establish its own experimental airmail route on which some actual operating experience might be obtained under favorable conditions. The fiscal 1918 appropriation act included $100,000 for this purpose.

But now the same European war that was giving aviation such a strong lift had caught the United States in its grip, and the Post Office found that the nation's entire production of airplanes was being taken by the War Department. A solution emerged early in 1918 when the Army, with the prodding of the National Advisory Committee, offered to do the actual flying for a scheduled airmail service in order to give its young pilots experience in cross-country navigation. The Post Office accepted, and its impatient leaders quickly began making plans.

Not everyone shared their enthusiasm. American soldiers were fighting overseas, people at home were buying bonds and enduring rationing and tightening their belts in other ways, and there was no perceptible demand from the public for airborne mail. Congress, already concerned over the slow pace of airplane procurement for the Army, had plenty of doubters. Almost on the eve of the first mail flights Senator William H. King of Utah denounced the project as "visionary, utopian and absurd." At one point, Representative Martin B. Madden of Chicago seized an opportunity to give Captain Lipsner a dressing down. "We are at the height of a war," he told him. "We are pressed for men and materials . . . I know of nothing that is more ridiculous or asinine than a venture of this sort. If I had my way about it, I would see that you were thrown into the federal penitentiary, and the key thrown away."

Even some Army officers had serious reservations. Two weeks before the scheduled start, Otto Praeger was visited by a group of influential military aviators, including a British colonel, who tried to talk him into abandoning the project on grounds that service couldn't be assured in bad weather. Praeger suggested in return that the Army stick to its bargain.

As the Advisory Committee suggested, the Post Office carefully selected the conditions for the experiment. The route chosen was a simple one, 218 miles long, over the level and well-populated strip that today is known as the Northeast Corridor. Flying would be done by daylight, six days a week with Sundays off. The Washington-Philadelphia-New York service wouldn't actually offer the public much in the way of time savings; trains made the trip in five hours, and ordinary first-class letters mailed early in the day in Washington were routinely delivered in New York the same afternoon. The aim was to prove that the mail could be flown between cities on a regular basis, regardless of the weather — although what was acceptable flying weather would later become a bone of contention between the Post Office and the Army — and to prepare the way for the transcontinental, and eventually transoceanic, flights which the true believers were certain would follow.

On February 27, 1918, Postmaster General Burleson announced that the tri-city service would begin April 15. Two weeks later he had to announce a delay of a month, explaining that the Post Office hadn't found suitable landing fields in New York and Philadelphia. Now the second deadline was nearing.

On March 1 — the same day the Army and Post Office agreed to terms for operating the airmail — a directive went out to the Equipment Division of the Signal Corps to provide six Curtiss JN-4H (Jenny) biplanes and six Curtiss R-4 biplanes, modified to carry mail instead of a passenger, along with spare parts. On April 30 Major Reuben H. Fleet, the Army's chief of flying training who had been designated officer in charge of the aerial mail service, reported by letter to Otto Praeger that the planes had been built and were being shipped for

**Postmaster General Albert S. Burleson, who believed firmly in the practicality of sending mail by air.**

assembly to the Army's Hazlehurst Field at Mineola (near the site, coincidentally, of Earle Ovington's pioneering flight). A memo to the major from R.M. Jones of the Equipment Division, dated May 8, advised him that "the last of the 12 planes . . . will ship from the Curtiss plant midnight Sunday."

Yet, years later, Fleet recited a curious story about a confrontation with Postmaster General Burleson on May 6 at which he told Burleson that "the Air Service had no airplanes capable of flying non-stop from Washington to Philadelphia or from Philadelphia to New York, and requested postponement to gain more time than eight days" to obtain them. "Burleson went into a rage over the suggestion for deferment," Fleet recalled, "stating he had already announced to the press that an Army aerial mail service would get started on 15 May, and that it had to start then, even if war work suffered." Fleet, according to his story, then phoned Air Service Production and asked for a rush order of six Jennies, modified to haul mail, to be delivered by May 14. But the documentary evidence to the contrary casts considerable doubt on this entire anecdote.

Jenny, the plane that would launch the airmail service, was the twin-seat trainer in which virtually all U.S. and Canadian combat pilots had learned to fly. She was unbeautiful — people called her "a bunch of parts flying in formation" — and she had been known to shed fabric or even wings during high-stress maneuvers. Unforgiving of errors, she had taken a high toll of lives at the Army's training bases. Early in 1918, for example, five people were killed in Jennies in a single week at Benbrook Field in Texas. One of them was the famous dancer Vernon Castle, then a flying instructor with Canada's Royal Flying Corps, who crashed while trying to avoid a collision with another Jenny piloted by a cadet. However, Jenny was in plentiful supply — she was the only plane the U.S. managed to turn out in quantity during the war —and the Army deemed her suitable for the relatively short, straightforward hopscotching called for by the first airmail route. The fact that she could land at 45 miles per hour or less meant pilots in an emergency had a good chance of putting her down safely if they could find a flat spot — an important consideration in an era before the parachute had become part of a flyer's standard equipment.

Jenny was conceived when U.S. air pioneer Glenn H. Curtiss commissioned a young British aircraft designer named B. Douglas Thomas to create a new plane that he could manufacture in quantity. Thomas devised a two-seat biplane that had a front-mounted motor, in contrast to the pusher-type motors that had dominated aircraft design since the Wrights flew at Kitty Hawk a scant dozen years earlier.

Soon afterward, Curtiss combined the best features of this so-called "J" model and an "N" model of his own design, and the hybrid that resulted was designated JN. Fitted out with the Curtiss eight-cylinder OX-5 engine, the planes began coming off the line at Curtiss' Buffalo plant in the fall of 1915. By the end of the World War, plants owned or licensed by Curtiss had turned out 6,072 Jennies for the United States at $5,000 apiece and more than 2,000 for other Allied governments. Hundreds of them would be sold as surplus after the Armistice to barnstorming stunt men and fly-for-hire pilots who would ride them in and out of cow pastures and county fairgrounds all over America during the 1920s.

Jenny was a two-seater, made of spruce, with a fabric hide that was treated with coats of dope until it clung to her wooden skeleton like a drumhead. Her thin wings were braced by wooden struts (collectively termed a "cabane") and elaborately rigged with turnbuckled wires. Because the two wheels were so close together, landings often were wobbly, and sometimes one wing would dig into the ground, with considerable breakage resulting. To prevent this, large semicircular wing skids were added.

Other refinements came as the designers learned from experience — aircraft design was a highly empirical science then — and the plane progressed through a series of model designations: JN-2, JN-3, JN-4, JN-4A and so on. The models ordered by Major Fleet for the airmail were labeled JN-4H; the H indicated that they carried the 150-horsepower Hispano-Suiza ("Hisso") engine. The Hisso was a good exchange for the 90-hp OX-5, an engine whose many shortcomings included a tendency to break its camshaft in flight. With a Hisso, Jenny was capable of 93 mph at sea level, compared to the 75 mph of the OX-5 models, and could climb to 12,800 feet.

The airmail planes had some additional features. In place of the forward cockpit, the Army asked for a compartment covered by a hinged metal hood held shut by straps. Here up to 200 pounds of mail would be loaded. The Army also specified double capacity for fuel and oil, which Curtiss provided by simply installing an extra 19-gallon gasoline tank and 2½ gallon oil tank.

Six pilots were assigned from the Air Service Division of the Signal Corps to carry the mail. Four were satisfactory to Major Fleet: First Lieutenants Howard Paul Culver, Torrey H. Webb and Walter Miller and Second Lieutenant Stephen Bonsal. The other two, according to Fleet, had been specifically requested by the Post Office, and for reasons other than sheer merit.

One, Second Lieutenant James Clark Edgerton, was the son of the department's purchasing agent, who had played a prominent role in planning the airmail service. The other, Second Lieutenant George Leroy Boyle, was engaged to the daughter of "Judge" Charles C. McChord, chairman of the Interstate Commerce Commission. The ICC during McChord's time of membership dealt with several matters of interest to Postmaster General Burleson, including parcel post rates and package sizes and the rates charged by the railroads for carrying the mail. He was consequently a man with whom the Post Office wished to stay on friendly terms. *

Both Lieutenants Edgerton and Boyle were fresh out of flying school. Nevertheless, they were given high-visibility assignments. Boyle would fly the first mail out of Washington, in the presence of the president, the postmaster general and the other dignitaries; that was a role Fleet had contemplated for himself. Edgerton would wing south from Philadelphia, bringing the first incoming mail to the capital.

*—Coincidentally, both Burleson and McChord later died on the same day—November 24, 1937.

## Chapter Three

# The Rush

*"It is desired to begin printing these stamps this afternoon."*
**— James L. Wilmeth**

As the countdown proceeded, a thousand details were clamoring for attention. One was the question of how much to charge the public to use this new service.

The Post Office, with no experience on which to base estimates of demand and costs, arbitrarily fixed a price of 24¢ per ounce for letter mail. This included the 10¢ special delivery fee then in effect. If the letters arrived at their destination post office in time to make the last delivery, they would go out with the regular carrier. If they missed it, they would be dispatched by special messenger.

There are no records indicating who decided on 24¢, and why. Major Reuben Fleet claimed long afterward that the rate had been set on his recommendation. It's doubtful, though, that the Post Office would have been influenced on this point by the view of an Army officer whose expertise was in pilot training, not postal economics.

Some people expressed shock at the rate, eight times the cost of a first-class letter. During Senate debate on the bill to authorize the 24¢ charge, Senator Jacob H. Gallinger of New Hampshire warned: "If we are to establish a postal route on which it will cost 24¢ an ounce to transmit a letter, I think we might as well abandon the scheme at one time as another. It may amuse somebody for two or three days, but my impression is that it never will become a reality." (Gallinger died the following August, but he lived long enough to see the Post Office, on July 15, lower the rate to 16¢.)

In spite of such pessimism, the Senate approved the bill May 6. The House followed suit the next day, and President Wilson signed the measure into law May 10, five days before the scheduled first flights.

Meanwhile, officials were taking steps to make sure the public had something to stick onto its air letters. As late as April 25, the White House itself was dismissing speculation about a new stamp. ("It has been impossible to create a distinctive aeroplane service stamp in time for the inauguration of the service," Joseph Tumulty, the president's secretary, wrote to a correspondent.) However, at some point after this, the decision was made to go for one. The fact that there was no 24¢ stamp then in production may have influenced the decision, along with an understandable desire on the part of the Post Office for something out of the ordinary to accompany this dramatic new venture.

To hear Ben Lipsner tell it in his memoirs, he was the one who called the shots on the new stamps. "Just see that they have 'airmail' of some description on them," he quotes himself as saying, "and have them ready in time." Old soldiers, it would seem, not only never die, but also never understate their role in great events. Realistically, the Post Office would have been no more likely to turn to Captain Lipsner for advice on stamp design than to Major Fleet for help in setting rates.

Then, as now, the Post Office obtained its stamps from the Treasury Department's Bureau of Engraving and Printing, a large complex of buildings on Fourteenth Street in southwest Washington. The Bureau, already overtaxed by wartime demands, was now asked to do a rush job on the new airmail stamp. For special effect, the Post Office asked for a bicolor, in the patriotic combination of red and blue. It would be the first U.S. bicolored stamp since the Pan-American Exposition commemoratives of 1901. About a million stamps a month would be needed, the department estimated.

Today, U.S. stamps are produced by a variety of processes — intaglio (line engraving), photogravure, offset, or a combination of intaglio with one of the other methods — on high-speed equipment that turns out multicolor work on a continuous web of stamp paper. In May 1918, however, with the exception of some offset work to conserve steel for the war effort, the only process the Bureau used for postage stamps, or had ever used, was intaglio. And although webfed rotary presses were coming into use, the workhorse of stamp manufacture was still the slower, sheetfed flatbed press. It was on such a press, by intaglio, that the new 24¢ stamp would be printed.

Like all stamps, this would be a team effort. To execute it, the Bureau picked a trio of veteran craftsmen.

The design assignment went to Clair Aubrey Huston. Huston had designed most U.S. stamps since 1903 — including the only other one to show an airplane, that prophetic parcel post 20¢ in 1912 — and would continue to be the Bureau's most prolific designer until his retirement in 1933. Working from a War Department photograph of a Jenny, he created a horizontal arrangement showing the plane in flight from

**Clair Aubrey Huston, designer of the Jenny airmail stamp and dozens of other U.S. postage stamps.**

right to left, inside a frame carrying the standard information ("U.S. Postage 24 Cents 24") and some ornamental triangles and scrolls. Ben Lipsner's "instructions" notwithstanding, the word "airmail" did not appear.

Huston's model was etched onto metal, in reverse, by two engravers. Edward M. Weeks — later to become superintendent of the Bureau's Engraving Division — did the frame, numerals and lettering on one piece of soft steel. The Jenny, with a light cloud background, was reproduced on another piece of steel by Marcus Wickliffe Baldwin. Baldwin, 65, was one of the Bureau's, and the country's, most talented bank note engravers. He had come to the Bureau from the American Bank Note Company in 1897, and the following year he engraved the $1 Trans-Mississippi Exposition commemorative stamp, showing Western cattle in a storm, which many collectors to this day consider the finest U.S. stamp ever produced. His stamp credits also included the familiar Washington-Franklin head definitives that were still in use in 1918. The Jenny would be Baldwin's next-to-last stamp assign-

**Marcus W. Baldwin, one of the country's top bank note engravers, who engraved the Jenny stamp vignette.**

ment before he retired in 1920; the World War I Victory commemorative of 1919 would be his last. *

Surviving documents of the Post Office Department and the Bureau of Engraving and Printing reflect the uncommon haste in which the Jenny stamp was created. There is no record of the date the department formally requested the stamp or when designer Huston began work, but a Bureau document discloses that Edward Weeks started engraving die 663, the frame, on May 4. On May 7, James L. Wilmeth, director of the Bureau, sent to A.M. Dockery, third assistant postmaster general, Huston's model of the stamp, together with a photograph of it reduced to stamp size (87/100th of an inch wide by 75/100th of an

* A cover exists bearing a 24¢ Jenny stamp and autographed with the initials MWB (for Marcus W. Baldwin) and the signatures C.A. Huston and E.M. Weeks. Postmarked in Washington July 25, 1918, it was mailed by still another Bureau engraver, W.B. Wells, to a friend at the American Bank Note Company in New York. The cover sold for $380 in the 1971 auction of the collection of Henry M. Goodkind, airmail specialist and author of the first extended study of the Jenny invert.

inch deep), asking that it be approved if satisfactory and returned "in order that the work of engraving may be proceeded with." Weeks, however, had begun "proceeding" three days earlier.

On May 8, Marcus Baldwin got busy on the vignette die, No. 664. His personal diary entry for that date reads: "P. O. 664, 12. h until 10 o clock on Aviation 25 ct (sic) Stamp. for the new Airplane P. O. Service between Wash. & N. York." The May 9 entry reads: "P. O. 664 all day at stamp. Mr. Weeks did the lettering." In view of Baldwin's

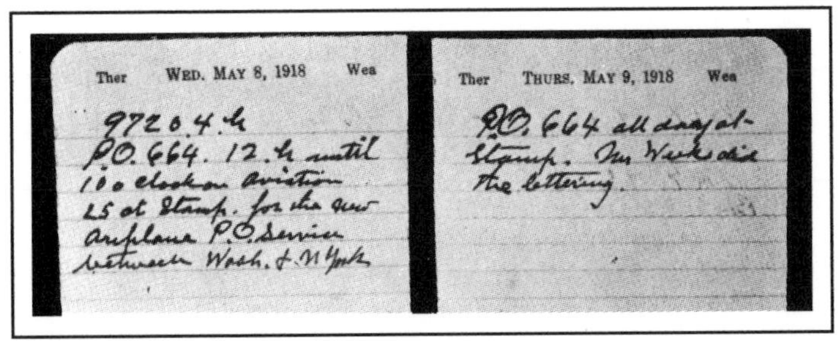

Ther WED. MAY 8, 1918 Wea

9720.4.h
P.O. 664. 12. h until
10 o clock on aviation
25 ct Stamp. for the new
airplane P.O. Service
between Wash. & N York

Ther THURS. MAY 9, 1918 Wea

P.O. 664 all day at
Stamp. Mr Weeks did
the lettering.

**Engraver Marcus W. Baldwin's diary pages recording his work on the vignette die for the 1918 24¢ Jenny airmail stamp.**

confusion over the denomination, it's probably just as well that Weeks was assigned to engrave that portion of the design.

On May 9, while all this was going on, and while the authorization bill was still awaiting the president's signature, the Post Office made its first public announcement of the new stamp. Despite the stamp's special nature, the public was told, it would be valid for ordinary postage as well as airmail; conversely, as a May 11 announcement explained, ordinary postage would be accepted for airmail, as long as the envelope was appropriately marked.

Back at the Bureau, the records show, the frame die was completed and hardened May 9 and the vignette die was completed and hardened May 10. But in another letter from Director Wilmeth to the Post Office's Dockery, this one dated May 9, Wilmeth transmitted "two proof impressions of the new 24¢ stamp" and asked Dockery to indicate which one he preferred "at the earliest possible moment as it is desired to begin printing these stamps this afternoon." A pencil notation on the letter reads: "1 proof blue background and red machine/1 proof red background and blue machine/the latter approved by (initials indistinct) 5/10/18." The revelation that the Bureau considered printing the stamp with the blue and red colors reversed is an interesting one, but the document raises the question of how a vignette proof could have been made May 9 when the die wasn't completed until the following day.

The urgency of the operation is further underscored by a follow-up letter from Wilmeth to Dockery dated May 16, three days after the stamps had gone on sale. "I enclose herewith two proofs of the new 24¢ postage stamp and have to request that one of them be approved and returned to this Bureau, and the other retained for the files of your office," Wilmeth wrote. "These proofs should of course have been approved prior to the issue of this stamp, but an informal approval was obtained owing to the great hurry in the production of the stamps and it might therefore be proper for these proofs to be approved as of date of May 11, the first delivery of the stamps having been made to your office on the 13th instant."

On May 21, Dockery's office replied that Postmaster General Burleson had indeed approved the proofs "as of May 11," thus completing the little piece of retroactive bureaucratic housekeeping.

Almost as an afterthought, Post Office purchasing agent J.A. Edgerton inquired as to how much the Bureau would charge his department for producing the new stamps. A dollar a thousand, he was told, compared to 65¢ for ordinary one-color postage.

Of all the minor mysteries surrounding the creation of the Jenny stamp, the most tantalizing is what might be called "the case of the prophetic number."

Engraved on the fuselage of the airplane on the stamp, so small that a glass is needed to see it, is the number 38262. This would turn out to be the number painted on the real Jenny that would fly the first

**The Jenny on the 1918 24¢ airmail stamp carries number 38262, the number of the plane that made the first mail flight out of Washington, D.C.**

mail out of Washington on May 15. Very neat. But how was it managed?

On May 7, Bureau designer Huston's stamp design went to the Post Office for approval. On May 8 and 9, Marcus Baldwin did the engraving of the plane. Somewhere along the line the five-digit number was incorporated in the picture. Obviously, the number was furnished to Huston (or possibly to Baldwin, to insert at the engraving stage) by someone who knew that it had been assigned to one of the mail planes. That person could hardly have known, however, that it would be the number of the first plane out of Washington; as we shall see, the selection of planes for specific flights would be by luck of the draw. And there is no other obvious reason why 38262 would have been chosen for the stamp. It wasn't the lowest number assigned to the Jennies that flew the mail (37944 would take the Philadelphia-to-New York leg on May 15) or the highest (38273-4-5-6 and 8 all participated during the first week.) The conclusion is inevitable that 38262 was selected for the stamp purely at random.

The situation would be clearer if certain key information and items were available. The records don't show, for example, how the assignment of numbers was made to the planes, and when. And neither the Post Office Department nor the Bureau can locate the original War Department photo of a Jenny from which Clair Huston worked, nor can they find Huston's completed model for the stamp from which the engravers worked. These would indicate at what stage the airplane number was introduced to the stamp design.

The original photograph would be useful to have for another reason. The plane on the stamp is of the modified design, with a mail compartment in place of the front cockpit. Yet the first of these custom-built Jennies wasn't actually assembled until May 14, a full day after the stamps themselves were first placed on sale. So either the War Department artistically modified a photograph of a normal Jenny before giving it to the Bureau, or artist Huston made the necessary changes while designing the stamp.

* * *

To create a plate of 100 subjects, the Bureau hardened the engraving, then placed it on a device called a transfer press which brought it in contact with a blank roll of soft steel mounted on an axle. Under increasing pressure, the roll was rocked back and forth until its malleable metal was forced into every line of the die, creating a positive impression, in relief, on its curved surface. The roll itself was then hardened and returned to the transfer press, where it served as the master to create the rows of negative impressions on a printing plate, 10 across by 10 deep. This job was done by a technician called a siderographer, or transferrer.

Only a year before, a siderographer had been responsible for a remarkable stamp error, unlike any other committed at the Bureau before or since. Because Robey, like other collectors, knew all about this error, and because it would be on his mind as he ventured forth to the post office May 14 and afterward, its story is worth telling here.

It happened in March 1917, when a new plate was being prepared for the standard 2¢ red Washington stamp. This stamp, which had also been designed by Huston and engraved by Baldwin, had been used for years on the country's first-class mail. It was printed on the flatbed presses in sheets of 400 which, during the perforating process, were divided into panes of 100 for distribution to post offices. (This quartering operation produced stamps with straight edges along two sides of each pane.)

After the new plate, numbered 7942, was made, the customary proof was taken to make sure all the transfers were satisfactory. Those with defects were marked with blue pencil on the proof so the siderographer could burnish them out and make fresh entries with the transfer roll. After final approval, the plate would be hardened and sent to the press.

Three flawed transfers were found on plate 7942: stamps 74 and 84 on the upper left pane, and stamp 18 on the lower right pane. The siderographer made re-entries, but instead of the transfer roll for the 2¢ stamp, he mistakenly used the 5¢ roll. The design of the two denominations was the same, although the 5¢ stamps were normally printed in blue, not red. Though images on transfer rolls were positives rather than reverses, the technician looking at the figure "5" may have absentmindedly taken it for a reversed "2."

Whatever the reason for his error, it was compounded by the failure of the person responsible for checking the corrected plate proof to spot it, and the plate went onto the press.

What came off the press as a consequence was a stack of sheets, each of which included among its cohort of red 2-centers three impostors — red 5-centers. Between March 9 and April 1, 1917, plate 7942 produced just under 50,000 sheets of 400 stamps each. After they were separated into the standard panes of 100, one of every four panes contained two examples of the error, adjacent vertically; another pane contained one error, and the remaining two out of every four were error-free. The panes were bundled in the usual manner and sent out to the post offices.

One appealing story had it that the mistake was first spotted in late April by the postmaster of a small Virginia town, who sent a copy

**The 5¢ red error — a 5¢ stamp in a sheet of 2-centers — was on Robey's mind when he purchased the inverts.**

of the red 5-center to the department with a plaintive request not to mix denominations on the sheets, as he already had enough trouble keeping his accounts straight. However, the chief of the Stamp Division, W.C. Fitch, asserted that the error was first brought to his attention by the proprietor of a Washington drug store that had a postal substation.

The department in its May 3 *Official Bulletin* advised all postmasters of the error and asked them to retrieve any copies they could find from their stock — or from the public, "for redemption at 2¢ each." (At least one stamp actually was turned in for the 2¢ refund, by a conscientious customer in St. Paul.) The announcement failed to make it clear that postmasters were to look for individual 5¢ stamps buried in panes of 2-centers rather than full panes of 5-centers printed in red, and so a fair number of errors escaped the dragnet at first.

At the department, the error stamps were carefully removed from the panes and the panes then returned to circulation. By April 1918 the Post Office had reported the recovery and destruction of 23,021 of the red 5-centers.

During the run of plate 7942, the Bureau was completing a changeover of its perforating wheels from the coarse gauge of 10 holes per two centimeters to an easier-to-separate 11 holes. It also turned out a small number of imperforate and uncut sheets of 400 for sale to companies that cut them into strips for use in stamp vending machines. Thus the error existed in three different varieties. Of the three, the imperforate was by far the rarest; only 50 sheets, containing a total of 150 copies of the 5¢ red, reached collectors' hands.

* * *

Now, in May 1918, the Bureau scheduled its new airmail stamp, as a bicolor, to be printed on a small hand press used for making bank notes. This press, instead of producing large sheets of 400 stamps, produced sheets of only 100 stamps each. But nobody announced that

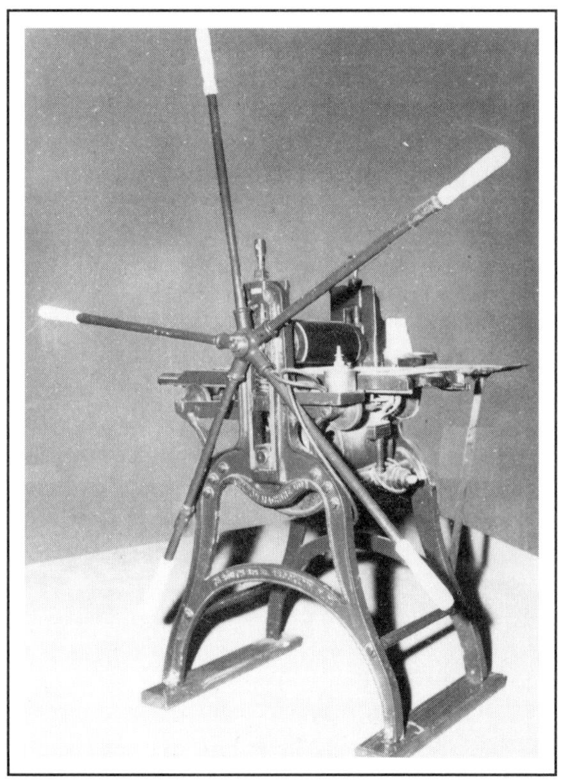

**An old-fashioned "spider" hand press of the kind used by the BEP to print the Jenny airmail stamps.**

in advance, and Robey and most other collectors assumed that the airmail stamp plates contained 400 units, like the regular plates. This misunderstanding would influence Robey's actions in the days after he found the sheet of inverts.

Each sheet of 100 airmail stamps, as it came off the press, was surrounded by a margin, or selvage, of varying width. The margins on two sides were trimmed off before the sheets left the Bureau; otherwise, the sheets would have been too large to fit the shipping packages, whose size was tailored to the dimensions of post office stamp drawers. But all four margins contained various markings of interest to philatelic specialists.

There were the two plate numbers, both in the top selvage: a red 8492 above the seventh stamp, identifying the plate which printed the red frames, and a blue 8493 over the fourth stamp, for the plate that printed the blue vignettes.

There were pairs of red diagonal lines, laid out like arrows pointing into the sheet, halfway across the top and bottom selvage and halfway down the left and right sides.

There were registration markings, shaped like heavy "T's" with beveled tips. Both plates had them, centered just above the top row and beneath the bottom row of frames or vignettes. On a perfectly registered sheet the blue markings would be superimposed on the red, inside the red arrows at the top and bottom.

There were siderographer Samuel DeBinder's initials — "S. DeB." — under the first stamp in the bottom row on the red plate. Since 1906, Bureau siderographers had stamped their initials onto plates on which they had worked. For some reason, however, no initials were placed on the blue plate for the Jenny stamp.

On the blue plate only, however, were engraved two additional "T" registration markings. These show up on the certified proof of the plate, far out at the sides, about 4½ stamp widths from the outer vertical rows of Jenny vignettes. What purpose they served is conjectural. John S. Meek, a specialist in marginal markings, has suggested that these extra "T's" didn't print on the sheets of stamps themselves, but rather were used by the printer's assistant to help center each half-finished sheet face down on the blue plate for its second pass through the press.

Within the sheet itself were other functional markings.

Red guidelines connected the opposing arrows, to help with the lining up of the perforating machines. These ran horizontally and vertically across the sheet, quartering it into sections of 25 stamps each.

Finally, there were the blue position dots. When the siderographer made the blue plate, he tapped 100 tiny dots into the metal, in 10 rows of 10 dots each, to guide him in laying down the 100 airplane images with the transfer roll. These dots showed up on the printed sheets. Each one was approximately six-tenths of a centimeter below the corresponding blue vignette, so that normally it would appear just within the top red frame line of the stamp beneath, between the "O" and "S" of "POSTAGE." The top row of stamps, therefore, showed

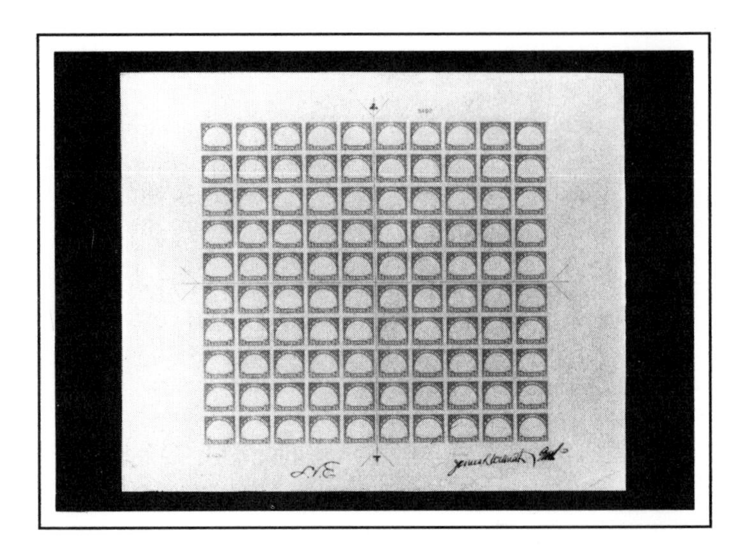

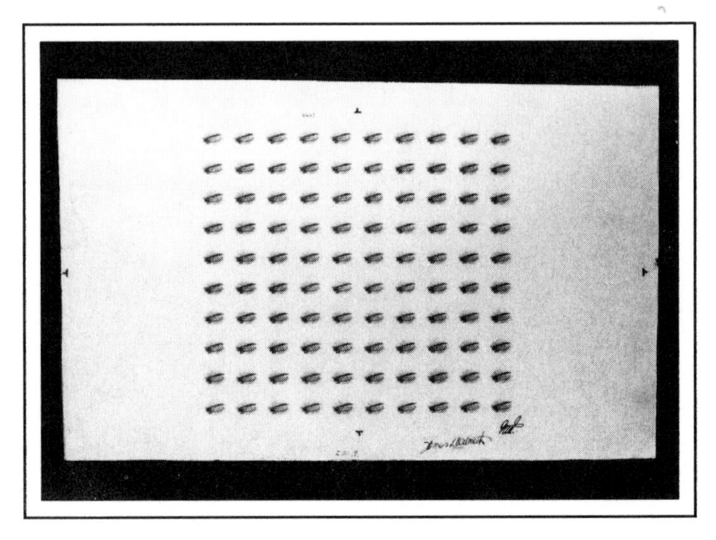

**Plate proofs of the Jenny stamp frame (top) and vignette (bottom), signed and initialed by Bureau of Engraving and Printing officials.**

no dots at all. Most of the dots can be seen with a magnifying glass, but a few were made so lightly that they are virtually undetectable.

The two steps required to print the stamp were time-consuming. "The border or frame is printed first," Joseph Leavy explained to readers of the *Philatelic Gazette*, "the sheets then examined and counted and delivered to the presses to have the center or medallion printed;

any defective sheets having been thrown out, the sheets are dampened the same as if they were blank and are ready to be fed to the press.

"In printing from a hand press the plate is removed after one impression, placed on a heated block, re-inked, wiped, and then returned to the press for the next impression; this is all done by the plate printer. The plate printer's assistant feeds and removes each sheet to and from the press, her hands being clean; in feeding, the sheet is taken between the thumb and forefinger with the thumb just below the registering T and placed on the plate with the thumb just below the registering T on the plate." If John Meek's theory is correct, the assistant used the additional registering "T's" at the outer edges of the blue plate for guidance in positioning the sheet for this second printing operation.

This primitive method of registry led to considerable variation in the placement of the Jennies within their arched frames. At least three sheets reached the public on which some of the aircraft flew so low that their landing gear broke through the bottom frame line and into the word "CENTS." These so-called "grounded plane" varieties, though not considered errors, came to be valued by collectors of philatelic oddities. *

**Poor registration of red and blue plates produced this "grounded plane variety" of the Jenny stamp.**

More basic was the small variation that existed in the siderography on the frame and vignette plates. The horizontal rows of airplanes on the blue plate were laid down a fraction farther apart than the frames on the red plate. Thus, even on a normal sheet of 100, if the planes are centered properly in the frame arch of the stamps on the top row,

* — A "grounded plane" single sold for $750 in the Philip Silver collection auction in November 1985, six times the price fetched by a normal single in the same sale.

they will be slightly low on the stamps at the bottom of the sheet.

The final step was perforating. This was done on line machines, one for the vertical rows and one for the horizontal. For each operation there was a set of 10 parallel wheels, one-half male containing 176 pins, the other half female with holes to mesh with the pins. However, just as the two plates didn't line up precisely with each other, the distance between the rows of perforations varied slightly but perceptibly across each sheet.

It was during this step that part of the selvage was trimmed away. At the edges of the perforating mechanism were knives that sliced off the top and right selvages of each sheet, taking with them both plate numbers, the top and right arrows, and the top registering "T" marks. The bottom selvage was trimmed so close to the bottom row of horizontal perforations that the "T" marks there were lost as well.

From the viewpoint of philatelists, the trimming process had two unfortunate results. Straight-edged stamps are less popular with collectors than fully-perforated ones, and the process created 19 of them along the top and right sides of the sheet (stamp number 10 in the top row was a double pariah, with straight edges on two sides). Collectors do like plate number blocks, however — blocks of stamps with attached selvage bearing the plate number or numbers — but these numbers, on the Jenny stamp, were eliminated by the cutting knife.

The Bureau began printing from the frame plate, 8492, on Friday, May 10. The next day, at 4 p.m., it began putting frame-printed sheets onto the vignette plate, 8493. There is no record of whether printers worked on the new stamps on Sunday, but by Monday, May 13, enough of them had been produced to permit an initial delivery to the Post Office Department. At 3:30 p.m. that day, the stamps were placed on sale at Washington's main post office. *

* — Three covers exist with the May 13 first day postmark. One is an envelope with a 3 p.m. Washington handstamp, addressed on a typewriter with an Old English typeface to "Hon. Morris Sheppard, United States Senator, Father of the U.S. Air Mail, Washington, D. C.," and with the words "The First U.S. Air Mail Stamp" typed in the upper left corner. The others are postcards, one from New York, the other from Philadelphia, each bearing a machine cancellation with the slogan "Food Will Win the War/Don't Waste It."

The New York cover, a commercial postcard, is postmarked 11 p.m. and hand addressed to a Mr. Albert Schuckert, Indianapolis. The Philadelphia item is a Post Office Department postal card bearing the 1¢ green Abraham Lincoln imprinted stamp then current. It is postmarked 4 p.m. and is addressed to a Mr. Arch LaMont. Each card in addition bears a May 15 first flight handstamped postmark from its respective city.

Who prepared and mailed these three covers is a mystery, and even more puzzling is how the New York and Philadelphia covers were created in view of the fact there is no official record of the stamp being sold in those cities on May 13. All three covers turned up in October 1956 in the sale of a single collection; until that time they had been unknown to philately. The Philatelic Foundation, one of the major stamp expertizing organizations, has given the New York cover its blessing with its certificate 22620 ("first day cover with genuine cancellations"). The Foundation has declined a formal opinion on the Washington cover, however, because of what it called "insufficient criteria." So far as is known, the Philadelphia cover has never been submitted to the Foundation for its opinion.

Two specialists in the Jenny airmail stamp, the late Henry M. Goodkind, who at one time owned the Washington cover, and Philip Silver, who owned the New York cover, were convinced that the items were authentic.

The Philadelphia cover was auctioned April 13, 1965, in a lot with first day covers of two later Jenny airmail stamps (16¢ and 6¢) for $5,250. In 1967 it was reportedly sold individually for $2,500. The Washington cover brought $3,500 at the 1971 auction of the Goodkind collection. In the November 1985 sale of the Silver collection, the New York cover was sold in a lot with 16¢ and 6¢ first day covers for $70,000 plus a 10 percent buyer's fee.

Chapter Four

# The Mistake

*"More likely . . . the plate printer reversed his plate . . ."*

**— Joseph B. Leavy**

Printers making bicolored stamps were unusually vulnerable to Murphy's Law, which holds that if it is possible for something to go wrong, it will.

It happened as early as 1854, when the East India Company issued a lithographed 4-anna stamp for colonial India bearing a profile of the young Queen Victoria in red within an octagonal blue border. At least one sheet escaped with the royal countenance upside down. The error is considered one of the choice rarities of philately, with an estimated 30 specimens in existence today.

In the United States in 1869, the National Bank Note Company printed some exquisite miniature bicolor pictorials for the Post Office, and in the process permitted sheets of the 15¢ (landing of Columbus), 24¢ (signing of the Declaration of Independence) and 30¢ (eagle and flags) to slip out with colors inverted. Numerous revenue stamps printed for the Treasury Department by private contractors in the early 1870s were found with inverted centers.

The Bureau of Engraving and Printing, after it took over stamp production, was not immune. In 1901, when it printed the Pan-American Exposition commemoratives with black vignettes inside colored frames, it created inverts of the 1¢ (lake steamer), 2¢ (express train) and 4¢ (electric automobile).

With the airmail stamp, as Robey had realized, conditions were ripe for another error. The printers would be working on a tight schedule in a shop that was operating night and day. They would have to hand-feed each sheet through the presses twice, removing and replacing the printing plate after each pass.

And so it happened. It happened not once, but nine times in the course of the printing of the Jenny stamps. The printer, or his assistant, had a lapse of concentration and a sheet emerged from the second pass with the airplanes upside down. Eight of these were intercepted and destroyed. Robey's sheet was not. Through the perforator it went and out the other side, with the blue plate number 8493, which was supposed to disappear with the top selvage in the trimming process, partially surviving in the shallow bottom selvage instead. Into a pad of normal sheets it went for shipping. The day it happened was probably Saturday, May 11, the first day the blue vignette plate was employed.

Precisely what misstep produced the sheet of inverts can only be surmised. There is no evidence that the Bureau ever staged an internal investigation to determine the cause or the culprit. The most plausible theory is contained in the first detailed public description of the printing of the stamps, which was written in June 1918 for *The Philatelic Gazette* by its new issues editor, Joseph B. Leavy of Washington. Leavy was philatelist for the U.S. stamp collection at the Smithsonian Institution (the title later became "curator") and undoubtedly had access to official sources. He wrote:

"The inverts could have occurred by the assistant feeding the border sheets to the press in an inverted manner, but as the sheets are all sorted and arranged in a normal manner it would require an awkward, unnatural movement to invert the sheet in feeding; it is therefore not probable that the assistant was responsible for the errors, but more likely that the plate printer reversed his plate in returning it to the press after inking and wiping, very easily done in the rush under which the printing was conducted and requiring no awkward nor unnatural movement to accomplish.

"Of course the examiner was directly responsible for the inverts being delivered, but whether normal or inverted the aeroplane is at the same angle in the frame, and to one possibly not conversant with the construction of an aeroplane the matter of the landing wheels being at top would not be an important point. Those fortunate enough to have seen the inverts realize how easily they could have been passed in hurried examination."

Leavy didn't mention another argument strengthening the case for the "inverted plate" as against the "inverted sheet" theory. If it had been the sheet that was rotated 180 degrees between the red and blue printings, it would have had to be rotated again before it went through the perforator-trimmer. Otherwise the knife that sliced away the top selvage would have taken off the blue plate number and left the red one, instead of vice versa. The odds against the same sheet being turned twice would seem to be extraordinarily high.

Interestingly, the Post Office itself in later years couldn't decide which scenario it favored. In 1938, an inquiring citizen was told that "an employee at the Bureau of Engraving and Printing inadvertently reversed the plate containing the central design." In 1946, however, a similar query was answered this way: "Upside-down frames are caused by reversing the direction of the sheet in the second printing operation."

And the card that accompanies an inverted Jenny die proof that is now on permanent display in the U.S. Postal Service's Hall of Stamps also dispenses the inverted-sheet theory: "The error occurred when the paper was turned the wrong way for application of the second color."

Not only was Robey's sheet the only one to reach the public with the planes inverted; it was, for a time, the only one with a plate number — the partial blue 8493 that appeared inverted in the bottom selvage. This led Henry M. Goodkind, author of the first extensive study of the Jenny error, to speculate that Robey got his inverts only because he had asked the stamp clerk for "plate number blocks or sheets." The clerk searched through his stock, according to Goodkind's theory, and came up with the only sheet he could find that bore a number — the sheet of inverts. The trouble with this scenario is that in none of Robey's own accounts of his visit to the New York Avenue branch post office does he even suggest that he had asked for plate numbers.

There was one other, though minor, side effect of the inversion. On the inverts the tiny blue position dots placed on the plate by the siderographer appeared not within the red frame of each stamp but centered in the bottom margin of each one, between the frame line and the perforations. Stamps from the bottom row of the invert sheet showed no dots.

As soon as officials learned that an invert sheet had gotten into circulation they took steps to prevent it from happening again. The next day, May 15, the Bureau of Engraving and Printing added the word "TOP", in capital letters with serifs, to the blue vignette plate, in the top selvage above the third stamp, just to the left of the plate number. The idea was that inspectors thumbing through the stacks of finished sheets could look for that key word and be assured that the airplanes were right side up.

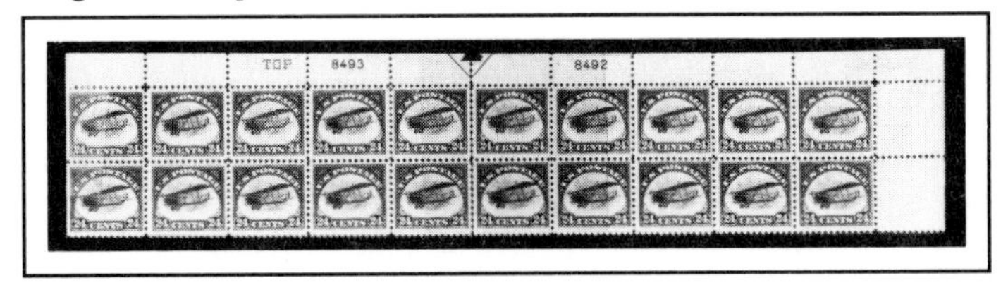


**The second printing of the 24¢ Jenny airmail stamp carried the word "TOP" once, in blue, in the upper selvage.**

Of course, it was also necessary to reset the knives on the perforating machine so that they would leave the top selvage in place on the finished sheets. Consequently, sheets sold to the public from this "second printing" carry a top selvage — and, at the bottom, a straight edge rather than a selvage. The top selvage contained, in addition to the blue "TOP," both the red and blue plate numbers, the red arrow and the red and blue registration marks. For some reason, the other trimming knife was switched from one side to the other during the second printing, so that some sheets were produced with selvage on the left side and straight edges on the right, and others had them reversed.

Soon thereafter — the date isn't recorded — Bureau officials decided to play it safer still. They added the word "TOP" to the red frame plate as well; this one was in slightly smaller capitals, and without serifs.

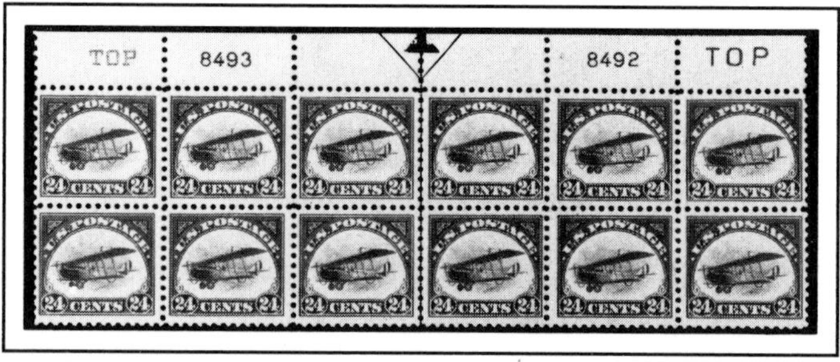


**In a third printing of the Jenny stamp, an additional "TOP," in red, was added to help inspectors spot any further inverts.**

Thus, if inspectors saw both words in the top selvage, there could be no possibility of any inverts. As with the second printing of the Jenny stamp, all the sheets of the third printing were issued with the top selvage intact. Unlike the second-printing sheets, however, those of the third printing were all made with selvage at left and straight edge at right.

Because the second printing of the stamp was so brief, examples are extremely rare today. In fact, it was a year and a half before philately was fully aware that sheets existed with only a single, blue "TOP." Joseph Leavy, in the August 1918 *Philatelic Gazette*, reported the addition of the word "TOP" to the "plates" — note the plural.

Finally, in November 1920, Edward Stern of the Economist Stamp Company called the one-"TOP" sheets to the attention of Philip H. Ward, new issues columnist for *Mekeel's Weekly Stamp News*. Ward, an electrical engineer who would later become a prominent stamp dealer and buy and sell numerous Jenny inverts, speculated that these sheets were the result of an error of sorts. They were "evidently the result of some sheets being partially printed at the time the plates were inscribed 'TOP' and then were later finished with the changed plate," he wrote. *

For the next 20 years, whenever the Bureau printed a bicolored stamp it followed the Jenny precedent of adding the word "TOP" to one or both of the printing plates.

Speculation began almost at once as to how many inverted Jenny sheets had been printed. In his June 1918 article in the *Philatelic Gazette*, Joseph Leavy reported that "in the small stock of the first printing which remained in the vaults of the Bureau, three sheets of inverts were found, each stamp of which was heavily blue penciled before being consigned to the macerator."

Robey himself, in his first, brief account of his discovery in the June issue of the *Collectors' Journal*, also asserted that three more sheets had been found in the Bureau and "were cancelled with a pencil and thereby spoiling same for postage." Robey's source for this was almost certainly Leavy.

The authoritative word, however, came in January 1919 from the director of the Bureau, James L. Wilmeth. *Mekeel's* columnist Philip Ward had submitted a series of written questions about the Jenny stamps to the director, and one was, had additional inverts been found? Wilmeth relayed the question to his staff and received this memorandum from the chief of his Stamp Perforating Division:

"Eight other sheets were found on different days in perforating and canceled by hand with pen and ink so as to entirely efface the stamp and then they were delivered as mutilated to Custodian of Paper for destruction July 11, 1918." Wilmeth duly reported this information to Philip Ward.

Possibly Joseph Leavy's information about three other invert sheets being found was correct as of the time he received it; the other five sheets could have been produced later — the last border printings were made June 5, the last vignette printings June 12 — and spotted because a "TOP" was missing from the upper selvage.

The answers Philip Ward had solicited were intended for an article for *Mekeel's*, but no such article can be found. And though the chief of perforating's memorandum and at least two copies of Wilmeth's letter

* — At least two full sheets still exist from the second printing, as do a small number of blocks of 12 or more stamps with attached top selvage showing both plate numbers and the single "TOP." At several auctions a second-printing sheet with selvage at top and right has been sold, at widely varying prices; quite possibly it is the same sheet. In 1964, at the sale of the Thomas A. Matthews collection, it brought a remarkably low $850. In a 1973 auction, as part of a lot that included sheets of the two other Jenny stamps, it fetched $8,250. Two years later, the same three-sheet lot brought $18,000. In 1980 the 24¢ sheet alone sold for $37,250. Then the price plunged precipitously — at a 1981 auction to $25,000 and at a 1982 sale to $10,500. Meanwhile, another sheet, with selvage at top and left, was offered at sales in 1981 and 1982 by another auction house.

to Ward have been in government files since they were written, they were apparently never seen by later writers. Henry M. Goodkind, for instance, asserted that Leavy's account of three sheets destroyed in the Bureau "has never been confirmed to our knowledge. Lacking any official word or documentation, a matter like this must remain one of conjecture." The "official word" had been theoretically available since 1919.

Wrote Captain Ben Lipsner in his memoirs:

"At the time (of the printing) I knew nothing of philately, but I certainly wish I had, for I could easily have purchased an inverted sheet." That comment suggests only that Lipsner, decades later, still didn't know much about philately, and also had a greatly exaggerated notion of the privileges available to a temporary postal official.

Even the Smithsonian Institution couldn't coax any extra inverts out of the Post Office. In June 1918 — no doubt at the suggestion of Joseph Leavy, the government philatelist — this hopeful letter was composed by one W. deC. Ravenel, administrative assistant:

"The National Museum is desirous of securing for the official collection of postage stamps a sheet of the new 24¢ stamp with the inverted aeroplane in center, and I beg to inquire if you can furnish one for the purpose mentioned . . . The general and philatelic public are at the present time greatly interested in the matter of representation of 'war stamps' in the official collection, and since the aeroplane stamps are essentially of that character, it is particularly desirable that they be placed upon exhibition with the Government collection."

The Post Office's reply isn't available, but needless to say it was negative, and it would be nearly 40 years before the Smithsonian ob-

**In 1901 the Post Office Department deliberately created 400 4¢ Pan-American Exposition inverts.**

tained even one copy of the Jenny invert.

Actually, there would have been a precedent for a reprinting. An earlier invert, the 4¢ Pan-American Exposition stamp of 1901, existed only because the Post Office had ordered 400 of them to be deliberately printed on the basis of an erroneous report that some had been created accidentally and sold to the public. Accordingly, it decided to make a few for its own files. Most of these artificially created "errors" eventually found their way into private hands. This time, in contrast, the error was genuine, but the Post Office chose not to deliberately recreate it. The department did, however, order some die proofs of the invert made later on, and these will be described in a later chapter.

The reduction in the airmail postage rate to 16¢ July 15 ended any real need for the 24¢ stamp, and a new stamp was issued for the lower rate. It used C.A. Huston's Jenny design, but was printed in only one color, green. Still later, on December 15, the rate was cut again, to 6¢, and the automatic special delivery service was eliminated. This called for a third Jenny stamp, which was printed in orange. Of the 24¢ stamp, a total of 21,986 sheets, or 2,198,600 stamps, were printed, and 2,134,988 were distributed.

**When the airmail rate was lowered by the U.S. Post Office to 16¢ and later to 6¢, new Jenny stamps (in single colors) were issued.**

## Chapter Five

# The Pursuit

*"A novice might have been scared . . ."*
— **William T. Robey**

William Robey had been introduced to stamp collecting by a fellow employee at Hibbs and Company about two years before fate, and the Bureau of Engraving and Printing, put his name into the hobby's history book. He had other diversions; for instance, he and Caroline enjoyed dancing and partying with a theater crowd they had met through the manager of the local B.F. Keith theater. But after Caroline became pregnant in the summer of 1916, they cut down on socializing, and stamps helped fill Robey's spare time.

Robey was born April 21, 1889, in Cockeysville, Maryland, and grew up on a farm near what is now the town of Potomac, near Washington. He attended the University of Maryland before going to work for Hibbs. When he was 23 he met 17-year-old Caroline Scott of Washington, and a few months later, on June 18, 1913, they eloped. The marriage was performed by a Methodist minister they had chosen as a compromise — he was Catholic, she Episcopalian.

Once Robey had discovered stamp collecting, he pursued it with enthusiasm. Henry M. Goodkind has described him as a kind of ill-informed beginner at the time he bought the inverts, but the evidence is clear he was anything but that. He knew stamps, he bought and sold them, he was well aware of errors and their value, and when dazzling luck came his way he knew how to make the most of it.

Shortly before that happened, Robey had progressed enough in the hobby to place an ad in a stamp publication offering to buy the 5¢ red Washington error in singles, pairs, blocks or sheets. That required no unusual financial resources — the error, which had originally sold for more than $100, now could be bought for about $2.50 because of the discovery of a substantial number of additional copies — but it indicated that the young collector was no neophyte.

Correspondence discovered a few years ago between Robey and Elliott Perry, a well-known stamp dealer of Westfield, New Jersey, shows how seriously he took philately. In his earliest letter, written in January 1917, Robey asked Perry for help in classifying two copies of the U.S. 5¢ Jefferson stamp of 1857, part of a series on which Perry was an authority. At the same time he confided that he didn't intend to bid at an upcoming auction by J.C. Morgenthau, a New York auction house, "as from past experiences I can say I do not like the way they do business."

Later letters to Perry contained orders for unused official stamps, postage dues, a complete set of India-paper proofs or surcharged specimen stamps for the various executive department issues of the 19th century, and revenue stamps. There are references to payments in amounts of $18.50, $17.85, $12.50 and $11.50. On December 31, in a letter that began "Happy New Year!" (little did he know), Robey submitted a want list for 23 U.S. stamps in "O.G. (original gum) blocks of 4 with your best price on approval."

Another letter enclosed a check for $38.85 to pay for stamps which Robey had sold to a fellow collector on Perry's behalf. On March 23, 1918, he boasted to Perry that he had bought a block of the 5¢ Zachary Taylor stamp of 1879 for $6 and sold it for $12, "which gave me a good profit on same," and in a letter dated May 11 — the same day the Jenny error was being committed down at the Bureau of Engraving and Printing — Robey offered Perry another block of the Taylor, "perfectly centered with the American Bank Note imprint at the bottom. This is another one I have recently picked up and will accept $15.00 for same if you can use it." (A pencil notation by Perry at the bottom of the letter reads: "$15.00 too much. Interested at $12.00.")

In an earlier note, Robey had briefed Perry on his collecting interests, and how they were influenced by his sense of the stamp market:

"I have never started to make a collection of anything but the U.S. stamps. Not even the colonies and think it will be sometime before I start on these as I believe money put in the old U.S. stamps now will in a few years be worth much more and will prove a good investment for anyone procuring same now. This is the reason I have never started a general collection of all countries. My collection is nearly complete from 1869 to date except some of the revenues."

Now, on May 14, 1918, back at Hibbs and Company with what looked very much like the ultimate "good investment" in his hands, Robey was eager to share his news.

He telephoned a Washington stamp dealer, Hamilton F. Colman, whose office in the Second National Bank building was a gathering place for collectors, but Colman wasn't in, so Robey told the story of the inverts to one of the regulars, Catherine L. Manning. Mrs.

Manning, known as "Miss Kate," was assistant to Joseph B. Leavy at the Smithsonian, and would later become curator of the government stamp collection herself. "For some unknown reason," though, as Robey put it, she didn't believe him.

Robey also phoned a collector named Harry B. Mason, who came to the Hibbs office and, Mason later recalled, became "one of the few to hold the sheet of inverts." Another collector, Albert E. Gorham, also saw the sheet that day.

The fellow employee whom Robey had first told of the discovery came back, unsuccessful in his search for more inverts. All he had managed to do was put the Post Office on Robey's trail by giving Robey's name and address at one or more of the branches he visited. Within an hour after Robey returned to work, two postal inspectors called to see him. Robey described the "very interesting" visit in the account he wrote 20 years afterward:

"At first they wanted to know if I had purchased the sheet of the 24¢ airmail stamps with a purported inverted center. Upon informing (them) that I had, they asked me to let them see it, which I refused to do.

"Well, the conversation was hot and furious from then on and ended in their making the statement that the government would confiscate the sheet. This in no way intimidated me and I informed them that they had said enough. Also, I said that '. . . before they tried to confiscate the sheet which I had purchased at the face value from the post office, they had better start confiscating the 1869 inverts, the Pan-American inverts, and all of the 5¢ errors. After securing them, it was then time to talk about confiscating my property.' No doubt," Robey concluded with obvious self-satisfaction, "a novice might have been scared into relinquishing the sheet."

Later that afternoon, dealer Colman visited Robey to see the sheet and offered him $500 for it. Robey said no, and Colman said he didn't blame him. After work, Robey took the sheet to Colman's office at 509 Seventh Street N.W., where Mrs. Manning, Joseph Leavy and some others were assembled. No one would venture a guess as to what the find was worth.

Then, according to Robey's recollection, a piece of misinformation was floated that would cause him much concern and strongly influence his actions for the next few days.

Joseph Leavy said that because the stamps were printed in sheets of 400 and cut into post office panes of 100, there obviously were three other panes of inverts in circulation. That was wrong, of course, and if Leavy in fact believed it he would soon find out otherwise because, as we have seen, he wrote in his June philatelic column an accurate description of how the stamps were printed.

But he and the others could be excused for not knowing on the afternoon of May 14 that the printing hadn't been done on the conventional 400-stamp plates. The Post Office hadn't revealed that information, or indeed much else, about the new stamps. And, as everyone could see, Robey's sheet had two adjacent straight edges, the kind made by cutting knives quartering large sheets into small ones at the Bureau of Engraving and Printing. (Apparently, though, Robey never did realize that the stamps were printed in sheets of 100, for in his 1938 memoir he reported Leavy's erroneous statement without comment.)

In any case, the possibility that other invert sheets were out there to be found added an element of urgency to the situation. Robey himself was well aware, from his own venture into the deflated market for the 5¢ red error, how values could plunge when a rarity suddenly becomes less rare.

The Post Office, alerted no doubt by the call made by Robey's window clerk, stopped the sale of the new stamps at all points in Washington, Philadelphia and New York so stocks could be examined. The communication advised postmasters that a sheet had been found with the airplane "reversed" (raising the diverting possibility that some who received it set to work looking for planes that were flying from left to right). The interruption — which in Philadelphia lasted from 4 to 6 p.m., according to Robey's friend Malcolm Ganser — was made without any explanation to the impatient collectors and dealers waiting to buy the stamps.

At some point in this busy day, Robey completed his original mission, which was to obtain some (normal) copies of the new stamp and use them on letters for the next day's first flight. What is most likely is that on his first visit to the branch post office he did indeed buy some stamps — as he said he had done in one of his earlier accounts —and had posted the letters then, before returning to the post office during his lunch hour.

At least one of these covers survives in philatelic hands. It is on a Hibbs and Company business envelope, and it bears the typed notation "Airplane Mail" and the address: "W. T. Robey, c/o Malcolm H. Ganser, 1509 Arch street, Norristown, Penna." The Jenny stamp is canceled with the special handstamped postmark that was used on all mail scheduled for air transit May 15: a circle about 1¼ inches in diameter, bearing the wording "Air Mail Service Wash. N. Y. Phila." around the inner circumference, "May/15/1918/First Trip" horizontally in the center, and "Washington" at the bottom, with four short parallel "killer" bars to the right. Identical postmarks, except for the city name, were used in New York and Philadelphia. *

* — A few specimens of the postmark are known with variations in the components, such as "10 AM" or "11 AM" in place of "1918," or "3 PM" or "4 PM" in place of "First Trip."

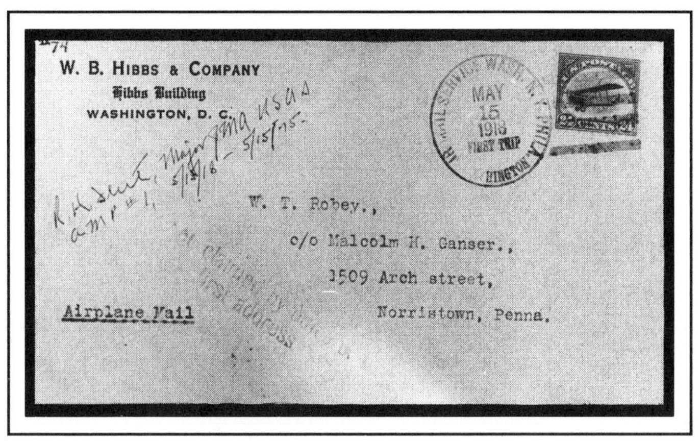


**First flight cover prepared by Robey and mailed to himself in care of Malcolm Ganser. (Autographed by Major Fleet in 1975.)**

Robey, perhaps on the advice of his friends at Colman's office, also began letting the outside world know of his discovery. Probably he telephoned the *Washington Post*, which the next morning carried the first published news of it. On an inside page, in the "jump" from the page one story about the new airmail service that would commence that day, was this paragraph:

"As soon as the first aerial mail stamps were put on sale in Washington yesterday, William T. Robey, employed at the W.B. Hibbs & Co., bought a sheet of 100. After examining the stamps carefully he discovered that the aeroplanes were upside down. He made an attempt to buy more, but didn't succeed."

Robey also sent a telegram to Percy McGraw Mann, then the author of the new issues column in *Mekeel's*, telling him of the inverts and asking him to "give proper notice of same" in his column. He also sent telegrams to Mal Ganser in Norristown and to Elliott Perry in Westfield, reading: "Look out for sheet 8493, aeroplane. They are inverts."

Both those wires arrived that evening and caused great excitement. To Ganser, who suddenly understood why Philadelphia had shut off sales of the stamp for two hours that afternoon, it was a stimulus to head again to the city's central post office; alas, the clerk on duty "only had two single stamps left," both normal.

Perry, too, was inspired to go hunting. He visited three large post offices in New York the next day, "but only a few stamps seemed to be in stock and they would sell only as many as you could show addressed letters to stick them on." Perry had a few envelopes with him, and he mailed one to Robey.

Meanwhile, Caroline Robey was spending the afternoon of May 14 wheeling their daughter Louise, then 13 months old, around Meridian

Hill Park, two blocks down 16th Street from the apartment, because the neighbors in the building had complained about the child's crying. She was puzzled when her husband didn't come home at 5:30, as he usually did, to take his turn at pushing the buggy while she prepared dinner. Later she took Louise with her to visit her parents, and when they returned she found two men waiting at the apartment. They introduced themselves as postal inspectors and asked where Robey was.

"I told them I expected him any minute, but after waiting a while they left," she recalled. "I was pretty tired of pushing that buggy by 9 o'clock, when Billy arrived and told me all about what had happened."

Robey told her that he had asked permission to keep the stamps in the office safe overnight, but his boss had refused for fear he would get in trouble with those postal inspectors who showed up earlier. So, after leaving Colman's stamp office, Robey rode around town on streetcars for three hours, carrying his stamps in a briefcase, waiting until he could slip back to the apartment under cover of darkness.

The Robeys were "a little disturbed" about keeping the stamps at home, according to Caroline. They had no place to lock them up, "so we turned out the light, pulled down the shades and stuck the briefcase under the mattress at the foot of my side of the bed."

## Chapter Six

# The Takeoff

*"We are losing a lot of valuable time here."*
**— President Woodrow Wilson**

While William and Caroline Robey tried to sleep above their odd little collection of airplane pictures, others were working feverishly to make sure the actual planes were ready and in the right places.

The pressure had been building since the afternoon of the day before, Monday, May 13, when Major Reuben Fleet and five of his pilots took delivery at Hazlehurst Field, Long Island, of six Jennies, fresh from the factory, in crates and unassembled. Working with crews of mechanics through the night, they succeeded in getting two planes put together and in shape to fly.

Curtiss had not done itself proud. "The machines were in very bad condition," Fleet reported. "In one of the JN4-Hs, the motor had a bad knock in the first cylinder, and it had to be pulled out of the airplane and another motor from Hazlehurst Field was installed in its place. The gasoline tank in one of the JN4-Hs had a leak in it the size of a lead pencil, at one of the joints. Fuselage wires in two of the other JN4-Hs were broken. The safety valve on the air pressure did not work in any planes, and in some of the planes the control wires were too long, and in some too short. The gravity tank feed pipe on all the JN4-Hs did not feed properly, and had to be taken out, and new pipes made with 'T' fittings leading direct to the carburetor, which piping had then to be installed with a control arrangement."

On the late afternoon of May 14, in fog and low clouds, Lieutenant Edgerton and Lieutenant Culver took off for Philadelphia in the two assembled planes. Major Fleet accompanied them in a regular Jenny trainer borrowed from Hazlehurst. The other mail pilots stayed behind to finish putting together the remaining aircraft.

Today, any amateur pilot with a few hours of cross-country training can fly from New York to Philadelphia, safe in the arms of modern technology. But for the three Army pilots on that day it was a leap into the unknown. Two of the aircraft had barely been flight-tested. Daylight was fading. Their maps were rudimentary, but the ground was mostly invisible anyway. They had no radios. Using the magnetic compass mounted in front of the cockpit required considerable skill; after a banking maneuver the instrument required a certain amount of time to recover, and sometimes the needle was affected by the metal in the plane. Finally, no one was quite sure where the airport in suburban Bustleton was. They knew only that it was some 11 miles northeast of downtown Philadelphia. *

In spite of all this, the two lieutenants made it safely. However, Major Fleet's unmodified trainer ran out of gas in midair. He landed in a New Jersey field, bought five gallons of ordinary gasoline in a milk can from a farmer, spilled perhaps two gallons of it pouring it into the tank without a funnel (and without a chamois skin to strain the impurities customarily found in the poorly refined product), took off, ran dry again a short distance from Bustleton, landed on a golf course with damage to a wheel, hitchhiked to the airport and sent Culver and Edgerton back with more gasoline and a spare wheel.

The plane was then flown to the field, which had for a while been lighted by a fleet of automobiles commandeered for the purpose. Unfortunately, the owners decided after waiting for a reasonable period of time that the pilot had deferred his trip until daylight, and went home. Lieutenant Culver, at the controls, coming in toward Bustleton in darkness, put the trainer down in an adjacent plowed field by mistake and broke the propeller. One can almost picture one of these young pilots tossing his scarf over his shoulder, lighting a cigarette and drawling: "Other than those trifling details, there were no problems, really."

But that night there was no time for striking poses and no rest for the weary. The officers worked all night to put the mail planes into better shape. At 4 a.m. it was discovered that, inexplicably, there was no oil at the field, and Fleet managed to secure two barrels from the Atlantic Refining Company in South Philadelphia so the planes could take off that day.

By 8:40 a.m. No. 38262 was pronounced ready, and Fleet departed in it. He was headed for the Washington end of the route, a field called the Polo Grounds, located in Potomac Park, between the Potomac River and the Tidal Basin. Here the plan called for the plane to be loaded with the first northbound mail out of the capital, after which George Boyle, the young lieutenant with the friends in high places, would fly it back north at 11:30 a.m. At Philadelphia, Lieutenant Culver would

* — The present Northeast Philadelphia Airport is on the site.

**The ground crew members help maneuver the Jenny 38262.**

be waiting with a fresh plane, Pony Express style, to relay the mail to New York.

At the same time Boyle was leaving Washington, Lieutenant Torrey Webb would depart with the southbound mail from the infield of Long Island's Belmont Park Race Track, loaned to the Post Office by the Westchester Racing Association, and head for a linkup with Lieutenant Edgerton in Philadelphia. The complete 218-mile trip each way was expected to take three hours, beating the train by two. Mail destined for other points would be transferred to trains on carefully worked-out schedules.

American industry was on the job, too, to help the pilots hold to their exacting timetable. The Hamilton Watch Company, proclaiming in quarter-page newspaper ads that "Hamilton is the watch of U.S. mail aviators," had arranged to present each pilot with a military aviation model Hamilton to carry aloft. (Fifty years later, Major Fleet would report that his watch still kept good time.)

* * *

May 15 dawned bright and clear in Washington, to the great relief of Captain Lipsner; the temperature would reach the mid-70s that day. But that disposed of only one of the officer's concerns. He would feel even better when he saw Major Fleet arrive at the Polo Grounds with that indispensable element, the mail plane. There was no backup craft, and through a sleepless night one of the thoughts that had haunted him was that he would have to say to Woodrow Wilson: "I'm sorry, Mr. President, but the plane didn't get in from Philadelphia — so you've wasted an hour of your valuable time."

Fleet came through, however. At 10:35 a.m., standing on the Polo Grounds by the strip of turf that served as a runway, Lipsner heard the welcome sound of an engine overhead, and shortly afterward Jenny 38262 touched down and rolled to a stop. The major greeted the captain, removed a map which he had strapped to his thigh for easy reference in the cockpit, spread it out on the fuselage and invited Lieutenant Boyle to go over the route with him. Then he helped strap the map to Boyle's leg.

**Major Reuben Fleet (left) and Lieutenant George L. Boyle examine the route map before Boyle's departure in the Jenny.**

The Polo Grounds was an oval field about 900 feet long, surrounded by trees, with a hangar at one end, a covered bandstand at the other and water on either side — not the ideal place for planes to land and take off. Major Fleet had personally improved it four days earlier by ordering mechanics to cut down a lone tree that had been blamed for causing a crash. Secretary of War Newton D. Baker asked him whether he knew that it was necessary to get Park Commission approval before removing a tree in Washington. "I told him," Fleet recalled, "the Park Commission had said it would take them three months to act, so I acted."

By now a crowd of several hundred people had gathered, and soon it was augmented by the arrival of the official party. At its head was President Wilson, his left hand bandaged because he had burned it at an Army tank demonstration when he inadvertently touched a hot exhaust pipe. Mrs. Wilson was there, too, along with Postmaster General Burleson and his wife, Secretary of the Navy Josephus Daniels, Senator Morris Sheppard, the derby-hatted Postmaster General Kamara of Japan, and several lesser officials, including a young assistant secretary of the Navy (and stamp collector) named Franklin Delano Roosevelt.

Into one of Boyle's four mail bags, alongside some 5,500 other letters destined for New York, Philadelphia and connecting points, President Wilson personally placed a special item. It was a letter of greeting from Burleson to Postmaster Thomas G. Patten of New York. The envelope bore what purported to be the first of the new stamps to be sold, purchased by the postmaster general himself, and indeed the stamp was from the lower left corner of the sheet, with the bottom selvage still attached.

**At Potomac Park May 15, 1918, from left, Otto Praeger, M.O. Chance, PMG Burleson and President Wilson.**

The original idea had been for President Wilson to initial the stamp, but ultimately it was decided to crowd onto the stamp's selvage the initials of six postal officials, including Burleson, Otto Praeger and A.M. Dockery, and have Wilson autograph the envelope. The curving

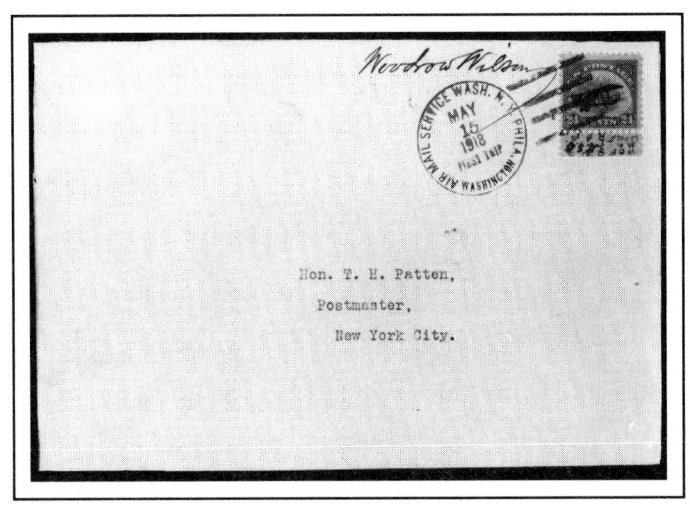


**First 24¢ Jenny to be sold adorns this cover autographed by President Wilson. Cover later sold for $1,000 to benefit Red Cross.**

flourish that ended his signature fell just short of the edge of the stamp. The special first-flight postmark completed the cover.

This collector's item was the inspiration of Noah W. Taussig of New York, president of the American Molasses Company and a stamp collector for half a century. Taussig on April 22 had written to the president to say that if he would create such a memento, Taussig would auction it off for the benefit of the American Red Cross, whose second nationwide war relief drive was scheduled to begin May 20. He would personally start the bidding at $1,000, Taussig said. *

The bags were stowed aboard. Boyle accepted a bouquet of red roses and a kiss from his fiancee, Margaret McChord, then climbed into the cockpit and hit the switch ("Contact!") as the ground crew pulled the wooden propeller through a half-turn.

Then ensued what could well be called the Great Gasoline Fiasco.

The engine failed to start.

Four times the ritual was repeated, with the same result.

Lipsner directed his mechanic to clean the spark plugs. They were clean. He personally examined the fuel gauge. It registered full.

Minutes ticked away. Lipsner, his nighttime fears of disaster coming true, heard the president behind him saying to Mrs. Wilson: "We're losing a lot of valuable time here."

Then a thought struck the officer. The gas gauge was made to read

**Lieutenant George L. Boyle lifts off from the Polo Grounds on the ill-fated first airmail flight May 15, 1918.**

* — The auction was held at the Collectors Club in New York June 11, 1918, by J.C. Morgenthau. To Taussig's disappointment no one topped his opening bid, and he obtained the cover for $1,000. In 1977 the Taussig family donated the item to the National Philatelic Collection at the Smithsonian Institution.

in level flight, but on the ground the plane sat at an angle. He ordered a dipstick inserted into the tank. It showed nearly empty.

No one had fueled the plane upon its arrival from Philadelphia. Even more dismaying, there was no aviation gasoline readily available.

However, there were other planes parked at the field, and fuel was siphoned from them and poured into the Jenny's tanks. On the next try the Hisso engine roared to life. The crowd cheered. The president smiled. Boyle taxied out a short distance, turned into the wind and took off, barely clearing the trees at the end of the runway. It was 11:46 a.m. *

The dignitaries got into their cars and other onlookers began to disperse, but Lipsner, as he told it, stood watching Boyle's plane as it climbed into the sky.

"I watched him for some minutes trying to figure out what he was doing," the captain recalled. "Finally I realized that he was taking a course that was almost opposite to the one he had been instructed to fly.

"The first scheduled air mail was in the air — but it was flying in the wrong direction."

* * *

Captain Lipsner returned to his office with a feeling of frustration, tempered by the hope that somehow the rookie pilot would get himself turned around. The first telephone call received at headquarters brought good news.

* — Who was responsible for the Great Gasoline Fiasco? Major Fleet was quite sure he knew: It was Captain Lipsner.

In a written report three days later to the chief of the Air Service Division, Fleet asserted that Lipsner had personally assured him May 8 after a tour of the three landing fields that 1,000 gallons of gasoline and 300 gallons of oil would be on hand at each field May 10. Nevertheless, there was no gasoline at the Polo Grounds, just as there had been no oil at Bustleton.

Years later, Fleet brought up the subject again, telling a 1966 convention of the Air Mail Pioneers that Lipsner had "failed in his mission" to have aviation gasoline at the Polo Grounds as instructed. Twice in the speech Fleet noted that Lipsner was "not a pilot"; the sniff of condescension is almost audible.

Lipsner, in his own book published in 1951, didn't address the question of who was to blame for the lack of gasoline, but Fleet's speech sent him into a fury. By now, of course, both were old men looking back on their great moments with vision distorted — as we have already seen — by time and vanity. Lipsner's personal copy of a reprint of the Fleet speech is heavily annotated with angry comments. "A tissue of lies!" he scribbled at the top. Virtually every assertion in the text is challenged with such interjections as "not true," "bunk," "this is absolutely false" and "ha! ha!" Over Fleet's statement that he had directed Lipsner to have fuel available, Lipsner wrote in block letters: "He never did. Fleet was NOT my superior." Technically this was true; Lipsner, although he was outranked by Fleet, was on temporary assignment to the Post Office Department. "Fleet the ferry pilot came in 38262 from Phila empty of gas," Lipsner added. Alongside the major's account of his forced landings of May 14, Lipsner wrote triumphantly: "Fleet got lost."

**Captain Benjamin B. Lipsner, who as a civilian would become first superintendent of Aerial Mail Service.**

Lieutenant Torrey Webb, one-time mining student at Columbia University and now a reluctant mailman (he wanted to fight Germans instead), had departed from Belmont Park on schedule, a gift horseshoe from a well-wisher nailed to his plane. His two bags contained 2,457 pieces of mail, including a letter to President Wilson from Governor Charles S. Whitman pledging New York's support for the Red Cross fund drive. Webb arrived at Bustleton at 12:30 p.m. The mail for Washington was transferred to the waiting plane and six minutes later Lieutenant Edgerton took off.

No call came reporting Boyle's arrival in Philadelphia, however. Instead Boyle himself called, from the town of Waldorf, Maryland, barely 20 miles from his takeoff point, and almost due south. His Jenny, No. 38262, the plane on the stamp, was lying in a field — upside down.

It was an extraordinary case of life imitating art.

How Boyle ended up in that unlikely spot and ignominious position he attempted to explain later on his pilot's daily report form:

**At Belmont Park, New York Postmaster Thomas G. Patten hands the mailbag to Lieutenant Torrey Webb.**

**Lieutenant Torrey Webb takes off from Belmont Park infield in the Jenny 38278, headed for Philadelphia.**

"In leaving Washington relied on compass and veered from proper course. When aware of this fact landed near farm house to ascertain position. Here three people gave their different ideas of direction but said I was 35 or 40 miles *South West* of Washington. Unable to rely on this information and not confident of compass, I took off and landed near Waldorf Md. Purpose was to ascertain from Post Office my real position. Landed in good looking large field. Field was soft however and machine nosed over after having made good landing, slightly tail low. Propeller and (blank space) were broken. Otherwise ship O.K. Reported by phone immediately to Major Fleet and started with mail to Wash. by automobile. Machine repaired by mechanics sent from Wash. Took it back, and arrived Wash. 8:05 P.M."

PILOT'S DAILY REPORT.

Plane No. 38262 Date 5-15-18
Temp. 70°
Weather Fair
Condition of field good 2nd Lt. G. L. Boyle (Pilot) A.S.S.R.C.

| | TRIP. | | TIME. | |
|---|---|---|---|---|
| | From— | To— | Started. | Landed. |
| 1 | N.Y.<br>Phila. | Phila.<br>N.Y. | | |
| 2 | Phila.<br>Wash. | Wash.<br>Phila. | 11.45 AM. | 8.05 P.M. |

Mark "X" after any of the following questions NOT found O. K.
Does engine lack power?
Does engine hesitate when accelerating?
Does engine misfire?
Any leaks? Gas Oil Water
Does carbureter spit?
(a) In normal flight?
(b) In accelerating?
Any tendency to turn? Right Left
Is balance correct? Slightly nose heavy
Water temperature normal? Yes
Any excessive vibration?
Any strange noise?
Are instruments recording?
Landing gear Tires Skids
Structural parts? Fuselage Wings

Note.—Use other side for forced landings, time lost, causes of delay, remarks, etc.

2209

Remarks:
In leaving Washington relied on compass and veered from proper course. When aware of this fact landed near farm house to ascertain position. Here three people gave their different ideas of direction but said I was 35 or 40 miles south West of Washington. Unable to rely on this information and not confident of compass I took off and landed near Waldorf Md. Purpose was to ascertain from Post office my real position. Landed in good looking large field. Field was soft however and machine nosed over after having made good landing, slightly tail low. Propeller and were broken. Otherwise ship O.K. Reported by phone immediately to Major Fleet and started with mail to Wash. by automobile. Machine repaired by mechanics sent from Wash. Took it back, and arrived Wash. 8:05 PM.

**Lieutenant George L. Boyle's May 15 pilot's report describes how he lost his way after leaving Washington, D.C.**

Fleet elaborated on the damage in his own summary report May 18: "He broke his propeller in landing, and turned the ship over on its back, breaking also the cabane struts." By coincidence, the field where Jenny 38262's maiden flight came to an end was near the country residence of Otto Praeger.

The local weekly newspaper provided its own arch account of Boyle's misadventure under the headline "Air Craft Loses Way":

". . . Instead of bearing northward, the craft came south, and finding he was lost, its pilot made his first landing on the Griswald farm, near Pomfret. Not succeeding in being properly directed, the aviator soon arose and made a short flight to Waldorf. Doubtless mistaking the latter city for that of New York, he made his second landing, this time breaking his propeller, which kept him on earth until aid could be procured."

Some later accounts had it that Boyle had followed the wrong railroad tracks out of Washington, but Boyle himself didn't make that claim, and Postmaster General Burleson's own explanation agreed with the young pilot's — that he was confused by "the vibration and spinning of the plane's compass."

As soon as Washington heard of Boyle's accident, word was flashed to Lieutenant Culver, who was waiting in Philadelphia to relay the Washington mail north to New York (and doubtless casting frequent glances at his new Hamilton watch). Culver promptly took off at 2:20 p.m., carrying 350 letters that had originated in Philadelphia. By this time Edgerton, flying south, was almost to the capital; he landed in

Potomac Park at 2:50, some 20 minutes behind schedule, but close enough to please postal officials, and was greeted by his mother and younger sister Elizabeth, who presented him with the inevitable bouquet of roses.

**Lieutenant James C. Edgerton receives roses from his sister after bringing first airmail to Washington May 15.**

A waiting truck rushed his mail bags to the city post office, where 190 Boy Scouts stood by to distribute the mail throughout Washington; they reportedly completed the job in 33 minutes. President Wilson got his letter from Governor Whitman, plus 18 other items delivered to him at the White House.

And what of the 140 pounds of mail that went astray with Lieutenant Boyle? After it was returned by car to Washington, there was some discussion of sending it north by train. A few accounts — including Lipsner's memoir — erroneously assert that this is what was done. In fact, however, it was decided that the mail should be held for the next day's air trip because of the "souvenir nature" of much of it. No doubt postal officials were thinking particularly hard of that letter which the president had autographed for the benefit of the Red Cross, and how inappropriate it would be to put it on an old-fashioned mail train.

Lieutenant Edgerton, who made the flight north from Washington the next morning, was emphatic afterward in saying that he had taken both the May 15 and May 16 mail with him, and this is borne out by the fact that all covers postmarked in Washington May 15 bear May 16 backstamps from Philadelphia or New York. *

Back in Waldorf, mechanics arrived later on Wednesday and fixed Lieutenant Boyle's propeller. "As soon as this was finished," the local weekly reported, "the modern mail carrier ascended again on his flight. In the meantime about 600 people had gathered around Waldorf to witness the proceedings, and as the plane gracefully arose above them, a mighty cheer went up." It was, the paper explained, for "many Charles Countians . . . their first close observation of a modern aeroplane."

In Washington, where Lieutenant Boyle returned with Jenny 38262, the enthusiasm was more restrained. He was treated sympathetically by the daily press, however. No reporter referred to him as "Wrong Way Boyle," or even pointed out that when he aborted his brief flight he was south of the capital instead of north. At least two newspapers even declared that his propeller had somehow broken while he was in flight, and that is why he had to land.

Two days later Boyle tried once more to carry the mail from Washington to Philadelphia in Jenny 38262. This time Lieutenant Edgerton escorted him north in another plane to the vicinity of Baltimore. "Lieutenant Boyle waved OK," Edgerton wrote on his pilot's daily report, "and was headed on correct course when I last saw him."

Once on his own, though, Boyle again became hopelessly disoriented. He finally landed at 2:45 p.m. on Cape Charles, Virginia, some 125 miles south of Washington, near the mouth of Chesapeake Bay. All that stopped him from going further, as Major Fleet put it, were "the Atlantic Ocean and lack of gas."

Boyle found fuel, got his bearings and took to the air again. This time he made it almost to the airport at Bustleton at dusk before he ran out of gas again and crash-landed on the grounds of the Philadelphia Country Club, hitting a fence and breaking both right wings, the left lower wing, landing gear, center section and various struts and wires.

To reporters he explained that his problem after leaving Washington was "fleecy, heavy clouds" that hid the earth from view. (Lieutenant Edgerton's own report on his escort mission described the weather as "clear" and visibility as "very good.") Again the press was sympathetic.

* — Thus both May 15 and May 16 airmail out of Washington qualifies as "first flight" mail. In fact, on a handful of May 16 covers the postmark was applied with the "First Trip" legend, before someone at the post office took note and removed it. These few covers have an added value to collectors.

**Unhappy ending of Lieutenant Boyle's second flight May 17 in Jenny 38262 — wrecked on grounds of Philadelphia Country Club.**

PILOT'S DAILY REPORT.

Plane No. 38274 Date May 17, 1918
Temp. ..........
Weather Fair
Condition of field Good Lt J C Edgerton (Pilot)

| | TRIP. | | TIME. | |
|---|---|---|---|---|
| | From— | To— | Started | Landed |
| 1 | ~~N. Y.~~ | ~~Phila.~~ | | |
| | ~~Phila.~~ | N. Y. | | |
| 2 | ~~Phila.~~ | Wash. | | |
| | Wash. | ~~Phila.~~ Baltimore | 11.30 a m | 12.15 p m |

Mark "X" after any of the following questions NOT found O. K.
Does engine lack power? ..........
Does engine hesitate when accelerating? ..........
Does engine misfire? ..........
Any leaks? Gas .......... Oil .......... Water ..........
Does carbureter spit? ..........
(a) In normal flight? ..........
(b) In accelerating? ..........
Any tendency to turn? Right .......... Left X
Is balance correct? ..........
Water temperature normal? ..........
Any excessive vibration? ..........
Any strange noise? ..........
Are instruments recording? ..........
Landing gear .......... Tires .......... Skids ..........
Structural parts? .......... Fuselage .......... Wings ..........

Note.—Use other side for forced landings, time lost, causes of delay, remarks, etc.
2209

Remarks: Left field Potomac Park at 11.30 with Lt Boyle, accompanying him to within ten miles of a point on course opposite Baltimore. Left field at elevation of 3000'. Left Boyle at 7000'. An Offshore breeze blowing. Corrected course ten degrees to west of north.
Altitude — 7000'
Wind — Offshore
visibility — very good
Compass Course 330°
Weather — Clear
Lt Boyle waved O K and was headed on correct course when I last saw him.

**Lieutenant Edgerton's report tells of escorting Lieutenant Boyle as far as Baltimore May 17. Boyle then lost his way again.**

"Lt. Boyle was thrown from his machine when he crashed but was uninjured," said the *Philadelphia Bulletin.* "He manifested a laudable devotion to duty by leaping to the fuselage . . . dragging out the mail sacks . . . and impressing a motorist from the club to rush them to the postal employees at the Bustleton fields."

Fleet, in his own summary report the next day, took pains to point out that he had had "no voice in the selection of this pilot for this service, this officer being ordered to report to Washington for this duty by the Office of the Chief Signal Officer." He "could not have been chosen because of his ability as a flyer," Fleet added tartly, "as the records of the Air Service Division show that he has had less than 60 hours of flying," and he had now broken two airplanes, one of them "so badly damaged that it will undoubtedly have to be rebuilt." As a matter of fact, it was the same airplane that Boyle had broken twice, poor 38262; a review of the daily reports filed by the pilots shows that it wasn't repaired after its second accident and returned to service until July 10.

The conclusion had been reached, Major Fleet wrote in his report, "that the best interests of the service require that Lt. Boyle be relieved from this duty, and he has been relieved and directed to report to the Chief of the Air Service Division for assignment to other duty."

Two days later a memorandum went out from the office of the chief of Air Service to his Personnel Section, quoting Fleet's report and concluding: "It is requested that you furnish this office any information you have showing why Lieut. Boyle was detailed on this work." It would be fascinating to read the reply; unfortunately, that document cannot be found.

Little could be discovered about the later career of this unlucky aviation pioneer. After leaving the Army he married Margaret, fathered a daughter and practiced law for a few years in Washington, with offices for a brief time in the Southern Building, only a half block from the Hibbs Building, where William Robey worked. Later he and Margaret separated, and he died at a young age, around 1935.

George Boyle wasn't the only pilot to have problems that first week, however. Lieutenant Stephen Bonsal Jr., flying from New York to Philadelphia May 16, the second day of operations, lost his way in a fog and landed in Bridgeton, New Jersey. His mail got to Washington at 8:42 p.m., some six hours behind schedule. As was done at Bustleton two days earlier, the Polo Grounds was illuminated by the headlights of borrowed automobiles to help guide the pilot coming in from Philadelphia (it was Lieutenant Edgerton, making his second flight of the day).

Major Fleet in later years took a more tolerant view of such incidents. "Pilots of this early day," he said, "had to have a natural sense to fly between given points at a designated hour irrespective of weather. We should, therefore, not criticize Lieutenant Boyle too severely for his failures. He simply lacked enough training to do the job."

The other "political" appointee to the aviator corps gave no cause for complaint, however. Lieutenant Edgerton, 22, was clearly the star of the group. He made 52 trips during the time the Army flew the mail, covered 7,155 miles and logged 106½ hours of flight time, far more than any of the other original pilots, and he was the only one to get an "excellent" rating at the end of his tour. From the first day his pilot's daily reports, unlike those of the other flyers, carried meticulous descriptions of flying conditions: altitude, weather, turbulence, clouds, visibility, wind, compass course and drift allowance. In December 1918, as a civilian, he was made chief of flying operations for the Post Office Department.

From those first days of mixed success, the airmail evolved into a permanent and expanding institution. It did not remain a joint operation for long, however. The Post Office quickly became disenchanted with what it considered an excessive reluctance on the part of the Army pilots to fly in bad weather. Colonel E.A. Deeds, the chief signal officer, had "assured us," Otto Praeger complained after a month, "that the mail routes would be flown daily, rain or shine. He agreed that it would not be a pink tea flying affair . . . and that the Post Office Department need not give itself concern on that score."

Yet the Army had defaulted on 15 percent of its flights, Praeger went on, "because its aviators reported that the weather conditions more or less seriously affected the visibility of its fliers . . . Unless we can eliminate almost entirely the weather delays, the public will not place sufficient confidence in the service to use it for commercial purposes."

The upshot was an amicable separation, on August 12, with the Post Office taking over operations and flying with its own support team, planes and pilots — more intrepid fellows, in Praeger's view, willing to fly in storms or fog. Among the nine planes turned over to the Post Office — five Jennies and four R-4s — was 38262, back in service after recovering from the effects of George Boyle's second crash landing.

At the Post Office's request, Ben Lipsner was allowed to resign from the Army to become the first civilian superintendent of Aerial Mail Service. He held that post only until December, however, when he quit in a dispute with Praeger over hiring, aircraft procurement and other issues.

After the Post Office took over the service, the number of aborted missions due to weather dropped sharply, and at the end of one year the department was able to report an overall flights-attempted rate of 95.6 percent. The safety record continued to be good; no pilot died carrying the mail that first year, although on the ground one mechanic was killed by a propeller at Belmont Park.

On the first anniversary of the service all six original Jennies were still at work. In fact, on that date, May 15, 1919, No. 38262 (now designated No. 10 under a new numbering system) carried the mail out of Washington's new terminal at College Park, Maryland, as it had done from the Polo Grounds a year earlier when George Boyle was at the controls. *

The airmail safety record disintegrated, however, when in the second year service was extended from New York west to Cleveland and Chicago, and pilots began flying over the treacherous Alleghenies. The Curtiss R-4s and DeHavilland 4s were bigger and tougher than the Jennies, but they were far from foolproof, and the combination of imperfect aircraft, mountainous terrain and unpredictable weather began to take its toll. Between October 1919 and July 1921, 26 airmail service employees died in crashes, an average of more than one a month.

Nevertheless, the department and its courageous pilots pushed on, ever extending their reach. In July 1924, little more than six years after that shaky beginning at Washington's Polo Grounds, the first planes took off from New York and San Francisco to inaugurate transcontinental round-the-clock service, following routes marked with great beacons 25 miles apart that blazed a path through the night. The airmail was here to stay.

* — Where are those Jennies today? Alas, gone without a trace. Nowadays the National Air and Space Museum pounces on planes and space capsules that have historic significance, but when airmail was in its infancy no one had such foresight.

Chapter Seven

# The Sale

*"I will take your sheet . . . for $15,000."*

**— Eugene Klein**

As the four Army pilots struggled with varying success Wednesday, May 15, to keep their mail planes on course, William Robey was confronting the problem of how best to dispose of the treasure that had fallen into his hands.

Two things weighed on his mind. The first was the persistence of the postal inspectors. He was visited Wednesday by another inspector, he told Mal Ganser. The official announced that he had been sent by Postmaster General Burleson himself, and that unless Robey turned over the inverts, "the government will void them for postal use." If that was indeed the threat, it was a curiously weak one, but even so the government's tenacity was getting oppressive.

His other, more practical concern was the matter he had discussed with his friends at Hamilton Colman's on Tuesday — the possibility that other sheets of inverts would turn up, diminishing the value of his own. If the Jenny stamps had in fact been printed in sheets of 400, as Robey believed, then three other panes had to be out there somewhere, perhaps already in collectors' hands.

So it behooved him to sell the sheet quickly. At the same time, though, he wanted to make sure he got the highest price possible. Colman's $500 offer of the day before didn't fit that description.

Early Wednesday Robey dashed off a letter to Elliott Perry in Westfield; it went out with an 8 a.m. Washington postmark. "Did you receive my telegram?" Robey wrote. "I have secured a sheet of 100 with inverted center, the only one in existence at this date. Are you interested. Yours very truly, W.T. Robey."

Although Robey knew — if anyone did — that an Army plane was scheduled to take off from Washington that morning with mail

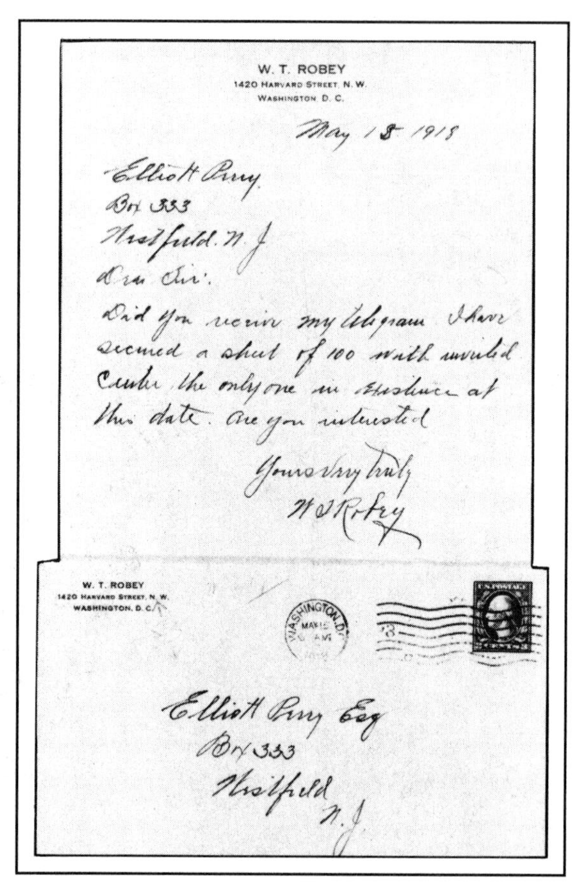
W. T. ROBEY
1420 Harvard Street, N. W.
Washington D. C.

May 15 1918

Elliott Perry
Box 333
Westfield N. J

Dear Sir:
Did you receive my telegram I have secured a sheet of 100 with inverted Center the only one in existence at this date. Are you interested

Yours Very truly
W T Robey

W. T. ROBEY
1420 Harvard Street, N. W.
Washington, D. C.

Elliott Perry Esq
Box 333
Westfield
N. J.

**William Robey's May 15 letter to Elliott Perry telling him of discovery of the 24¢ Jenny inverts.**

for New York, he chose to send the letter by first-class mail with an ordinary 3¢ stamp. That turned out to be a wise choice, of course; had he put a Jenny stamp on it instead, his letter would have ended up with Woodrow Wilson's cover and his own first-flight covers in Waldorf, Maryland, that afternoon, and not reached New York until the next day.

Instead, it got the swift handling routinely administered to mail of that era, was taken north by train, sorted at the main post office on New York's Eighth Avenue, routed by truck to New Jersey and delivered to Perry's home in Westfield shortly after 6 p.m., just as the dealer was leaving for a dinner party.

When Perry returned home he tried to telephone Robey at 10:30 p.m. He couldn't reach him, but was successful on another try after

11. At some point — perhaps before he made a decision to phone Robey — he penciled on the back of Robey's letter a draft of a reply:

"Yes am interested in sheet of inverts and would like you to forward it on approval at once, stating net price for all or any part. Will give you an immediate answer." These sentences are scratched out and the notation added: "Not sent."

Perry's understanding of their telephone discussion is recorded in a letter which he wrote Robey the next day, May 16:

"As a result of this conversation and of the fact that I was the first to answer your inquiry, and for other considerations of value, it is understood between us that you are not to dispose of the sheet, or of any part of it, without first affording me an opportunity to purchase, and that if I will pay an amount equal to the highest bona fide offer which you receive or obtain up to 11:30 p.m. Wednesday, May 22, 1918, you are to sell me the sheet.

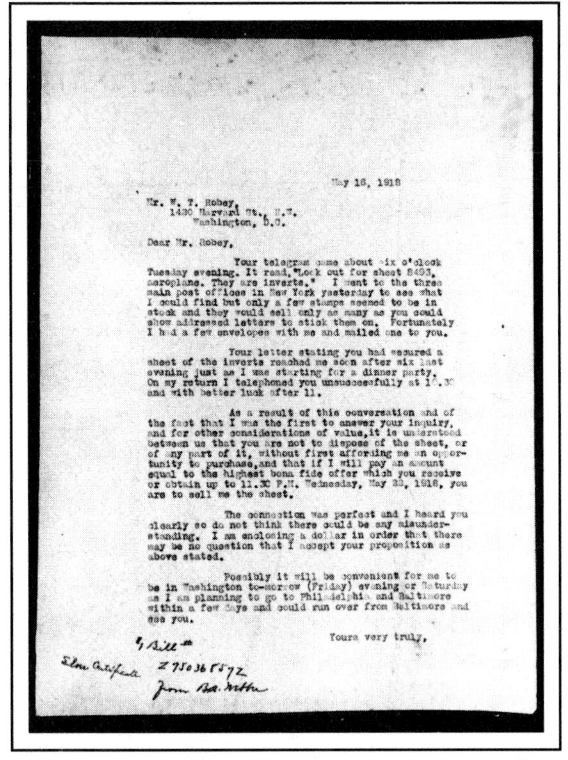

May 16, 1918

Mr. W. T. Robey,
1430 Harvard St., N.W.
Washington, D.C.

Dear Mr. Robey,

Your telegram came about six o'clock Tuesday evening. It read, "Look out for sheet 8493, aeroplane. They are inverts." I went to the three main post offices in New York yesterday to see what I could find but only a few stamps seemed to be in stock and they would sell only as many as you could show addressed letters to stick them on. Fortunately I had a few envelopes with me and mailed one to you.

Your letter stating you had secured a sheet of the inverts reached me soon after six last evening just as I was starting for a dinner party. On my return I telephoned you unsuccessfully at 10.30 and with better luck after 11.

As a result of this conversation and of the fact that I was the first to answer your inquiry, and for other considerations of value, it is understood between us that you are not to dispose of the sheet, or of any part of it, without first affording me an opportunity to purchase, and that if I will pay an amount equal to the highest bona fide offer which you receive or obtain up to 11.30 P.M. Wednesday, May 22, 1918, you are to sell me the sheet.

The connection was perfect and I heard you clearly so do not think there could be any misunderstanding. I am enclosing a dollar in order that there may be no question that I accept your proposition as above stated.

Possibly it will be convenient for me to be in Washington to-morrow (Friday) evening or Saturday as I am planning to go to Philadelphia and Baltimore within a few days and could run over from Baltimore and see you.

Yours very truly,

**Perry's May 16 reply to Robey's telegram and letter, asking for an option to purchase the sheet of inverts.**

"The connection was perfect and I heard you clearly so do not think there could be any misunderstanding. I am enclosing a dollar in order that there may be no question that I accept your proposition as above stated."

Even in pre-inflation 1918 a dollar was an extremely modest deposit to make on an item with the potential value of Robey's sheet of inverts. Still, Perry was serious enough about it to note in ink in the lower left corner of his carbon copy the serial number — 2750368572 — of the silver certificate he had enclosed.

"Possibly it will be convenient for me to be in Washington to-morrow (Friday) evening or Saturday as I am planning to go to Philadelphia and Baltimore within a few days and could run over from Baltimore and see you," Perry concluded.

In fact, Robey would see Perry personally in New York before he would receive this letter and its enclosure. Meanwhile, at some point Wednesday he received a reply to his telegram to Percy Mann in Philadelphia, saying that Mann was coming to Washington and would call on Robey the next evening.

When Mann arrived, he examined the sheet and told Robey he was prepared to offer him $10,000 for it. But Robey had been doing some thinking, and he told Mann he had decided to head for New York that weekend and personally seek a buyer there. He agreed to notify Mann by telegraph or telephone, however, if anyone in New York equaled or bettered his offer, so that Mann could consider making another bid.

(Mann duly noted the find, as requested, in his column in the next issue of *Mekeel's*, dated May 25. "We have seen the sheet of inverts," he wrote. He accurately noted that they were printed by plates of 100 subjects, but then reported erroneously that "investigation by the postal authorities discloses . . . that this is the only sheet printed with the center inverted." It was Mann's last column for the magazine; he was replaced by Philip Ward, and later that year he became editor of a brand-new monthly, *Hobbies*.)

Robey left for New York by train with his stamps on Friday afternoon, May 17, presumably after putting in his regular day at work, and arrived about 9 p.m. Awaiting him at the Hotel McAlpin were Percy Doane, a well-known New York dealer and auctioneer, and Elliott Perry. His own fame had preceded him, as Robey put it in his 1938 memoir, and Doane and Perry wanted to see the sheet. They asked if he had received any offers, and Robey told them about Percy Mann's $10,000 bid.

Curiously, this is Robey's only reference to Elliott Perry in any of his published accounts. He says nothing about his telegram of May

14, his letter of May 15, the telephone conversation that evening, or his later contacts with the New Jersey dealer. Nor does he mention the telegram which Caroline Robey sent on her husband's behalf to Perry at 5:20 p.m. Friday, probably about the time Robey was leaving for New York. "Mr. Robey will be at Hotel McAlpin New York tomorrow," the wire said. It was sent to Perry c/o Western Union in Philadelphia, where it was marked received at 5:48 p.m. Whether Perry was in Philadelphia that afternoon — before he was to meet Robey later that evening at the hotel in New York — and if so how Robey knew it is unknown. In any case, Perry obtained the telegram eventually if not immediately, and put it in his files.

"Bright and early the next morning," Robey wrote, he set forth with his stamps to seek a buyer. His first stop on this Saturday was the office of the famous millionaire and stamp collector, Colonel Edward H.R. Green, at 111 Broadway. Within a few days Green was destined to purchase the sheet, but not from Robey; he was out of town when Robey called, and the colonel and the cashier never met.

Robey next visited Stanley Gibbons Ltd. at 198 Broadway, managed by Eustace B. Power, a man who, Robey wrote in 1938, "has frequently condemned all Twentieth Century issues of stamps." This was hardly accurate; Eustace Power, known affectionately to his friends as "Useless," was an authority on 20th century U.S. stamps, and the author of a respected reference book about them.

"At that time Mr. Power was a great humorist," Robey went on. "Imagine him offering $250 for $24 face value of 'Twentieth Century trash.' He also stated that he knew of three other sheets of these stamps and was negotiating for the purchase of same at that time. Wonder why he never bought them?"

Robey then went to the Scott Stamp and Coin Company, but the best he could get there was an offer to sell the sheet on commission.

"Feeling rather low and disgusted with my failure to secure a decent offer for the sheet," Robey wrote, "I returned to my hotel and found waiting for me Mr. John J. Klemann (of the Nassau Stamp Company), who after examining the sheet offered me $2,500 for it. When I told him that I had already refused $10,000 . . . he stated that I was crazy and anyone offering such a price was also crazy."

That evening Robey telephoned Percy Mann in Philadelphia and told him he was returning to Washington the next day, Sunday. Mann's offer of $10,000 hadn't been matched, he told him, but he had decided not to sell the sheet at that time. He didn't explain, in his memoir, why he had come to that decision; it may simply have been his frustration speaking. Mann asked him to stop off in Philadelphia and talk with him further, and Robey agreed.

On Sunday, May 19, Mann met him at the Philadelphia station and took him to the home of Eugene Klein, the city's leading dealer and a major figure in American philately (along with Percy Doane, Eustace Power, John Klemann and others, he had served on the executive committee of the country's first international stamp exhibition, the New York show of 1913). Klein looked at the sheet and asked Robey to name a price. Robey said he wouldn't take less than $15,000; how he arrived at that figure is undisclosed. Klein consulted Mann and then asked Robey for an option at $15,000 until 3 p.m. the next day, Monday, May 20. Robey agreed, took his stamps and proceeded home to Washington.

The final letter from Robey in Elliott Perry's files was dated May 20. It was sent by registered mail (but, again, not by airmail) from the

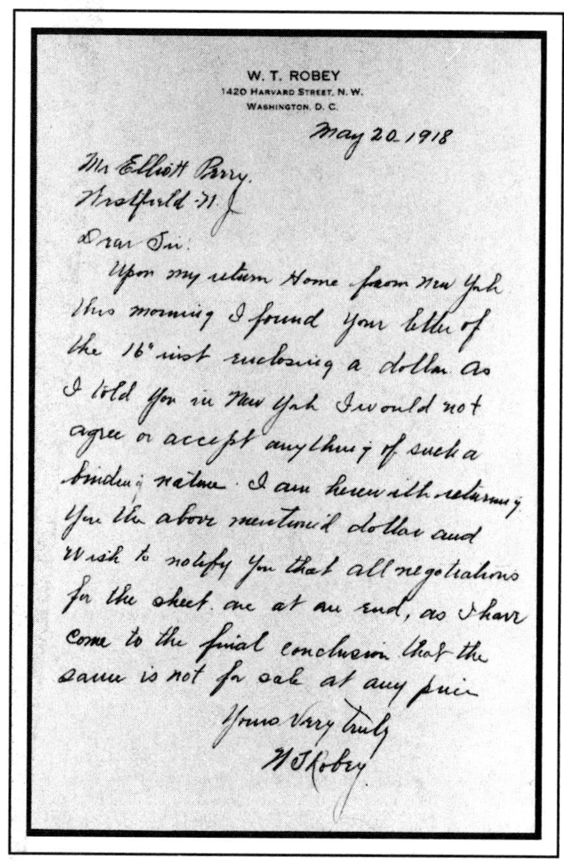

W. T. ROBEY
1420 HARVARD STREET, N. W.
WASHINGTON, D. C.

May 20 1918

Mr Elliott Perry.
Westfield N. J.

Dear Sir:

Upon my return Home from New York this morning I found your letter of the 16th inst enclosing a dollar as I told you in New York I would not agree or accept anything of such a binding nature. I am herewith returning you the above mentioned dollar and wish to notify you that all negotiations for the sheet are at an end, as I have come to the final conclusion that the same is not for sale at any price

Yours Very truly
W T Robey

**Robey's May 20 letter to Perry rejecting his request for an option and declaring that the sheet was not for sale.**

same New York Avenue branch post office where the inverts had been purchased. It read:

"Dear Sir: Upon my return home from New York this morning I found your letter of the 16th inst enclosing a dollar. As I told you in New York I would not agree or accept anything of such a binding nature. I am herewith returning you the above mentioned dollar and wish to notify you that all negotiations for the sheet are at an end, as I have come to the final conclusion that the same is not for sale at any price. Yours very truly, W.T. Robey."

Why Robey asserted that the sheet wasn't for sale at a time when Klein's option to buy was still in effect is a mystery. Perhaps, again, it was done out of frustration. Robey may have been regretting the fact that he hadn't demanded more than $15,000 from Klein. That morning he also received a telephone call at home from Hamilton Colman with an offer to buy the sheet for $18,000; he may already have received that call when he wrote his letter to Perry. That bid from Colman was exactly 36 times what the Washington dealer had offered only six days earlier. But Robey had to say no. "I told him that I had given Mr. Klein an option on it until 3 p.m. and if he did not exercise same by that time I would get in touch with him," Robey recalled. But shortly before the deadline the call from Klein came. Yes, he would buy the sheet at the agreed-on price, and would Robey deliver it to him as soon as possible?

Either Robey later incorrectly remembered the expiration time for the option, or there was a second telephone conversation that Monday afternoon, for Caroline Robey's scrapbook contains a special delivery registered letter from Klein to Robey dated May 20, "confirming our telephone conversation at 4:30 p.m." (not 3 p.m.) and continuing: "I will take your sheet of inverted center 24¢ airplane stamps for $15,000, which you agreed to deliver at my office tomorrow. I am looking forward to your arrival at about noontime, tomorrow, as stated. Very truly yours, Eugene Klein."

Robey was accompanied to Philadelphia by his father-in-law, Mr. Scott, according to an interview Caroline Robey gave many years later. "They didn't want to attract attention, so the stamps were carried in a shoebox," she said. The fastidious collector will shudder at the thought. As Robey's daughter, Louise Birch, remembered hearing the story, the shoebox, with the stamps "very carefully rolled and inserted," was carried by Scott, while Robey carried an empty briefcase as a decoy. As far as we know, Robey had resorted to no such subterfuge when he took the stamps to New York the preceding week; still, a little paranoia at this point is probably forgivable, with the payoff, as it was, virtually in sight. "They didn't know who might be ready to snatch

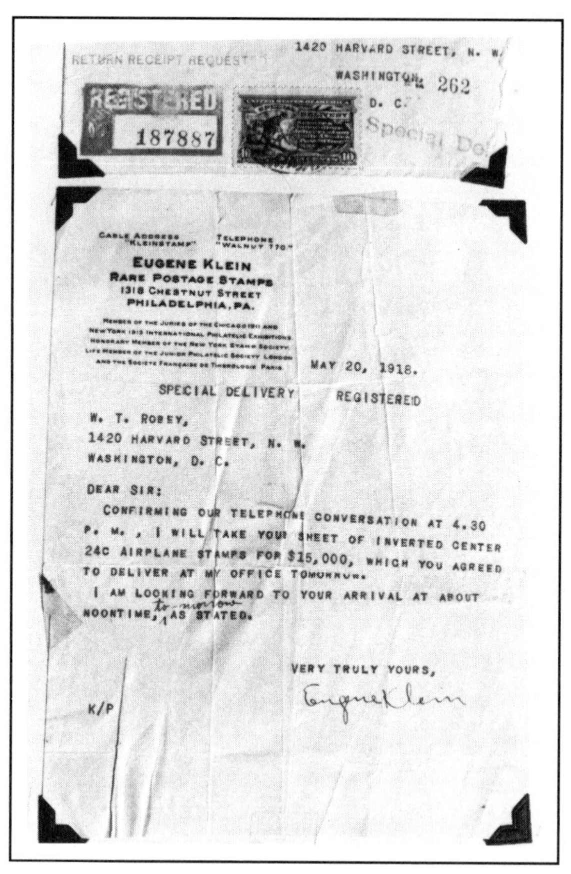

RETURN RECEIPT REQUESTED

REGISTERED 187887

1420 HARVARD STREET, N. W.
WASHINGTON, D. C.

Special Del

CABLE ADDRESS "KLEINSTAMP" TELEPHONE "WALNUT 770"

EUGENE KLEIN
RARE POSTAGE STAMPS
1318 CHESTNUT STREET
PHILADELPHIA, PA.

MAY 20, 1918.

SPECIAL DELIVERY REGISTERED

W. T. ROBEY,
1420 HARVARD STREET, N. W.
WASHINGTON, D. C.

DEAR SIR:

CONFIRMING OUR TELEPHONE CONVERSATION AT 4.30 P. M., I WILL TAKE YOUR SHEET OF INVERTED CENTER 24C AIRPLANE STAMPS FOR $15,000, WHICH YOU AGREED TO DELIVER AT MY OFFICE TOMORROW.

I AM LOOKING FORWARD TO YOUR ARRIVAL AT ABOUT NOONTIME, to-morrow AS STATED.

VERY TRULY YOURS,

Eugene Klein

K/P

**Eugene Klein's May 20 letter to Robey exercising his option to buy the sheet of 24¢ Jenny inverts for $15,000.**

the stamps," Mrs. Birch explained. "The postal inspectors had told him they were going to get them back."

"Promptly at noon," Robey himself wrote, "the sheet was delivered to Mr. Klein at his office in Philadelphia, receiving a certified check in payment. Thus, within one week, stamps that originally cost $24 were sold for a profit of $14,976." Individual Jenny stamps and blocks, as we shall see, would be sold and resold at ever higher prices through the years that followed, but never again would a seller come close to realizing the 62,400 percent profit which William Thomas Robey collected on the first investment.

Henry M. Goodkind, in his 1956 study of the Jenny inverts, related an anecdote about the sale which he heard from Klein's daughter, the late Mrs. Jay (Dolores) Hertz of New York. It was, Goodkind wrote, a story "she said her father often told her when remembering his famous 1918 purchase."

"Robey came into Klein's office carrying a briefcase that contained his sheet," the writer continued. "After Klein had agreed to purchase the sheet and was preparing to make payment, Robey took his sheet out of the briefcase. But Mr. Klein, careful to keep this valuable sheet from damage and not having anything before him for this purpose, asked Robey to return the sheet to his briefcase and turn over the whole thing to him. Robey balked. He asked for extra payment for his briefcase, which was described as neither new nor in good condition. Robey asked Klein for $20 or $30 extra for his briefcase. Mrs. Hertz recalls her father later often laughing about this episode, when he thought back to this $15,000 transaction in 1918 with the seller demanding a few dollars more for his second-hand briefcase."

Robey's daughter Louise Birch said that her mother resented this story when it was published and called it inconsistent with her husband's character. (Goodkind didn't interview Mrs. Robey or Mrs. Birch, and only mentioned in a footnote that he had been told that Robey's widow was alive and living in Baltimore.)

The story sounds like one Eugene Klein would have enjoyed telling, but it is anybody's guess what truth there was in it. It could have stemmed from a joking exchange between the two men. One must say that it would be surprising if Klein, long experienced in stamp transactions, and waiting in his office to receive a prize of this magnitude, would have had no secure container set aside to hold it.

Klein and Robey must have stayed in touch, at least for a while, because when the second Jenny airmail stamp was issued in July in the new 16¢ rate, Robey sent a first-flight cover addressed to himself in care of Klein in Philadelphia.

As for Elliott Perry, he continued to regret the one that got away. A letter he received from Harry L. Lindquist, publisher of *Stamps* magazine, dated October 9, 1933, contains this paragraph: "I did not know you had any part in that 24¢ air mail invert find and it certainly was unfortunate that Ackerman did not fall for it as there was a beautiful chance to make a clean-up. However, I doubt if he would have been as liberal with you as Green was with Klein." Ackerman was U.S. Representative Ernest R. Ackerman, Republican, resident of Perry's hometown of Westfield and one-time acting governor of New Jersey. He apparently had been Perry's candidate to put up the money to buy the sheet from Robey. (When Ackerman died in 1931 he left a prodigious collection of stamps and proofs — including a block of four Jenny inverts.)

Perry replied October 10: "My connection with the matter was before

Robey went to Philadelphia and closed the deal there. I have always had a feeling that if I had shoved $11,000 under his nose that night in New York he would have grabbed it. He did not talk to me as tho anyone in New York had offered $12,000 — he seemed to be disgusted because nobody seemed to think the sheet was so wonderful as he did. They all expected there would be plenty more.

"I am quite confident E.R.A. often tried to be generous with me and occasionally he succeeded. But he was so suspicious that whenever he got scared — and that was often — he'd be likely to do some fool thing that would make it hard for me . . ."

In a letter to Harry L. Jefferys of Ardmore, Pennsylvania, December 29, 1943, Perry added another detail. "Robey had been a customer of mine and had not been collecting long," he wrote. "When he got the sheet he notified five people including myself and I was the first to answer. All he wanted was $50,000 for the sheet. I had dinner with him at the Commodore when he brought it to New York and had it in my hands. New York was scared because the bottom had just dropped out of the 5¢ error and they thought Robey was wrong and there would be plenty of the sheets. My own customer (Ackerman?) was out of town and I was helpless."

That $50,000 figure — unmentioned in any of Robey's writings — can also be found on the back of the May 15, 1918, letter from Robey to Perry, along with the figure $500, both penciled by Perry. This pair of figures, Perry wrote in a 1957 letter to Ethel B. McCoy, another one-time owner of a Jenny invert block, "I believe was Robey's price for the invert sheet and the average price for each of the 100 stamps necessary to make the total price for the sheet." The $500 could also have been Perry's notation of the sum which Hamilton Colman had offered Robey for the sheet on the afternoon of May 14.

Perry had in mind writing an article about his involvement in the invert story. Harry Lindquist wrote to him February 18, 1938 — no doubt after reading Robey's own memoir in the February 19 issue of *Weekly Philatelic Gossip*, in which Perry was barely mentioned — to say: "I will be looking forward with interest to your article on the 24 cent airplane invert, and any additional light thrown on the subject should be welcomed rather than otherwise." The next day Perry wrote back with this cryptic comment: "Probably won't release the 24¢ air mail invert story until the U.S. stamp catalog is fixed up so it doesn't contradict itself so often." Perry died in 1972 with his story still unwritten.

Chapter Eight

# The Resale

*"We are selling those stamps too cheap."*
**— Col. Edward H.R. Green**

Eugene Klein of Philadelphia played a leading role in American philately for more than three decades. Hungarian born, he was reportedly literate in Hebrew, Arabic, Turkish and Persian, plus a half dozen modern languages. He was an expert on such varied postal topics as the stamps of Hungary and Heligoland and the packetmarks on mail carried on U.S. waterways. He served a term as president of the American Philatelic Society.

He was also an able businessman, as shown by the fact that of all the dealers who had a chance to buy William Robey's sheet of inverts between May 14 and May 20, only Klein was bold and resourceful enough to swing a deal for it — a deal that netted a quick $5,000 profit.

Unfortunately, Klein, who died in 1944, never wrote his own account of the transaction. He did, however, give an interview, albeit a rather superficial one, a dozen or so years afterward to stamp writer Charles J. Phillips. * He first learned of the invert sheet, he said, from Percy Mann and Joseph A. Steinmetz. "Mann phoned Robey to give him first refusal of the sheet," Klein said, "and then went to see Joseph Steinmetz and they came to see me. We three agreed to combine."

The career of Joseph Steinmetz — philatelic and otherwise — was an oddly mixed one. A mechanical engineer, Steinmetz was fascinated by aviation from its earliest days. Before the Wright brothers flew at Kitty Hawk, Steinmetz was helping their rival, Samuel Langley, produce parts for his aircraft engines. He was also an enthusiastic stamp collector, and this once got him in big trouble.

* — Phillips was also the one-time owner of the grand old British stamp firm of Stanley Gibbons and Company. As a young man in 1899, he had made a Robey-like discovery of his own when he found a pair of the world's first inverts, the 4-anna India of 1854, while sorting through a batch of envelopes.

**Eugene Klein, the Philadelphia dealer who headed the three-man syndicate that bought Robey's sheet of inverts.**

Steinmetz allegedly worked out a scheme with the acting third assistant postmaster general, Arthur M. Travers, by which Travers would take stamp rarities from the Post Office vaults, pass them on to Steinmetz to sell, and replace them with common stamps. Early in 1911 the Philadelphia Stamp Company, of which Steinmetz was an officer, began advertising some of these rarities, including two types — the 4¢ and 8¢ Washington stamps of 1909 printed on experimental bluish paper — that had never reached the market before. An investigation followed, and in April both Steinmetz and Travers were indicted by a federal grand jury on the odd-sounding charge of conspiring to sell postage stamps above their face value. Travers was also charged with embezzlement and fired by the Post Office.

Steinmetz, who was freed on $500 bail, denied any criminal intention, saying he had no reason to think Travers hadn't acted legally.

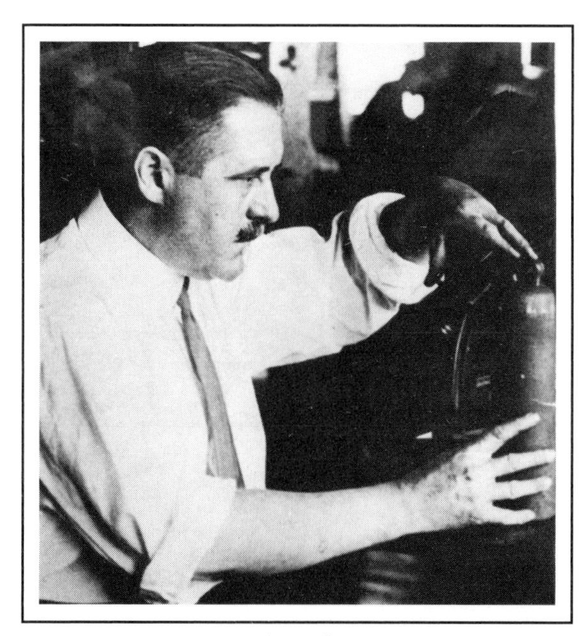

**Joseph A. Steinmetz, mechanical engineer, inventor, aviation authority and stamp collector.**

*Mekeel's Weekly Stamp News* favored him with a sympathetic editorial ("The standing of Mr. Steinmetz in philately is high and because of his services for the welfare of the pursuit he has the regard of philatelists generally.") Nevertheless, he was stigmatized by the indictment and was forced to resign as president of the Red Cross in Pennsylvania.

The case dragged on for 19 months, until finally in October 1912 Travers was allowed to plead *nolo contendere* and settle for a fine of $1,500, supposedly the amount he had netted from the scheme. The following month the U.S. attorney's office in Washington dropped the charges against Steinmetz, and that was the end of it.

Steinmetz rallied from this misadventure to regain distinction in both his profession and hobby. The very next year, 1913, he won the prized Visitor's Cup at the International Philatelic Exhibition in New York, awarded by the votes of the showgoers, for "a Wonderland Collection," consisting of items "selected for their quaint, striking or human interest," such as the world's smallest stamp.

Early in World War I he developed antiaircraft devices for the Allies, including aerial mines and a hook-bomb on a wire which French planes could use to "fish" for German dirigibles. By war's end he was a major in the Army Ordnance reserve and later he was promoted to lieutenant colonel.

As first president of the Aero Club of Pennsylvania, he was chairman of the arrangements committee for the May 15 ceremonies accompanying the debut of the airmail at Bustleton Field.

Eugene Klein told interviewer Phillips that Robey telegraphed him from New York: "If you will pay $15,000 for the sheet I will stop off at Philadelphia on my return home." "We decided to telegraph him to stop," Klein continued. "Steinmetz tried to bargain but Robey said that he had got $12,000 offered and would not take less than $15,000. Eventually we decided to purchase at his price and a certified check was given him. After this I went up to New York and sold the sheet to Col. Green for $20,000."

This version of the syndicate's negotiations with Robey differs from that of Robey, who wrote that Percy Mann had asked him to stop in Philadelphia on his way home to Washington. Furthermore, Klein's account of the sequence of purchase and resale of the sheet is refuted by the evidence.

The evidence is a news story that appeared Tuesday, May 21, in the New York morning papers, including the *Times, World* and *Tribune.* All used virtually the same wording, indicating that they came from the same wire service story or press release. The longest version was in the *Times,* on page 13, and it is quoted here, beginning with the headline:

"$20,000 BY COL. GREEN/FOR AIR MAIL STAMPS/Sheet with Plane Inverted/Sold Over Post Office/Counter for $24./OTHERS WERE CANCELED/Buyer Will Keep Some of Pur-/chase for His Collection and/Give Rest to Friends.

"A sheet of 100 of the new postal airplane stamps, but with the airplane turned upside down through an error made by the Bureau of Engraving and Printing at Washington, has been purchased for $20,000 by Colonel E.H.R. Green of Texas, son of the late Hetty Green. Over a window counter at the Post Office in Washington this sheet sold for $24.

"So far as is known this is the only sheet that escaped the vigilance of the Washington postal authorities. Three other sheets were discovered and were pen-canceled so that their postal value was nullified, and these probably will be destroyed.

"The stamps bought by Colonel Green were turned back by a Washington citizen at the stamp window because the airplane was inverted. In the line behind this citizen was a man who sensed the philatelic value of the sheet, and purchased it at its face value, and it reached the hands of a Philadelphia stamp dealer, who today received a bid of $12,500 prior to the higher offer made by Colonel Green.

"Colonel Green said yesterday that he planned to retain a portion of the sheet for his collection, and dispose of the other stamps among his friends. It is predicted by philatelists that if the sheet proves to be the only one in existence outside of Government ownership the stamps will attain a philatelic value of $250 each."

The "today" at the end of the third paragraph was a logical impossibility in a story that appeared without a dateline in a morning paper. Presumably the original wire-service story or handout carried a May 20 dateline, which the *Times* copy editor struck out. The editor then changed the "today" references in the copy to "yesterday" but overlooked this one.

This hasty news account contained at least one inaccuracy that would become part of the mythology of the Jenny invert — that some witless customer in line ahead of Robey had rejected the error sheet. But one thing is quite clear from it: Before agreeing on Monday afternoon to pay $15,000 for Robey's sheet, Eugene Klein had nailed down a deal to resell it for $20,000, and the deal was with a man whom Robey himself had tried unsuccessfully to see on Saturday: Colonel Green.

A writer who knew both Klein and Green asserted that the colonel was traveling in Texas that weekend and "only by chance" was Klein able to track him down and get a commitment to buy the sheet for $20,000. Another acquaintance of both men reported that Colonel Green mistakenly thought he was buying a sheet of the 1901 2¢ Pan-American Exposition inverts. No record can be found of the details of how and when the Klein-Green deal was struck — or of how, why and by whom the news of it was released to the press before Robey had even delivered the stamps to Klein.

As Robey boarded the train in Washington Tuesday, May 21, with his sheet of inverts in a shoebox, the morning papers in New York were already on the newsstands with the announcement of Green's purchase, and the hometown *Washington Evening Star* was preparing to go to press with it. There is no reason to believe, however, that Robey knew then — or, indeed, ever — that his stamps had by then already been resold to the colonel. In fact, in his 1938 article he mistakenly wrote that Green had entered the picture "later."

Klein muddied the waters with a pair of ads which he placed in successive issues of *Mekeel's*. Among those misled by the ads was Jenny researcher Henry M. Goodkind.

The first one appeared in the issue dated May 25, 1918 (but whose actual date of publication, and deadline for receiving copy, fell earlier). Printed in the upper left corner of page 1, where Klein's ads customarily ran, it read:

"A NEW U.S. INVERT. 24¢ carmine and blue with inverted airplane in center. A few of the remaining copies of the only sheet found for sale at $250.00 each. Copies with one straight edge $175.00 each. Collections of United States, Twentieth Century and War Stamps will be incomplete without this great rarity. Eugene Klein, 1318 Chestnut Street, Philadelphia, Pa. Cable Address: Kleinstamp."

(The $250 figure was the same one which "philatelists" cited in the *New York Times* story May 21 had predicted the stamps would attain, leading one to suspect that Klein had been the source of that original news release.)

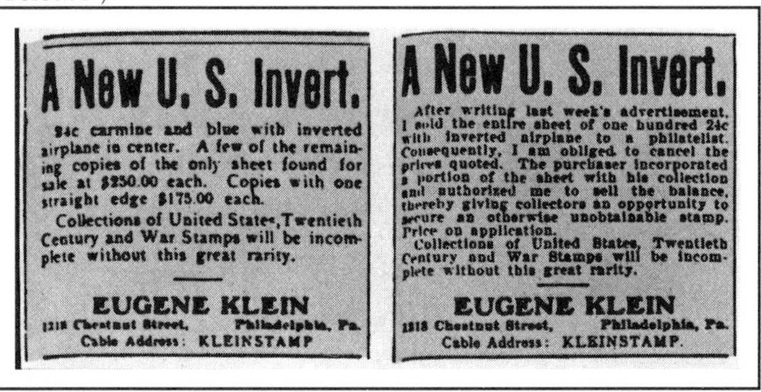


**Klein ads in *Mekeel's* May 25 (left) and June 1 concealed that Klein had arranged from the beginning to resell the sheet.**

The next issue of *Mekeel's*, dated June 1, carried this revised Klein ad:

"A NEW U.S. INVERT. After writing last week's advertisement, I sold the entire sheet of one hundred 24¢ with inverted airplane to a philatelist. Consequently, I am obliged to cancel the prices quoted. The purchaser incorporated a portion of the sheet with his collection and authorized me to sell the balance, thereby giving collectors an opportunity to secure an otherwise unobtainable stamp. Price on application. Collections of United States, Twentieth Century and War Stamps will be incomplete . . ." and so on.

The third week, the ad read: ". . . A few of the remaining copies of the only sheet found for sale. Price on application . . ."

One wonders what was going on here. Klein had to have placed the first ad knowing he had already resold the sheet "to a philatelist"; the same May 25 issue of *Mekeel's* which carried it also carried a news account of the purchase of the sheet by Colonel Green, citing the *New York Tribune* as the source. Possibly Klein was testing the market on Green's behalf with the first ad.

But Henry Goodkind, taking the ad at face value, concluded that Klein "probably did not buy the sheet as Colonel Green's agent." He went on: "He may have bought it with him in mind, because Colonel Green was well known at this time for his fabulous investments in stamps. But the sheet was sold to Hetty Green's son between May 25th and June 1st." That, of course, was incorrect, as the newspapers of May 21 attest.

The news of the discovery and sale of the Jenny inverts created a sensation in the stamp world. *Mekeel's* hailed it editorially:

"It came sooner than expected and it was introduced with a fanfare of trumpets that would make the ranking star of the circus satisfied with life. The Associated Press was generous in its treatment of the momentous discovery and detected the human interest in the episode and played it up with a master's touch. Aerial post, aeroplane on stamp upside down, and Colonel Green, son of Hetty Green, were an ensemble that was worthy (of) the eye of the best of managers and the refreshing result rejoices philatelists."

The find inspired jokesters. Dealer W.H. Henshaw displayed four normal Jenny stamps in his window with the sign "All I have — $500." *Mekeel's* quoted a conversation it claimed took place in a Boston stamp shop: "Customer — 'Say, I would like to own one of the inverted aeroplane stamps.' Dealer — 'I can sell you one.' Customer — 'Can't afford to buy it now.' Dealer — 'I'll sell you one on margin.' Customer (seriously) — 'No, I want it well centered.' "

It also sent people on futile searches for more inverts. These included two of Robey's associates, Hamilton F. Colman, who had offered him $500 for his sheet back on May 14, and Joseph Leavy, who had also seen the original sheet and who later sought unsuccessfully to obtain another one, through official sources, for the government collection.

Colman enlisted the help of an old friend, Army Captain A.C. Townsend, who was in charge of the military post office in Hoboken, New Jersey, through which passed all of New York City's mail to servicemen overseas. At the dealer's request, the captain got permission from New York Postmaster Thomas G. Patten to go through all the 24¢ Jennies in his stock. The next day Townsend and Joseph Leavy sat at a table in a hot post office vault breaking the wrappers on package after package of airmail stamps and riffling through the sheets looking for upside-down airplanes. Their search was in vain.

Some found fault. The *New York Times*, for instance, tut-tutted editorially about the Green purchase. "Even for a set of stamps as 'hard' as that — to use the word of boy collectors — $20,000 does seem too much," the paper said. "And if the giver of that astonishing price had not been a man notable in the financial world for his sound and practical sense of values, the impulse of most of us would be to call him mad . . . Some critics are sure to opine . . . that at this time there are several better uses for $20,000 than the purchase of a set of stamps which, except for a printer's error, would be worth in the open market just $24."

Another sour note came from the *Albemarle Stamp Collector*, a Virginia publication edited by Charles H. Mekeel, who had founded the publication that carried his name. "The Bureau of Engraving and Printing has recently become famous of its 'errors' so these inverts are only in keeping with its bad record," the editor wrote. If the reports were true that Colonel Green had paid $20,000 for the sheet, "which there is good reason to doubt, the stampic Col. got badly stuck. He has probably got wise to stamp conditions in the U.S. and takes better care of his money than to pay at the rate of $200 per copy for such a cheap thing as a U.S. Bureau error, but if he really did make the investment he has bought experience as well."

That comment brought a reply from Eugene Klein himself. "As far as Colonel Green is concerned," Klein wrote to the magazine, "he not only did not get stuck but will have the advantage of owning unique blocks which will cost him a nominal price and have practically all his money back for the balance of the sheet, which is being sold."

Klein elaborated somewhat in his interview years later with Charles Phillips. When he "delivered" the sheet to Colonel Green in New York, Klein said, Green asked: "How will that fit in my books?" Klein continued:

"I said, 'Colonel, I was told that when I turned the sheet over to you I should request you to have compassion on your fellow stamp collectors and give them an opportunity to also obtain a few of these stamps. If you keep the whole sheet it will probably never be worth much more than you are paying for it. If you break it up it will enhance the value of the stamps and you could get your money out of it in time.' Colonel Green replied, 'Well, that is reasonable,' and agreed to keep a block of eight as being the largest block in existence, that is a block with the plate number at the bottom. He also kept the center line block and two arrow blocks, twenty in all."

Either Klein or his interviewer was mistaken here. The 20 stamps Green kept in block form were the plate number block of eight, which was also the bottom arrow block; the left arrow block of four; the center line block of four and the lower left corner block of four, with siderographer DeBinder's initials in the selvage.

When these blocks came on the market years later, after Colonel Green's death, the left arrow block was separated into two horizontal pairs, and the plate number/bottom arrow block of eight had the upper left stamp detached. How did these mishaps occur? No one knows. Probably they were the result of mishandling by the colonel, but it is possible they occurred on that momentous but, alas, unrecorded occasion when Eugene Klein broke the sheet, along the perforations, to extract the blocks for his client. Did he do it with infinite care and preparation, like a diamond cutter about to cleave a rare gem, or casually, so that unique blocks were violated?

Klein's only reference to the procedure in his interview was this: "Before I broke up the sheet I numbered each stamp lightly on the back." The numbers, in pencil, appear very faintly on the gum in the lower right quadrant of each specimen. The action was an inspiration. Klein must have foreseen, correctly, that future philatelic scholars would want to trace the ownership of individual stamps from the sheet, and he deserves much credit for making that task easier.

"It was agreed," Klein continued in the interview, "I should advertise the stamps at $250 per stamp for perfect copies and $175 each for straight edges. I was to get $25 on each stamp that I sold. In a short time I sold ten copies, drew a check for $2,250 and took it to Colonel Green." Thus, the prices of the stamps, listed in Klein's second advertisement as available "on application," were the same $250/$175 prices he had quoted in his first ad.

Klein went on: "He (Colonel Green) was much amused at the way things were going and said, 'We are selling those stamps too cheap. Let us make the price $350.' This was agreed to and I sold the next ten at this price and gave the colonel $3,250. He said, 'What is that for? How many did you sell?' I said, 'Ten.' He said, 'I told you I wanted $225 each.' I said, 'Yes, but since then you told me to sell them at $350.' The colonel replied, 'Oh, yes, but I wanted you to keep the difference.' I therefore made out a new check.

"Then he said, 'John Klemann wanted some of these stamps. Let him have some of them at the original price.' "

Klein went on to say that "the next week the price was raised to $500 and shortly after that to $650." His memory may have betrayed him. In a letter he wrote to longtime collector Baldwin Schlesinger of New York dated July 26, 1918, a little over two months after he had sold the sheet to Colonel Green, Klein reported:

"I have just sold a copy yesterday for $325. I have two more left for which I expect to get between $350 and $400 apiece. After that I will have nothing but straight-edged copies. If I get an inquiry for a perfect copy, I will let you know and you can then decide whether you want to sell yours or not. In my opinion it will be $500 before long." * (Schlesinger decided not to sell. In a letter about the Jenny inverts which he wrote to the *New York Times* in 1928, he said he wouldn't take $1,000 for his copy.)

* — Ever the salesman, Klein added: "A good way to mount the stamp is to put it in the center of the page and surround it with the blocks of the various plate positions such as the arrow blocks, the plate number blocks and engraver's (sic) initial blocks. If interested in these I will gladly send you all the varieties, as I have a few sets on hand."

In his interview with Phillips, Klein concluded:

"Eventually Joseph Steinmetz, Percy Mann and I got together to share up the profit. Steinmetz said, 'Klein ought not to have one-third but he ought to have half the amount because he did the whole of the buying, the selling and the financing and we did not put up a cent.' This was agreed to. Percy Mann took three copies at the original price, and Steinmetz took a pair which 10 years later he broke and sold one of them, which is now in the collection of Insley Blair (a Tuxedo Park, New York, banker). With the proceeds of that stamp he purchased a grand piano for his wife. That piano is known in Germantown as the 'proceeds of one little stamp.' "

If Klein's recollection was accurate, Steinmetz must have broken the pair and bought the piano shortly before his death, which occurred at age 58 on July 11, 1928.

Soon after Colonel Green bought the inverts he authorized the sale of one copy for the benefit of the Red Cross. It was auctioned off June 29, 1918, by George R. Tuttle, a dealer on Manhattan's Nassau Street. The stamp, Tuttle predicted in his sale catalog, "will probably oversell the rare 2¢ Pan Am. inverted, before long." It brought $300; the buyer's identity is unknown.

Chapter Nine

# The Eccentric

*"I would place Colonel Green in a category all his own."*

— **Walter S. Scott**

William Robey's attempt to offer his sheet of inverts directly to the ultimate buyer, Edward Howland Robinson (Ned) Green, was unsuccessful. But it was based on sound judgment. In May 1918, if you happened to have a spectacular new U.S. stamp error to sell, Colonel Green was the man to see.

The colonel (his title, strictly honorary, was bestowed in 1910 by an old friend, Governor O.B. Colquitt of Texas) had been a stamp collector for only about as long as Robey had. However, as the son and heir of the late Hetty Green, the so-called "Witch of Wall Street" who was reputed to be the wealthiest woman of her time, he brought considerably more resources to the hobby.

**The eccentric millionaire Colonel Edward H.R. Green in one of his automobiles (left) and mother Hetty Green, known as the "Witch of Wall Street."**

A big man — he stood six feet, four inches tall and weighed some 300 pounds — with a right leg made of cork, Ned Green was a familiar figure along stamp dealers' row on Nassau Street in lower Manhattan. His philatelic *modus operandi* has been described many times, mostly at second or third hand, but a consistent picture emerges, that of an impulsive, free-spending accumulator. He would snap up whole collections at a time, with no haggling, and pay thousands of dollars on the spot. He was partial to errors, and owned more than half of the known sheets of 400 of the 5¢ red color error in imperforate form. The Jenny inverts were tailor-made to excite him.

Green's mother had inherited a fortune herself from her New England whaling and shipowning ancestors and had multiplied it many times. A tough, resourceful penny-pincher, Hetty shuttled between Brooklyn and Hoboken to avoid establishing residence and paying taxes while she was making millions in the stock market. She haggled over prices, dressed in rags and went unwashed to save on soap; she once reportedly spent hours looking for a 2¢ postage stamp she had mislaid in a carriage. She conducted her business from any desk she chose in the old Seaboard National Bank on lower Broadway, where she lunched regularly on oatmeal warmed on a radiator at a nearby broker's office. The cereal, she said, gave her the strength she needed "to fight those Wall Street wolves."

Though Hetty apparently doted on her son, it was her penuriousness that had caused him to lose his leg. He hurt it in a sledding accident as a boy and reinjured it several times, and she dosed him with Carter's Little Liver Pills and oil of squill and sought treatment at free clinics, too stingy to pay for proper medical care. Eventually gangrene set in and amputation was necessary.

Hetty died at 82 in 1916 — her husband, a gentle and retiring chap named Edward Henry Green, had left her a widow many years earlier — and she left to Ned, then 47, and his sister Sylvia an estate officially declared to be $67 million but estimated at well over $100 million. Her son immediately got to work spending his share.

"Before the year 1916 ended," wrote a biographer, "the colonel . . . took a 16-room corner suite in the Waldorf-Astoria at an annual rental of $28,000 and spent $150,000 on its decor; bought Mabel" — handsome, red-haired Mabel Harlow, his companion for some 24 years — "a diamond-studded chastity belt for $50,000; hired a personal staff of 14 young ladies including two 'masseuses' and a half-dozen typists, although his office contained a single L.C. Smith; had plans drawn for a 60-room mansion, and placed an order for the largest yacht in the world." He also immediately proposed marriage to Mabel; Hetty had disapproved, but her opinion was no longer a factor.

It was then, too, that the colonel plunged into stamp collecting. In the 20 years of self-indulgence that followed, he also collected coins, currency, jewelry and first editions and dabbled in horticulture, radio, aviation, even jigsaw puzzles, pursuing all his hobbies with the same kind of impulsive dilettantism he brought to philately.

He is said to have discovered stamps when he went into the Scott Stamp and Coin Company on Madison Avenue in 1916 or early 1917 to buy a packet of 1,000 varieties and an album for the son of his laundryman. Next day he returned and told the manager, Hugh Clark, that the stamps had piqued his interest and he would like to begin collecting. Before he left he had bought a multi-volume general collection, paying $31,000 for it in $1,000 bills. Within four months he bought eight to ten other collections.

At the Economist Stamp Company, another firm that became a favorite, Green left a standing order for every new issue of the world, in singles and blocks of four. Among the collections he bought from Economist were C.F. Heyerman's inverted centers, for $12,500; a splendid specialized collection of Sweden, for $25,000; and J.K. Storrow's virtually complete collection of U.S., including special printings and pre-stamp postmaster's provisionals, for $77,500.

With Colonel Green, money was literally no object. "I have never achieved my ambition," he once told a young visitor, "which is to spend one day's income in one day." Finding that he had bought a stamp that had been repaired by having margins added, he contacted a manufacturer of optical equipment and asked for a glass that would magnify a stamp to four feet square with sharp definition. The custom-made instrument cost him $22,000 and was so big he had to have the framework removed from the door of his house at 5 West 90th Street, Manhattan, in order to get it inside.

His impulsiveness was sometimes improvident. He asked Economist's Sidney Barrett to make for him a set of albums for the stamps of Great Britain, with a separate page for each variety in the Stanley Gibbons catalog. This required some 40 volumes. Later Barrett asked Green how he was doing with the British collection. Green replied that the plan had turned out to be impractical; he had many more copies of some varieties than he could get on a page, and his blocks and reconstructed sheets were too big to fit. He scrapped the albums and put his British stamps in cardboard-pocketed stock books.

He could be impulsively generous as well. Robson Lowe, who later in London would build up one of the world's great stamp dealerships, came to New York in 1926, met the colonel through a mutual friend and was invited to spend a weekend at Round Hills, Green's Massachusetts estate. At the end of his visit, Lowe recalled, "the colonel gave me an envelope with strict instructions that I was not to sell the contents until I married. He had already learned that I was engaged to be married and had just had my 21st birthday.

"To my delight the content of the envelope was an inverted 24-cent. When I did get married, in 1928, I did sell the stamp for 70 pounds ($350) to David Field, a leading stamp dealer. I still use the table and the armchairs that I had made with the money."

Eventually, the colonel's interest in stamps waned and after 1927 was described as "slight." His principal hobby in the last few years of his life was his jewelry collection. He loved gems and frequently gave them as gifts, such as the diamond-studded pins modeled after Charles A. Lindbergh's plane, *The Spirit of St. Louis*, which Tiffany's custom-made for him at Christmas in 1927, the year of Lindbergh's flight to Paris. Between 1930 and his death in 1936, Green bought more than $10 million worth of jewels, most of them purchased as he sat in his limousine double-parked on Miami's Flagler Street examining the wares of dealers from all over the East who had followed him to Florida.

To stamp writer Ernest A. Kehr, a guest at his Massachusetts estate in 1934, he brushed aside questions about the Jenny invert, saying: "Don't remember. All my stamps are down in New York, locked up in the vaults of the Chase National Bank and in safes of my office at Trinity Place."

Veteran auctioneer Walter S. Scott was called upon after the colonel's death at age 67 in Lake Placid, New York, June 8, 1936, to organize his collection for sale. Scott wrote this about him:

"I would place Colonel Green in a category all his own. He certainly loved stamps, as is definitely evidenced by the great quantity he acquired, and undoubtedly if he had had competent philatelic assistance, his holdings could have been developed into the greatest single collection ever known. The material is there, but the mounting and classification is far from what it should be, although there are included many beautiful individual collections which he purchased intact, any one of which is in the gold medal class.

"That he had fully intended to gather this wonderful assortment into albums, properly mounted and philatelically annotated, is shown by the fact that blank quadrille pages had been laid out and lettered, awaiting only the mounting by an experienced hand."

An experienced hand seems to have been lacking all along. One acquaintance tells how Green treated the specialized collection of Belgian stamps assembled by Joseph Leavy. Leavy had made a lifelong study of the early issues and had carefully written up the many plate varieties and siderographer's re-entries he had acquired, in many cases determining and noting their positions on the plates. After Green bought the collection he gave it to one of the girls he hired from time to time to arrange his stamps. She took the stamps out of Leavy's albums, placed them in stock books under Scott catalog numbers and threw away the annotated pages.

In this way Colonel Green built a reputation as a stamp collector who did much more spending than thinking. At times he personally seemed to cultivate that reputation. One result was the wide circulation of stories about various bizarre fates which befell copies of the Jenny invert that remained in the colonel's possession.

Prominent among them was the waste paper basket story, which Green himself originated. Eugene Klein related it in his interview with Charles J. Phillips:

"(After Klein had been selling the inverts for a while) there were mostly those with straight edges left and only a few odd copies, and Colonel Green said to me, 'You know my blocks are up in my collection and I want some downtown. I want to show them to a friend who said that such things cannot exist.' I sent him some of the straight edges and the next time I went to New York, Colonel Green said, 'Do you know what happened to those stamps you sent? They disappeared. I had them here on this desk and I think they must have fallen into the waste paper basket.' There were 13 copies which were apparently lost and possibly there were four or five copies that he had that were also lost at the same time."

This account was accepted and repeated as fact by several stamp writers, including the respected Max G. Johl, who had no way at the time to disprove it. Very little was actually known about the colonel's collection during his lifetime, including how many Jenny inverts he owned. He didn't exhibit his stamps, and few philatelists were privy to what was in his albums and stock books.

The evidence that the waste basket disaster never happened didn't emerge until after the colonel's vast stamp holdings were inventoried and auctioned after his death, and researchers came on the scene who would systematically trace the travels and ownership of each of the Jenny inverts. These researchers in time established that all 19 of the straight-edge copies survived the colonel; thus, the 13 straight-edge Jennies that Klein had sent to Green didn't fly off his desk into a waiting waste basket at all.

Why did the colonel concoct the story? Whatever his reason, it wasn't the first whimsical yarn he had ever spun. Once, when he was 43 years old and Hetty Green was still alive, her son and heir planted a story in the *New York Telegram* describing his ideal bride ("Someone who can cook and sew and not be a parasite . . . a woman who wants a real home and children. I have been searching far and wide for this woman and I will not rest until I can find her"). He then seated himself in the lobby of the Waldorf-Astoria hotel, with a newspaper held in front of his face, and watched happily as crowds of excited women pushed their way in, demanding to know where Colonel Green's suite was located.

The earliest catastrophe story concerning the Green inverts developed out of the sinking of the colonel's yacht, the *United States*. Philip H. Ward Jr. reported in *Mekeel's* November 8, 1919:

**BEFORE: Steamship *United States* as it looked carrying passengers and freight on Lake Michigan. AFTER: Colonel Edward H.R. Green bought the ship and had it lengthened, adding an extra stack.**

"We learn with regret that Colonel Green's yacht has been sunk and we have been reliably informed that his wonderful collection of stamps were on board. Our informant states that this included 43 copies of the 24¢ aeroplane invert, his wonderful lot of plate numbers, the (Edgar) Nelton covers and other items too numerous to mention. We sincerely trust that if this is the case that the greater portions of his rarities are in waterproof safes."

The *New York World* added to the story November 18. "The stamps are said to be in two safes aboard the yacht," the paper said, "but water seeped in and it will require the services of an expert to ascertain the extent of the damage . . . 43 copies (of the airmail invert) are reported destroyed." The colonel, the *World* added, "could not be reached last night to verify the report."

Also carrying the story were *A.C. Roessler's Stamp News*, which put the number of lost inverts at 33, and the *Albermarle Stamp Collector*, which asserted that "the action of the salt water has severely damaged the stamps."

That Colonel Green's yacht sank is indisputable. The extent of philatelic damage, if any, is another matter.

The *United States* had been built originally to carry passengers and light freight on Lake Michigan. The colonel bought it, had it lengthened by 40 feet to a total of 255 feet, as big as some ocean liners, added a new upper deck and ended up with what the magazine *The Rudder* called "the largest, finest and costliest privately owned yacht in the world," one that required a full-time captain and crew of 71 to operate.

Unfortunately the colonel discovered on his honeymoon cruise that he hated the sea. Walking with a cork leg aboard a ship in motion proved to be painful. He soon decided to retire the floating palace to houseboat service in Buzzard's Bay, off South Dartmouth, Massachusetts, near his mother's ancestral home at Round Hills, where he had already decided to settle down and build an enormous mansion.

Here ill fortune befell the *United States*. Anchored some 50 yards offshore inside the Padanaram breakwater, early on the morning of August 21, 1919, with the sea calm, the yacht somehow swung around and struck a rock. Water began pouring in through a hole in the ship's bottom. Colonel Green, Mabel, their guests and the crew had 10 hours to reach shore (and salvage any treasures that weren't waterproof, such as stamps). By noon, however, the prize yacht was keeled to starboard in 16 feet of water, on an angle of nearly 50 degrees. One can assume that David Bosworth, the skipper, had a lot of explaining to do.

The ship was raised and towed to a Brooklyn shipyard. In January 1920 the press reported erroneously that the colonel had sold it to a South American syndicate to haul rubber on the Amazon, but three years later she actually was sold, to the Peninsula and Northern Navigation Company, to once again carry passengers and mail on the Great Lakes.

Did any Jenny inverts go down with the ship? Despite those "reliable" published reports, the evidence is against it. Charles J. Phillips, who as a leading stamp dealer had known Colonel Green, wrote after the colonel's death that Green had "stated there was no truth whatever" to the report that any stamps were lost. He didn't elaborate.

Nor does it seem likely that any inverts sank and were salvaged, which would have inevitably resulted in a loss of their gum. When Green's collection was sold, ony eight of the 41 Jenny inverts it contained were without gum, and all of these were straight-edge copies. The most plausible explanation for that is found in a letter which dealer Elliott Perry wrote to collector Harry L. Jefferys the day after Jefferys had bought one of the ungummed specimens at a Green auction:

"Walter Scott (the auctioneer) told me that he himself took the gum off the 'no gum' copies. They were found in an envelope stuck together and had to be soaked to separate them. Col. Green is said to have intended to prevent reperforating of the straight edges by taking them to the Collectors Club and publicly burning them. Evidently these were what he got together and carried in his pocket until they adhered."

The third oft-heard disaster story was apparently first related by Charles Phillips. This one wasn't attributed to the colonel or, for that matter, to anyone at all. Phillips wrote:

"How many airmail fans know there is just one used copy of this rarity? The story is as follows: One day Mrs. Green wished to send an airmail letter to her husband. She went into his study and noticed some of these 24¢ stamps on his desk and used one on her letter. Colonel Green spotted it, took it off the letter and had it inserted in a pendant which he wore on his watch chain."

This anecdote was repeated unquestioningly by other writers. No used copy of the Jenny invert has ever turned up, either in or out of a pendant, and people who knew Mabel Green scoff at the suggestion that she would be ignorant enough to use a rare stamp on a letter. The story could have originated in another of the colonel's jests.

**"Locket copy" of the Jenny invert.**

There was, however, an invert which Colonel Green did in fact place in a pendant — and gave to Mabel to wear. Its existence wasn't generally known about until long after the colonel's death.

It was an unused copy with a straight edge at the top, position 9 from the original sheet, and it was placed back to back with a normal copy of the stamp and sealed in a round glass case, transparent on both sides, with a gold rim and a small ring at the top for a chain. This invert in the locket probably became transformed, in somebody's retelling, into the fictitious "invert that Mabel used on a letter."

The first description of the actual locket and its contents was made in 1956 by the late George B. Sloane, a stamp dealer, auctioneer and writer. In his column in *Stamps* magazine, Sloane recalled how he had been asked to come to an unnamed midtown Manhattan bank one day in June 1950 to appraise a philatelic item.

When he arrived, lawyers and others were preparing to inventory the contents of the safe-deposit box of Mabel Green, who had died in Florida the previous April. Sloane was shown the locket containing the two stamps. He noted that the invert had a straight edge at the top, plus "light creases in the upper left and lower right corners . . . probably of little consequence." His column contained no other details, and for nearly 30 years after it was published the locket never resurfaced.

Then, in 1984, this writer located the owner of the locket. She was a Long Island resident, originally from New Bedford, Massachusetts. Through her parents, she had met Colonel Green and his wife when she was a child, and she became a companion of Mabel after the colonel's death. Finally, after Mabel died, she inherited the bulk of the widow's estate.

The owner, who asked that her name not be disclosed, agreed to make the locket available to be photographed at the Bank of New York at Fifth Avenue and 44th Street, Manhattan, where it was kept. She said she didn't know when Colonel Green had the item made or who fashioned it. As far as she knew, Mabel Green never wore it as an item of jewelry.

According to the records of the Suffolk County, New York, Surrogate, who probated Mabel's will in 1950, the locket with its Jenny invert was valued at that time at $900, presumably by George Sloane. The entire Mabel Green estate, containing many items of jewelry but no other stamps, was assigned a gross value of $865,846, the records showed.

Mabel hadn't inherited the estate of Colonel Green. Under a prenuptial agreement signed in 1917, she had waived all rights to her future husband's fortune in return for a guaranteed life income of $1,500 per month, to be paid out of a $600,000 trust fund. After the colonel died she went to court to try to invalidate that agreement, but was unsuccessful, and the estate went to the colonel's sister, Sylvia Green Wilks.

Green, like his mother, had kept on the move during his lifetime to confuse tax collectors. So successful was he in this effort that he never paid an income tax or personal property tax on intangibles in any state. All his life he insisted he was a resident of Texas, where he had once spent several years managing a railroad owned by Hetty Green (and where he had been awarded his "colonelcy"), but during the last quarter century of his life he had no home there and visited the state only occasionally.

After his death Texas, Florida, New York and Massachusetts competed to be declared his domicile in order to tax the estate, and it required two years of hearings before a special master appointed by the U.S. Supreme Court, with 385 witnesses testifying, to resolve the issue. Finally, in an opinion authored by Justice Harlan Fiske Stone and handed down in 1939, Massachusetts was declared the winner.

Chapter Ten

# The Dispersal

*"I got in early and bought one for $250. . ."*

**— Benjamin K. Miller**

When Eugene Klein broke up the original sheet of inverts for Colonel Green and began selling the stamps on his behalf, he began a diaspora unique in the history of philately.

Scarcely two years went by before the original Klein-Green customers or their estates began reselling. Copies of the invert have been appearing regularly on the market ever since.

The unique combination of characteristics of the Jenny invert has

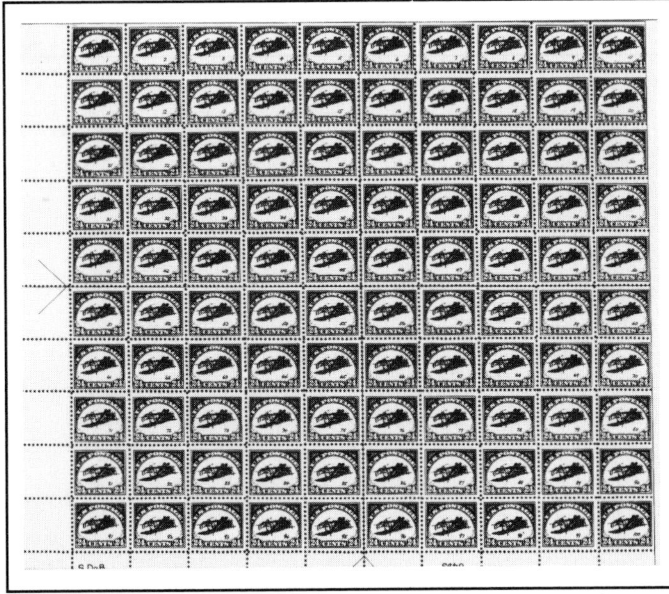

**Clifford C. Cole Jr. created this exact pictorial reconstruction of the original sheet of 100 of the 1918 24¢ Jenny airmail inverts.**

enabled researchers to account for, at one time or another, all but four of the original 100 stamps, and to trace the successive ownerships — what fanciers of rare collectibles call the provenance — of many of them. On at least three occasions these characteristics have made it possible for law enforcement officials, aided by these experts, to identify stolen copies, in spite of efforts by the thieves to disguise them.

Consider:

Here was a compact "family" of 100 stamps, each one originally identified as to position on the sheet by a number penciled on the lower right-hand corner of the back by the man who separated the sheet.

They appear to a casual glance to be as alike as peas in a pod, but, like peas, each has its own unique features and these are discernible to an expert. They make it possible to identify a position even when the pencil mark has disappeared, whether from excessive handling, gum loss or deliberate erasure.

There is, first, the minute mismatching of the two printing plates, which causes the placement of the airplane inside the frame to "sink," with each horizontal row of planes a trifle lower than the one above it. In the top row of inverts, the Jenny's horizontal stabilizer points squarely at the white dot before "U.S. Postage"; on each lower row it points progressively farther below the dot. Also, a slight counterclockwise twist in the registry causes the planes at the bottom right to seem lower than the planes at the bottom left.

Because the rows of perforating holes weren't spaced equidistantly, the centering of the stamps within their borders of perforations varies. For the same reason, the overall dimensions of the stamps vary; those in some vertical rows are narrower than others, those in some horizontal rows are shallower than others.

And, of course, 19 of the stamps were originally distinguishable from the rest by straight edges. These ran along the top for positions 1 through 9, along the top and down the right side for position 10, and down the right side for positions 20, 30, 40, 50, 60, 70, 80, 90 and 100. By the same token, 19 stamps from the left and bottom rows of the sheet originally had adjoining pieces of sheet selvage attached to them.

The very act of separating each stamp from its neighbors contributed another clue to its identification. As with all stamps, the invert's "teeth," or projections of paper between the perforations, didn't break off uniformly but varied in length, and this made each stamp a unique piece of the jigsaw puzzle. (One perforation in the original sheet, between positions 63 and 64, was "blind," or unpunched, which resulted in a single distinctively wide tooth on each of those stamps when they were separated.)

This assortment of characteristics enables an expert to match a Jenny invert, or a good photograph of it, with previous photographs of the same stamp where available. Even if one feature has been altered —if perforations have been added to a straight edge, say, or removed or modified, or if an attached piece of sheet selvage has been detached — the remaining features are almost always sufficient to allow a solid identification.

In a few cases, mistakes have been made or disagreements among experienced collectors have occurred. These have involved positions for which no clear, reliable photograph existed at the time. Federal law in 1918, when the dispersal of the Jenny inverts began, prohibited the publication of illustrations of U.S. postage stamps. That law wasn't changed until 1938, so for the first 20 years of the inverts' existence they couldn't be legally pictured in American auction catalogs, stamp books or periodicals. The average collector could only imagine what the "stamp with the upside-down airplane" looked like.

For the same reason, the early ownership of some of the positions is unknown. Few Jenny invert sales in the 1920s and 1930s were recorded by position number. Without pictures to go by, the present-day historian, although he may have the date of a sale, the names of the seller and the buyer, and the price, can't say for sure which stamp was involved.

As Eugene Klein announced, Colonel Green in May 1918 kept one block of eight and three blocks of four for his collection, and directed the dealer to sell the rest at $250 for fully perforated copies and $175 for straight edges. Shortly thereafter the copy which the colonel donated to the Red Cross was sold at auction for $300. As we have seen, Klein later raised the price for perforated specimens to the $350-$400 range. As for the straight-edge copies, Klein apparently was able to sell only two, positions 3 and 4; these were the only straight edges that were not later accounted for in Colonel Green's possession.

And soon the third-party sales began. In May 1920 stamp writer Philip H. Ward Jr. told of "a recent auction" at which a Jenny invert sold for $675. Ward, looking back years later, attributed this jump in the stamp's value to the reports of the loss of dozens of specimens when the Green yacht sank — reports which Ward himself had helped spread, but now acknowledged were mistaken. In any case, that $675 price beat the $580 fetched by a 2¢ Pan-American Exposition invert in the same sale — thus confirming auctioneer George Tuttle's prediction of two years earlier that the Jenny would soon be more valuable than the 1901 error.

For a while that record stood. On May 5, 1923, when auctioneer J.C. Morgenthau sold the U.S. collection of the late Clarence H. Eagle of Long Island, a Jenny invert described as "centering practically perfect, a superb mint copy" went for $610. But in January 1924 Eugene Klein advertised "a beautiful mint copy just released from a large airmail collection. Price $750."

Not long afterward, the general public got its first opportunity to see a Jenny invert. It was part of a magnificent collection of U.S. stamps donated in 1925 to the New York Public Library by Benjamin Kurtz Miller, a wealthy Milwaukee lawyer. Of the Jenny, Miller said: "I got in early and bought one for $250 and commission," which means it came from Klein.

If Miller could have foreseen what would eventually befall his stamps, including the Jenny, while in the library's keeping, he might well have chosen to dispose of them elsewhere — but more of that later.

The invert reached a price milestone in the spring of 1928 when a single sold for $1,000. That mark didn't endure long. The year 1929, when Wall Street's Big Bull Market soared to a record height of its own and then collapsed, saw another sharp increase in Jenny prices. Joseph A. Steinmetz had died the previous July, and in March Eugene Klein, his old partner in the purchase of the Jenny sheet, sold at auction for $1,060 the remaining specimen (position 11) from the pair Steinmetz had kept. In April, an invert in the collection of Reid S. Baker was sold by H.A. Robinette of Washington, D.C., for $1,500. And on December 2, 1929 — after the stock market crash — Walter S. Scott auctioned off the collection of the late John C. Williams of Morristown, New Jersey, and got $2,300 for a Jenny invert that was described as "never hinged, full original gum . . . One of the finest of known copies."

The worldwide depression that arrived with the 1930s and lasted through the decade failed to halt the upward movement of Jenny prices.

Eugene Klein sold a copy in January 1931 to the Nassau Stamp Company's John Klemann for $2,360. This was almost as much as the $2,500 which Klemann had offered William Robey for the entire sheet less than 13 years earlier. Klemann, by now a true believer, predicted that "in a few years" an invert would sell for $5,000. "This seems optimistic," Philip Ward observed, and he was right. For one reason or another, it would actually take 28 more years for the $5,000 mark to be reached.

In December 1932, insurance executive Joseph Frelinghuysen, another resident of Morristown, New Jersey, sold his collection through auctioneer George Sloane. Frelinghuysen was a former U.S. senator and, like Representative Ernest Ackerman, had served briefly as acting governor of the Garden State. Also, like Ackerman, he owned a Jenny invert (position 74), and at the auction the "full original gum, never hinged" copy sold for a record $2,750. The buyer, intriguingly, was identified only as "Mrs. F. of Morristown, New Jersey." Stamp writers later

**Position 74. Present owner has held it since December 1932, the ownership longevity record for an invert.**

identified her as Adaline Frelinghuysen, wife of Peter H.B. Frelinghuysen, a second cousin once removed of the senator.

"Mrs. Frelinghuysen is a member of the Havemeyer family," observed the editor of the *American Philatelist* — the reference was to Adaline's father, sugar magnate Henry O. Havemeyer — "and so had the required sugar to pay 11,000 times face for a stamp less than 15 years old."

Shortly afterward Mrs. Frelinghuysen transferred ownership to another person, who still owned the invert as of this writing, more than 53 years later (and, like many other Jenny owners before and since, insisted on anonymity). *

And more Jennies began to travel abroad, in the path of the copy that Colonel Green had given as a gift to Robson Lowe. H.R. Harmer and Company of London reported in its resume of its 1932-33 sales year that "two copies of the rare U.S.A. airmail 'invert,' the highest price air stamp in existence, were secured for English collectors." It accompanied the note with a picture of position 32 — British law permitted the illustration of U.S. stamps — and this, incidentally, was the last time that particular copy has been heard from.

* * *

Even more impressive in a stamp album than single copies of the Jenny — if a collector had a big enough bank account — were unseparated blocks.

* — Unless someone has owned one of the four "missing copies" for a longer period, this is an all-time longevity record for possession of a Jenny invert.

The four so-called position blocks which Colonel Green kept for his own collection weren't the only multiples to exist. Eugene Klein, in separating the sheet for the colonel, broke out some other blocks of four as well. These came from the south side of the sheet, row five and below, where the centering was generally better than in the upper half.

Philip Ward, writing in his house organ *Ward's Philatelic News* in April 1933, put the number of blocks sold by his fellow Philadelphian Klein on behalf of Colonel Green at four. If his information was correct, then a total of five blocks existed outside of Green's hands, since Klein kept one block for himself.

The Klein block comprised positions 47, 48, 57 and 58. It was well centered and was bisected by the sheet's red horizontal guideline. Several years after Klein's death in 1944, as a friend recalls the story, Dolores Klein Hertz and her husband Jay were summoned to Philadelphia from New York to pick up a trunk, contents unknown, storage charges prepaid, which a bank had been holding. Klein had left instructions that the trunk be turned over to his daughter after a prescribed time. When she and Jay opened it, the first thing they saw was the block of inverts. Underneath was a treasure in collections, individual stamps and covers. One collection, of early Hungary, was so impressive that the Hertzes later won a gold medal with it at a Budapest stamp exhibition.

One of the blocks Klein sold comprised stamps 65, 66, 75 and 76. Like his own block, it was a handsome item, well centered and bisected by a red guideline — in this case, vertically. This is generally assumed to be the block that was acquired by Arthur Hind, an upholstery manufacturer from Utica, New York, although no picture or description of the Hind block can be found.

Hind was the owner of one of the world's great stamp collections. In 1922 he had excited the philatelic universe by paying $27,500 for "the rarest stamp in the world," the one-of-a-kind British Guiana 1¢ of 1856, a little fragment of magenta paper that was homely and mutilated (its four corners had been clipped, giving it an octagonal shape) but possessed of an inexplicable charisma. To get it, Hind outbid a representative of King George V of Great Britain. Hind died at 77 in March 1933, and the following November most of his collection (but not the British Guiana) was put up for sale.

His was the first block of Jenny inverts ever to be sold at auction. The bidding was spirited between Hugh M. Clark of the Scott Stamp and Coin Company — the man who had started Colonel Green collecting stamps — and Nicholas Sanabria, another New York dealer and a man who not long afterward would begin publishing his own specialized annual catalog of airmail stamps. Clark's bid of $12,100 captured the Hind block.

Another block, comprising positions 61, 62, 71 and 72 and with the left sheet selvage attached, was sold to that frequent supplier of material to Colonel Green, the Economist Stamp Company. Someone at the firm, probably owner Edward Stern, marked each of the four stamps on the back with Economist's identifying handstamp. The block was acquired by Edgar Palmer, Princeton '03, chairman of the New Jersey Zinc Company, whose surname is perpetuated in Princeton in Palmer Stadium, where the Tigers play football, and Palmer Square in the heart of town. Four years after his death in 1943, his widow would give the block of Jenny inverts to the university.

**The horizontal guideline block of Jenny inverts, comprising positions 43, 44, 53 and 54.**

Still another block first came to public notice in February 1933 when it was sold by Philip Ward as agent for a New York bank to "settle the estate of a Western collector." The block, like Klein's block, was well centered and had a horizontal guideline; it comprised positions 43, 44, 53 and 54.

Dealer Emil Bruechig of New York bought it for $12,000 and resold it for $15,000 — the same price William Robey had obtained for the entire sheet less than 15 years earlier. The new owner of the block declined to allow the release of his name, and Bruechig would identify him only as a New York collector.

The *Philadelphia Bulletin*, reporting Ward's announcement of the sale, did philately a great favor by publishing a photograph of the block, apparently unaware that illustrating U.S. stamps was against the law. This made it possible later on to ascertain just which block it was.

Unfortunately, other published reports of the sale of Jenny blocks in the 1920s and 1930s were not so helpful. There were several such reports, but none was illustrated and none mentioned which positions the blocks had occupied on the sheet. Because of the highly limited number of possibilities, however, they must have involved one or more of the specific blocks mentioned above. The reports included:

• A statement in a book published in 1926 that a block of four inverts had recently been purchased by Kansas City grain dealer Allen Logan for $3,000, or $750 per stamp. When Logan's collection was sold in 1944, however, it contained no invert.

• Philip Ward's announcement, in the first issue of *Ward's Philatelic News* in November 1930, that he had been commissioned by the estate of Edward Randolph Wood Jr. to sell Wood's stamp collection, which included a Jenny invert block and single. Two years later, in November 1932, Ward announced that he had "sold a block last year," which was probably Wood's. Wood, a Philadelphia engineer and banker, had died in March 1930 in Paris at age 53. He had acquired many of his U.S. blocks in the 1925-26 sales of the collection of Wharton Sinkler of Philadelphia, Ward wrote, but Ward didn't specify whether the Jenny was one of them.

• Newspaper stories in July 1931 that said that John Aspinwall, a Newburgh, New York, banker, had bought a block for $15,000 at a private sale through Joseph Hoffmann of New York. Shortly afterward Nicholas Sanabria wrote of "the recent purchase and sale consummated in one day by myself" of a Jenny invert block for "a five figures dollar amount"; it was probably the same block.

• Philip Ward's further announcement, in April 1933, that a client had commissioned him to sell yet another Jenny block. "It is magnificent, perfectly centered and with full original gum," he wrote. This was probably a block that had been owned by Elliott Perry's old customer, Representative Ernest Ackerman, who died in 1931; the *New York Times* in May 1933 reported that Ward was offering Ackerman's block for sale on behalf of the estate.

There was also old-time dealer Eugene Costales' reported recollection, not long before his death in 1984, that as an employee of the Scott Stamp and Coin Company at the time of the inverts' discovery, he had bought two blocks from Klein for resale to collectors at $1,100 each.

* * *

Some time in 1936 Spencer Anderson, a New York dealer, sold the block comprising positions 65, 66, 75 and 76 — which is assumed to have been the block owned by Arthur Hind — to Mrs. Ethel Stewart of Newton, New Jersey, in a private transaction for $16,000. At $4,000 per stamp, it was of course another record. The following February Anderson paid $3,200, a record for a single, on behalf of a client at a Nicholas Sanabria auction. (Sanabria was quoted at the time as saying he had recently sold "a fine specimen" privately for $4,250, but no information about that transaction can be found.)

In October 1937 Sanabria auctioned the collection of Roger Steffan, vice president of National City Bank, and got $3,900 from Emil Bruechig for position 35, a well-centered, fully gummed specimen. The invert was upstaged in that sale, however, by a copy of the Honduras 5-centavo of 1925 that had been converted into an airmail stamp by the overprint "AERO CORREO" in red; this item, one of only 12 printed, went for $8,200.

Position 35 came on the market again twice within two years and, curiously, brought a lower price each time. In 1938 Harmer, Rooke and Company of London auctioned it ("by order of a prominent New York collector") for 725 pounds, or $3,603. And in September 1939 it again passed under Sanabria's hammer, fetching only $2,750.

Two months after that, though, another Jenny, position 38, broke through the $4,000 mark. The stamp was part of the premium-quality collection of the late Stephen D. Brown of Glens Falls, New York. Originally set for London, the sale was moved to Manhattan by Harmer, Rooke because of the war in Europe. It proved to be a beachhead that the company would expand into a U.S. operation that would flourish for more than 30 years. And the $4,100 the Economist Stamp Company paid for Brown's Jenny invert set an auction record for the stamp that would stand through the next decade.

* * *

Meanwhile, the first known attempt had been made to call the roll of the dispersed Jennies. Done by Philip Ward, it took the form of a list of current owners known to him, and accounted for 37 copies. It was dated February 26, 1938, only a few days after *Weekly Philatelic Gossip* had published William Robey's last and most detailed recollection of his experiences in buying and owning the sheet of inverts. One can assume that the appearance of this article had prodded Ward into making his inventory, just as it had no doubt stimulated the discussion of the invert in the letters between Elliott Perry and Harry Lindquist during the same period.

Ward's list has a certain credibility to it because of his long experience with the Jenny invert, first in writing about it and later in selling several singles and blocks. Unfortunately, he didn't indicate the positions of the individual stamps he listed, and in several cases he used initials

**Philip H. Ward Jr., one of the early chroniclers of the invert, who later bought and sold numerous copies.**

rather than names to designate owners, no doubt to satisfy their wishes to remain anonymous.

The list follows as Henry Goodkind reproduced it, with the number of copies owned by each individual preceding the name:

1, Mr. West, Phila., Pa.; 1, Mrs. Heathcote, St. Petersburg, Fla.; 1, Mr. Ewing; 1, Mr. Honeyman; 1, Dr. Cole; 4, Mrs. E.B. Stewart; 1, Dr. D.; 1, Mrs. McCleverty, England; 1, Mrs. FitzGerald, England; 1, Sir Everaad, England; 1, Mr. Hudson; 1, Mr. O.; 1, Mr. James Helm; 1, Mr. Hayden; 1, Mr. P.B. Frelinghuysen; 1, Dr. D.; 1, Mr. C.;1, Mr. Wilson; 4, Mr. Sinkler; 1, Mr. Sinkler; 1, Mr. Clatt; 1, Mr. L.; 1, Mr. C. Smith; 1, Mr. S. Brown; 1, Mr. Breuchig; 1, Mr. B.; 4, Mr. B.; 1, F.R. Vernon-Williams.

Three blocks or presumed blocks were listed — Mrs. Stewart's, Mr. Sinkler's and Mr. B.'s. The latter two collectors were also credited with single copies. Mrs. Stewart's is assumed to have been the former Arthur Hind block, and much more will be said about that item later.

Ward's list raises tantalizing questions. Who was Mr. B. and what block did he own? What became of the single credited to Mrs. Heathcote? When the Heathcote collection was auctioned in 1951, the Jenny invert in the sale — position 8, with false perforations at the top — was described as being the property of another owner, included in the sale by permission.

And what block did "Mr. Sinkler" own, and what became of it? As already noted, Philip Ward had referred years earlier to a 1925-1926 sale of stamps owned by Philadelphia's Wharton Sinkler. When more Sinkler stamps were sold by Eugene Klein in two sales in 1940, they contained no Jenny inverts. Sinkler himself, speaking to New Orleans dealer Raymond H. Weill in the early 1970s, said he had disposed of his entire collection by then.

There were minor errors in the list. "Everaad" was actually Sir Lindsay Everard. (Everard exhibited his invert, position 19, at the British Philatelic Exhibition of 1946, but when his collection of U.S. airmail stamps was auctioned in 1953, the invert wasn't included.) Emil Bruechig's name also was misspelled in the Ward list — at least, as it was copied by Goodkind. And "Clatt" doubtless referred to John H. Clapp, a Washington banker who owned Jenny position 5 and at least one copy of every other U.S. invert except the unique 5¢ proprietary (revenue) stamp of 1871.

Among the owners omitted completely from the list — in this case, quite understandably — was the Colonel Green estate. No one yet knew how many Jenny inverts were contained in the prodigious Green collection.

Chapter Eleven

# The Forty-One

*"Beyond a doubt the greatest show piece in all philately . . ."*

**— Harmer, Rooke catalog, Green sale XVII**

Six years went by after Colonel Green's death in 1936 before the first of his stamps were sold. Leading auction houses in the United States and Europe urged the executor, the Chase National Bank, to allow them to handle the assignment. However, the colonel's sister, Sylvia Green Wilks, was in no hurry. She chose to wait to see what effect the war clouds gathering over Europe might have on the international stamp market.

It wasn't until well after the outbreak of World War II, in fact, and the entry of the United States into the conflict, that the great collection finally went under the hammer. The sales had far-reaching effects, not the least of which was a high relative increase in the supply of Jenny inverts available for collectors. Within a span of three years, the number almost doubled.

In May 1942 the Green estate announced that a series of seven "experimental" auctions would be held to determine whether the wartime market was ready to absorb the collection at favorable prices. Like the Super Bowl of the future, the sales would be designated by Roman numerals.

The business was divided up among several dealers, under the general supervision of Walter S. Scott and Percy G. Doane: In New York, Harmer, Rooke and Company, Hugh C. Barr, Irwin Heiman, J.C. Morgenthau and Laurence and Stryker; in Boston, Daniel F. Kelleher.

The sales, held in the fall of 1942 with Walter Scott wielding the gavel, so pleased the executor and Mrs. Wilks that they decided to proceed with the disposal of the rest of the collection. This was done in a series of 21 additional auctions, ending in 1946 (one of them, No. XI, was in two sections three months apart). Two additional auction houses, Edson J. Fifield and Eugene Costales of New York, were included in the action. When it was over the Green stamps had brought a total of some $1,765,000 against a pre-sale appraisal of $1,200,000. Nearly 50,000 lots were sold, more than twice the number ever offered out of any other single collection at public sale.

In the process, the colonel's Jenny inverts emerged at last into the light of day. The 41 specimens in the sales consisted of the 20 he had kept in block form, 16 straight-edge copies (including three vertical pairs from the right side of the sheet) and five fully perforated singles. One of the latter — the most attractive one, in fact — had not been retained by the colonel originally but returned to his hands when he bought the collection of J.K. Storrow of Washington, D.C., from the Economist Stamp Company for $77,500.

The effect of dropping such a large number of inverts onto the market in a short time was predictable; it firmly stabilized prices. Although each Jenny single, pair and block attracted considerable attention as it was put up for sale, the stamps brought relatively modest sums, considering the steady upward price trend that the 1920s and 1930s had witnessed and the fact that dealers and collectors, like many other Americans, had a lot of money to spend during the war and not much to spend it on.

The top price paid for a single Jenny in the Green sales was the $3,300 fetched by the Storrow copy, position 39, an extremely well-centered, fully gummed specimen featured in Sale VIII. This was well below the $4,100 record set in 1939 by the Stephen Brown single. The lowest price paid for a fully perforated and gummed copy was $1,150, for the poorly centered position 26.

Nevertheless, the organizers of the sales professed to be gratified at how well some of the Jennies performed. Sale I, held by Hugh Barr September 23, 1942, offered position 5, the first straight-edge Jenny ever to be sold at auction. It brought $1,750 from an unidentified Baltimore collector.

Philip Ward, who had helped Walter Scott prepare the sales, wrote that they hadn't expected the initial Jenny to fly so high. "It was our estimate that it would possibly sell at $800 to $900 and that $1,000 would be the top limit," he recalled. "We were glad to find that we were wrong."

Position 6, in the second sale, brought $1,350. It too was a straight edge, and like the first one it still had its gum, but it also had what was described as a "light 16mm. corner crease" and a "thin trace in bottom right corner perforation." Later, the straight edges that had lost their gum brought from $750 to $1,030.

The four position blocks, which appeared beginning with Sale XVII on November 13, 1944, did somewhat better, in spite of evidence which two of them showed of some rough handling during Colonel Green's stewardship. All four blocks were purchased by dealer Y. Souren of New York City.

The dealer's real name was a tongue-twisting Souren Yohannessiantz. He was born in Armenia, the son of a merchant, and he liked to tell of escaping just ahead of the Bolshevik armies, posing as a peasant, driving a donkey cart with a precious collection of old clocks hidden under the hay. In New York he sold the clocks and went into the stamp trade, which he plied with brilliance and flamboyance.

He devised elaborate optical equipment for detecting stamp alterations, so effective that the Secret Service borrowed it on occasion for use against counterfeiters. At auctions he bid relentlessly for items he wanted; in 1938 he used an open transatlantic telephone line to buy the unique block of four of the U.S. 24¢ pictorial invert of 1869 at a Harmer, Rooke auction in London. Now, with the same kind of persistence, he went after the Jenny blocks.

The first to go was the bottom arrow/plate number block of eight. It was something less than it appeared, in that the upper left stamp — position 85 — had been separated and reattached, and both stamps

**Center line block, one of the choice "position blocks" retained from the original sheet by Colonel Edward H.R. Green.**

on the left side had thin spots. The Harmer, Rooke catalog somewhat feverishly described it as "a spectacular and gorgeous block, beyond a doubt the greatest show piece in all philately" and asserted that "a very conservative catalog value . . . would be $50,000." Nevertheless, it was knocked down for $27,000 to Souren, who bought it as agent for Amos Eno of Princeton, New Jersey, a collector of wide-ranging interests.

The remaining three blocks were not offered until 1946, in the postwar auctions that concluded the series. The center block of four where the guidelines crossed was described by Irwin Heiman, with an enthusiasm that rivaled Harmer, Rooke's, as an "outstanding and spectacular show piece . . . the gem of the . . . collection." In truth, it was a splendid block, nearly perfectly centered and unmarred by thin spots or creases. Souren bought it for $22,000.

The lower left corner block, with sheet selvage on two sides and siderographer DeBinder's initials in the bottom selvage, was also in beautiful condition and sold for $17,000.

**Lower left corner block of the Jenny invert, bearing the initials of siderographer Samuel DeBinder in the bottom selvage.**

The final block, the left arrow, as noted earlier had been separated along the horizontal guideline and was actually two horizontal pairs. It was offered by Harmer, Rooke as either two pairs or a block, depending on the highest offer, and was taken as a block by Souren for $13,750.

The Jenny inverts brought the Green estate a total of $108,475. Add to that the sum which the colonel had netted from the copies Eugene Klein

**Left arrow block of the Jenny invert, separated during Colonel Edward H.R. Green's ownership into two horizontal pairs.**

had sold for him, probably around $15,000; note that Mabel Green still owned a single copy, encased in a locket; and it is clear that Klein had been right back in 1918 when he insisted that the colonel, with his initial investment of $20,000, had not gotten "stuck."

The Jennies were only a small fraction of the Green holdings that were put into circulation through these 28 auctions. Also included were many other inverted centers, underscoring the owner's affinity for this type of error. Of the Pan-American Exposition inverts, there were 47 unused singles, including nine of the rarest one, the 2¢; 11 blocks of four, one of them a 2¢ (which sold for $5,750), and three used singles. His supply of the revenue inverts of the 1870s included two to five copies of each variety. Twenty-one uncut sheets of 400 of the 2¢ red imperforate of 1917, each sheet containing three copies of the 5¢ color error, brought prices ranging from $1,450 (Sale I) to $3,400 (Sale XXV). * The colonel's holdings of the 1909 experimental bluish-paper issue included 35 copies of the 4¢ and 28 of the 8¢, the two varieties that had gotten Joseph Steinmetz in trouble with the federal prosecutors many years earlier.

At Sale IX in 1943, Harmer, Rooke and Company gave to every successful bidder a reproduction of a die proof of Colonel Green's personal book plate, picturing the colonel as a bookworm in his library. The plate had been designed and etched for Green by none other than Marcus W. Baldwin, who as a Bureau of Engraving and Printing craftsman had engraved Jenny herself for the 24¢ stamp back in 1918.

* — One of these sheets of 400 sold at an auction April 14, 1984, for $28,000.

Even the Green auction catalogs would in time become collector's items. A complete set sold for $2,200 at an auction of philatelic literature in New York in December 1984.

Chapter Twelve

# The Memories

*"He never had a regret, he never looked back."*

— **Louise Robey Birch**

William T. Robey spent one week in the philatelic sun. In the three decades of his life that followed, he would recapture the attention of the stamp-collecting public only briefly and intermittently.

On May 26, 1918, five days after he sold his sheet to Eugene Klein, he wrote a 350-word account of his experience for the *Collectors' Journal* at the request of J.E. Guest, the editor. He concluded the article, which appeared in the June issue, with this paragraph:

"Much more could be told about these stamps and I will be glad to write about my trip to New York and my funny experiences there if your editor wishes me to do so."

Robey never got the chance to follow up on this offer. In a subsequent issue of the magazine, editor Guest announced that he had been called to military service and would have to suspend publication. He never revived the magazine.

Nearly 20 years later, however, Al Burns, editor of *Weekly Philatelic Gossip*, asked Robey to prepare a more detailed reminiscence. The 2,600-word piece that resulted appeared in the issue for February 19, 1938, under the title "The Story of the Discovery of the 24-Cent Inverted Center Airmail Stamps, told by the actual finder, W.T. Robey."

"During all of these years that have passed since I purchased these stamps," Robey explained to his readers, "I do not recall having seen an article that has given all of the details connected with the purchase and sale of the sheet. I have often thought that I would like to write all of these details in order that many of the present and all future generations of philatelists may know these facts. At the request of the *Gossip*, I have decided to acquaint the philatelic world with the details."

Indeed, in spite of its gaps and inconsistencies, the article remains the most complete source of information on Robey's experiences with his Jenny inverts.

Back in June 1918, in the same issue of the *Collectors' Journal* in which his first essay appeared, Robey was also represented wearing his dealer's hat. A display ad read:

"I discovered the airplane inverts. I have none of these for sale. Have other good things. Send along your want list. References necessary. W.T. Robey, Harvard Street, N.W., Washington, D.C." The same ad appeared in the July issue, along with another ad in which he quoted prices for mint blocks of "hard to get" U.S. stamps.

Robey also performed a little task at the request of Philip Ward. Outfitted with a camera, he returned to the New York Avenue branch post office where he had bought the inverts and took a picture of the building. Years later, when Ward had become a major stamp dealer in Philadelphia, he used the photo on the cover of an issue of *Ward's Philatelic News*, the house organ he published.

Robey continued to show a lively interest in philately. When the airmail rate was reduced to 16¢ in July he obtained for his collection not only first-flight covers of the new green Jenny stamp mailed on July 15, but also at least one rare July 11 first day cover. (This cover, addressed on a typewriter to Robey at his Harvard Street address, sold at a 1973 auction for $3,500.)

He also passed along to stamp publications tidbits of information, such as the news that the Bureau of Engraving and Printing was discontinuing the war emergency measure of printing stamps on the offset press.

In later years people would write to Robey and visit him, and some asked for his autograph. He spoke to local stamp clubs, and he appeared on a radio program or two to talk about his great adventure. But he never sought the publicity; self-promotion wasn't really in his nature.

He even disliked being photographed. The picture of Robey used in this book was one he couldn't escape — it was taken at his daughter's wedding in 1940 — and the only other portrait of him which has survived is a small identification photo made by the federal government. He would have been an ideal candidate for television's panel shows, "I've Got a Secret" or "To Tell the Truth," if they had existed during his lifetime, but he might not have agreed to appear.

Henry M. Goodkind, in his 1956 study of the Jenny invert, indulged in some speculation about Robey and relayed some reports that are of dubious reliability. There was Dolores Hertz's account of the "briefcase incident" in the office of her father, Eugene Klein, described in an earlier chapter. And, Goodkind wrote, Elliott Perry had told him that Robey was in a hurry to sell the sheet because he "feared that

**A rare picture of William T. Robey, discoverer of the Jenny inverts. He is shown with his daughter Louise at her wedding in 1940.**

if news accounts were published mentioning enormous profits, he would be reclassified and drafted into the Army."

Robey was, in fact, later called before his draft board, as he freely acknowledged, but his classification wasn't changed. And he obviously wasn't reluctant to publicize his profit himself. The account he wrote for the *Philatelic Gazette* five days after the transaction with Klein contained this self-satisfied conclusion: "The sheet I finally sold to a Philadelphia collector (sic) for the princely sum of $15,000, which was quite an investment on the outlay of only $24."

Some of Goodkind's other second-hand reports about Robey are impossible to confirm. Again crediting Elliott Perry, Goodkind described Robey as "highly nervous" during the time he owned the sheet, because "not long before May 14th, a shortage of funds had been discovered in the office . . . where Robey was employed. Although completely innocent, this shortage was found in the department where Robey worked. As a consequence, he was being subjected to an investigation, an unnerving experience."

Goodkind, who seemed predisposed to picture Robey in an unflattering light, summed up the discoverer's later career this way:

"It has been alleged in stories told to collectors that Robey's life was not too fortunate after he had sold his $24 sheet for a net profit of $14,976. This caused him and his family to expand their mode of living so that the money was soon spent. In time, he had little to show except the fame of his purchase in 1918. It is known that since his death in 1949, no stamp collection belonging to Robey has been advertised for sale or offered at auction. So possibly at the time of his death, he was no longer a stamp collector or perhaps his stamp collections were of nominal value."

Contrary testimony came from Caroline Robey in an interview after her husband's death. She told one writer: "Billy said if he could get a car, I could have the rest (of the money) to do with as I wanted. That was the bargain, and he bought our first car, a touring model . . .

"The salesman gave him a driving lesson, and on the way home everyone on the street managed to keep out of his way, but when he drove it into the garage and the back wall refused to budge, he drove right on through it. Well, he got it patched up and we had lots of wonderful times with Billy's car.

"My share? I bought a house, paid all cash, and some furniture to put in it, and there wasn't enough left to speak of."

The house that was bought with stamp money was located on Kenyon Street, a few blocks from the Harvard Street apartment and the neighbors who didn't appreciate daughter Louise's crying. It did more than provide the Robeys with a home, however. They were convinced that it saved Louise from being crippled.

On Easter Sunday in 1923 Louise, then 6, was stricken with polio. Before long she had lost all movement and feelings in her lower legs. The doctor suggested a program of treatment consisting of hot compresses and manipulation of the limbs. The Robeys borrowed against the house and hired private nurses to work around the clock with the child. After several weeks she regained partial use of her legs. The doctor then prescribed exercise therapy, and for two years William and Caroline Robey took Louise to dance classes — "a physical ordeal for me, a financial ordeal for them," she remembered.

Eventually, her recovery was complete. Her mother would say afterward: "I don't care how many others made money on those stamps. They helped us when we needed it most. What more could you ask?"

William Robey agreed. As the years went by and the Jenny inverts climbed in value, people would ask him if he was sorry he had sold his sheet. "He would say, 'No, not at all.' He never had a regret, he never looked back," his daughter said. "He would say to me, 'If I hadn't sold it, where would you be?' " In his 1938 memoir he noted with a touch of pride that a Jenny invert — it was banker Roger Steffan's copy — had recently fetched $3,900 at auction.

Still, in later years, when Louise was grown, friends would send her clippings whenever another Jenny was sold for a high price, and always the question was implicit: "Don't you wish you still had some of them?"

Louise became a schoolteacher and later a principal. In 1940 she

**Louise Robey Birch and her husband Merritt in 1982, looking at her mother's scrapbook of Jenny invert memorabilia.**

married Merritt Birch, an insurance executive, and they had two children of their own. In their home in Towson, Maryland, in later years, they treasured the reminders of her parents. There was the scrapbook her mother kept after "Billy's" death, full of clippings and other memorabilia about the Jenny invert. It was a retirement gift from one of Caroline Robey's fellow workers, and it was embossed in gold "WTR and CAR, May, 1918," the month and year of the discovery. There were Oriental objects which Robey bought at auction on the family's vacation trips to Atlantic City. Outside the Birch home were peonies and other flowers which her father, who loved to garden, started for them years earlier. "Every time I move someplace," Louise said, "I take his flowers with me."

She described her father as she saw him in memory: a youthful looking man despite prematurely gray hair, of slender build, fastidiously dressed, and with the half-smile he characteristically wore. Not too long before the interview she had come across letters her mother had received after he died, "from Texas, the Midwest, people who had known him or had worked with him, saying what fond memories they had of him. He was just a nice, down-to-earth person."

He was also a devoted father, she said, always on hand at school recitals that involved herself or her younger sister Carolyn, who was called "Jackie," always available to take the girls to and from Sunday school, although he wasn't a regular churchgoer himself.

Robey made his livelihood with figures, first as a cashier for Hibbs and later as an auditor with the U.S. Department of Agriculture and after that the War Department. He had the right kind of mind for it, organized, systematic, and he had an unusual ability to quickly calculate sums in his head.

He continued to collect U.S. stamps and regularly bought new issues. As can be imagined, he always scrutinized his purchases closely, and shortly after discovering the Jenny error he found some 13¢ regular Franklin-head stamps with freak perforations — which he duly reported in a note to *Mekeel's* — but he never again found a bona fide error at a stamp window. He was a member of the Washington Collectors' Club.

Robey's love for stamps was transmitted to his younger daughter, and he and Jackie spent many evenings with their heads together over his collection. Jackie was like her father in other ways: She was quiet, she was good at mathematics and she was interested in a banking career. Attending accounting school on a scholarship, she helped some of the adult members of the class compute their income taxes. She also had a flair for dancing, using steps she had picked up as a child while watching her sister practice. It was a cruel blow to her family when she died, suddenly and unexpectedly, at 17 on February 27, 1939.

They buried Jackie in Washington's Rock Creek Cemetery. Afterward, William Robey couldn't face his stamp collection. "Every time he sat down with the stamps it brought her back to mind," Louise said. He sold at least part of the collection and used some of the money to buy a rose quartz stone from Finland for her grave.

During World War II Robey's assignment as an auditor was to the Chemical Warfare Service's fiscal division, and he traveled frequently by rail and air to such outposts as Huntsville, Alabama, and Provo, Utah.

In time his interest in stamps returned. He saved sheets and plate number blocks, and eventually he accumulated several thousand dollars' worth in face value alone, Louise said. On his wartime travels he would stop at small-town post offices looking for obsolete items. His favorite hobby workplace was the dining room table after dinner, and he would study his stamps with a glass, commenting whenever a bit of engraving or color struck his fancy, calling anybody near over to see it.

He continued to dabble in the stamp business — by now he saw it as a possible retirement career — and he set up a couple of display cases in a corner of his son-in-law's insurance office. "Daddy was not a businessman," Louise said. "If you came in to look at some stamps, he would spend all the time talking with you about them."

Over the years the Robeys traded up in housing, moving from

Kenyon Street to Quincy Street to 5618 North Capitol Street, all in Washington. After the war, Louise and Merritt moved to Silver Spring, Maryland, and in early 1949 the Robeys, impressed by the new house, bought an almost identical one two blocks away, at 9503 Wire Avenue. But William Robey would live in it only two weeks.

He had suffered from gall bladder illness, but had put off a recommended operation. In September 1948 he had a severe attack at his desk and collapsed, striking his head on a file cabinet as he fell. In December he had the surgery, which was successful, and he returned home Christmas Eve, but now he was complaining of headaches, worse than the migraines he had sometimes suffered in the past. On a visit to Jackie's grave in January he almost rammed his car into a stone pillar at the cemetery entrance, and only his wife's scream snapped him out of his daze. A few days later, complaining of "a headache like nothing I've ever had," he went to his doctor, who examined him and found signs of mental impairment; the man with the calculator-like mind couldn't count to 60.

The doctor ordered him to the hospital the next day for tests, but that night he was working with his stamps as if everything were normal. His daughter phoned her husband, who was in New Orleans, and asked him to return. Early in the morning Merritt Birch arrived from the airport by taxi and William Robey said: "Is that you, Merritt? Oh, I'm so glad you're here."

Those were the last words he spoke. The deterioration was by now so rapid that he couldn't speak, couldn't dress himself and could barely wave goodbye to his young granddaughter, Carolyn, as his wife and son-in-law helped him to the car. The diagnosis at George Washington University Hospital was a brain tumor — possibly related to the blow on the head the previous autumn — and the next day he underwent a seven-hour operation. Two days after that, on February 5, 1949, he died at the age of 59 without recovering consciousness.

William Robey was buried beside his daughter. A few months later his second grandchild, Douglas Birch, was born. Caroline Robey, reacting to the sudden void in her life, took a job with the Internal Revenue Service and worked during the next few years in IRS offices in Washington, New Jersey and Philadelphia, examining tax returns. In time, she began to collect stamps herself ("Wouldn't your father be surprised?" she said). She didn't do it systematically, as he had; she accumulated whatever struck her fancy, foreign stamps, U.S. first day covers, "anything pretty."

When Caroline Robey retired she moved in with Louise and Merritt in Towson. She struck up a friendship with Sol Glass of Baltimore, a leading authority on U.S. stamps who had known her husband and had owned a copy of the Jenny invert himself. They would often reminisce about William Robey and his great discovery. When she finally decided, in 1962, to sell Robey's stamps, Glass helped her find the right buyer, a Baltimore dealer.

Caroline Robey's own health failed in time, and she died May 8, 1972. While she was still active, however, she did something she had long wanted to do. She accompanied her daughter and son-in-law and two grandchildren to the Smithsonian Institution. They headed for the philatelic section, where the Smithsonian's Jenny invert was on display, and Caroline showed the children what their grandfather had found so many years before. Louise Birch smiled at the recollection.

"There was one woman standing there, looking at the stamp and reading the card," she said. "And when we walked up to the case, Mama said to the children, 'Now, see, this is the stamp I wanted you to see.'

"As the woman was ready to leave, she turned to Mama and said, 'Can you imagine owning that stamp?'

"And Mama said, 'Yes, I can.' "

Chapter Thirteen

# The Climb

*"We are actually prepared to go much higher."*

— **Roger Weill**

In the years since the Green sales, many philatelic dealers have bought and sold Jenny inverts or provided the necessary auction services. A few, however, have been identified particularly closely with the stamp.

One is the Raymond H. Weill Company of New Orleans, co-owned by the Weill brothers, Raymond and Roger. Another is Irwin Weinberg's Miner Stamp Company of Wilkes-Barre, Pennsylvania.

**Raymond (left) and Roger Weill, who have owned and sold more Jenny inverts than any other stamp dealers.**

Dominating the consignment business for Jennies have been the New York auction houses of Robert A. Siegel, H.R. Harmer and Harmer, Rooke and Company.

Of them all, Raymond and Roger Weill (pronounced Weel) clearly have the greatest personal affinity for the invert. "It has always been one of our favorites," Raymond says.

Operating out of a tiny shop on Royal Street, in the French Quarter's famous Antique Row, the Weills have bought and sold Jennies dozens of times since World War II, often at prices that set new records. It was they who, in 1958, donated a Jenny invert to the Smithsonian Institution at the request of Franklin Bruns, then the Smithsonian's curator of stamps. This Jenny is position 70, one of the ungummed straight-edge copies that was in Colonel Green's collection at his death; the Weills had obtained it from a Michigan collector. They have been especially partial to Jenny blocks, and have owned seven of them — all the blocks, in fact, that have come on the market since they began playing in the philatelic major leagues.

The Weills — bachelors who are now in their 70s — are more than dealers, though they have traveled the globe for years to buy and sell philatelic gems. They are first of all stamp lovers. "When Roger and I see a rare stamp, we gush over it like a mother with a newborn baby," Ray Weill says.

Similarly, he admits they feel "a great dejection" when they part company with one of their treasures. They sell only to bona fide collectors if possible; Ray said of one potential customer, "We've never sold him a stamp because we knew the purpose of his buying was for investment and we didn't want to be responsible if his investment didn't turn out the way he expected." Often they will buy a choice item just for the pleasure of owning it, without a specific customer in mind, and will hold it for years before selling.

Their most spectacular buy was made in 1968 when, from the back row of an H.R. Harmer auction, they went after a pair on cover of the 1-penny orange Mauritius of 1847. The stamps were from plates engraved by a jeweler on the island so the wife of the governor general would have something novel to use on invitations to a party, and this cover contained one of those invitations.

Auctioneer Bernard Harmer declared the item sold to Roger Weill for $280,000, then discovered he had missed a prearranged signal from another bidder. The Weills agreed without argument to a reopening of the bidding. When the hammer fell again they had won the cover for exactly $100,000 more — $380,000, the highest price paid up to that time for a single philatelic item. At last report, they still owned it.

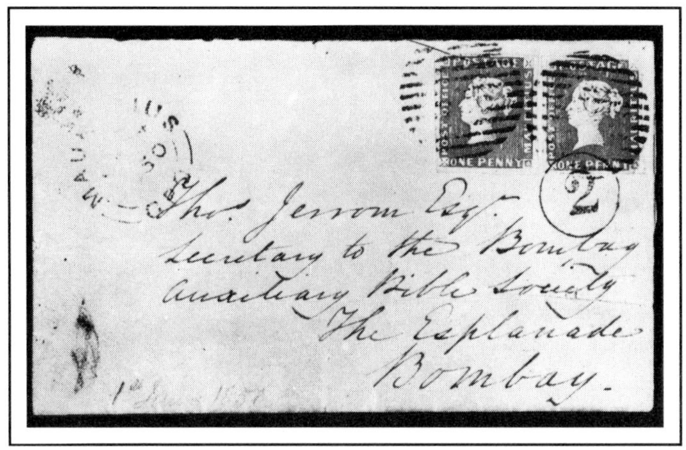


**The Mauritius cover, bought by the Weill brothers of New Orleans.**

As befits old pros in a business where discretion is essential, the Weills keep confidences, and they guard the names of even long-dead clients if those clients, when alive, had wanted anonymity. Unfortunately for the historian, this includes several people to whom they have sold Jenny inverts.

Irwin Weinberg, who began dealing in stamps as a teenager, went on to build one of the world's best-known stamp businesses in the old coal mining town of Wilkes-Barre. Over the years he has bought and sold Jenny inverts dozens of times, beginning in 1948 when he purchased a straight-edge copy from a Dr. Von Prichard of Pittsburgh for $1,200 and resold it not long afterward to another dealer for $1,800. He is best known as head of a syndicate of businessmen who for a decade owned the world's most valuable stamp, the 1¢ British Guiana black on magenta that had been the centerpiece of Arthur Hind's great collection in the 1920s.

Weinberg bought the British Guiana at Robert Siegel's annual rarities auction in 1970 with a bid of $280,000 (the Weill brothers dropped out of the bidding at $250,000). His group held the stamp exactly 10 years, and during that time Weinberg, fulfilling what he termed a duty to philately, exhibited it at stamp shows all over the world, in Paris, Tokyo, Prague, Hamburg, Berlin, New Delhi. In 1980 the group sold it, again at a Siegel rarities auction, for $850,000. The unnamed buyer also paid a 10 percent commission to the auction house, bringing his total cost to $935,000 — the highest price ever paid for a single philatelic item.

The Siegel firm dates to 1930. Harmer, Rooke and Company was founded in London early in the century, and began its operations in

**The world's most valuable stamp, the British Guiana 1¢ magenta of 1856, sold for $935,000 at auction in 1980.**

the United States in 1939 with the great Stephen Brown collection sale at which a Jenny invert first topped the $4,000 mark. And what is now Harmers International was begun in 1918 by Henry R. Harmer, an internationally known British philatelist, and eventually opened branches in San Francisco and Sydney to supplement its London and New York operations, under the overall direction of the founder's son, Bernard D. Harmer.

* * *

For a decade and a half after the Green sales, prices paid for the Jenny inverts remained level or, in some cases, actually declined. To some extent this reflected the general state of the stamp market, but the sudden availability of 41 new copies of the invert unquestionably had a depressing effect on the investment value of that specific stamp.

For example, position 28 was sold in 1940 with the collection of George R.M. Ewing of New York for $2,750. It sold again in 1947 as part of the collection of Cuban match magnate Alberto Perez for $3,550, then began losing ground, selling in 1949 for $2,700 and in 1950, its last recorded sale to date, for $2,600.

The shopworn position 93, which was creased and regummed, was auctioned for $2,100 in 1939 with the collection of Dr. Philip G. Cole of Tarrytown, New York (it was described then, probably inaccurately, as having "original gum"). It brought only $1,650, however, at auction in 1956. Mrs. William Deyo's slightly thinned position 34 sold for $2,550 in 1941, but fetched only $2,050 when it came on the market again in 1947.

The best recorded price for a Jenny invert during this period did no better than equal the all-time high, set before the war, of $4,100. This amount was paid by Roger Weill in June 1952 for position 39 — the copy that had brought the best price of all the inverts in the Green sales — at the auction of the collection of Henry Close, a food corporation executive.

Then, on July 30, 1959, came a breakthrough.

The preceding September, Frederick H. Douglas, a 79-year-old stockbroker from Rumson, New Jersey, had boarded a Jersey Central commuter train for his once-a-week trip to Wall Street. The train plunged through an open liftbridge and into Newark Bay, killing Douglas and 47 other passengers and crew members. Douglas, a stamp collector, years earlier had bought a beautifully centered Jenny invert, reportedly from Eugene Klein himself; now the stamp, position 77, never hinged, was put under the hammer for the estate by auctioneer John A. Fox of Floral Park, New York.

In a vigorous auction, Raymond Weill found himself competing in the rarefied atmosphere above $5,000, with six other dealers still in the bidding. Weill finally prevailed at $6,100, some $2,000 above the old record for a Jenny invert. John Klemann's prediction back in 1931 that a Jenny would sell for $5,000 had finally come true, but it took something more than the "few years" he had mentioned to make it happen.

The new record didn't last long, however. In December 1959 Robert Siegel auctioned position 68, also never hinged, from the collection of industrialist Theodore A. Stevens of Columbus, Ohio, for $6,400. Another major jump came in December 1960 when Harmer, Rooke sold the handsome position 94, with bottom sheet selvage attached, from the collection of the late Major T. Charlton Henry of Chestnut Hill, Pennsylvania, for $9,200. The buyer was Erwin N. Griswold of Belmont, Massachusetts, dean of the Harvard Law School and later to be solicitor general of the United States.

The record ratcheted up again the following June with Siegel's sale of another bottom-row copy, position 96, with half-arrow showing in the selvage, from the so-called "Brothers Collection" for $9,750. The buyer, West Coast collector Richard Engel, bid by phone, competing against floor bids starting at $8,000.

Prices were proving to be as volatile in the 1960s as they had been static in the 1940s and 1950s, and records fell almost yearly, sometimes more than once in a year. In October 1964 Siegel sold position 67 to dealer Ezra Cole for $10,500. The very next month H.R. Harmer auctioned the beautiful, never-hinged position 84 from the Thomas A. Matthews collection to the Weills for $15,500, the highest price ever realized for a U.S. stamp. In February 1966 the Weills pushed the record up to $18,000 in order to obtain position 35.

In March 1969, barely three years later, the same position 35 was sold to Ezra Cole for $27,000 at another Siegel auction. And in May of that year Harmer auctioned position 84 again, this time to stamp broker Myron Kaller, for $31,000. The specimen had exactly doubled its price in less than five years. The amount paid was, of course, another record for a U.S. stamp.

Not every sale was setting a record; position 60, for example, sold in March 1968 and April 1970 for the same $20,000 price. Still, for the top quality specimens, well centered and with little or no trace of hinging on the gum, the seemingly irresistible climb went on. November 1969, position 69, $33,000; March 1970, position 39, $34,000; March 1971, position 78, $36,000; January 1973, position 78, $37,000; March 1974, position 57, $41,000; May 1974, position 84, $47,000; March 1976, position 47, $47,500.

And that was only the beginning.

* * *

Meanwhile, the blocks were following their own remarkable courses.

The Weills have not been the only *aficianados* to combine a particular fondness for these blocks and the means to indulge it. Colonel Green, of course, had owned all four of the so-called position blocks. Dealer Y. Souren bought all four in the Green sales and resold them all in the few years before his death, at age 57, in 1949.

Then there was a Weill customer whom the brothers will identify only as "an Eastern collector, Mr. B," who at one time owned four different blocks. (This was almost certainly not the Mr. B. whom Philip Ward had included on his 1938 list as the owner of a block; the Weills' Mr. B acquired all four of his blocks through their firm, and long after 1938.) The items he owned were the left arrow, the plate number and the center line blocks and the "Klein-Hertz" block — the quartet of inverts which Eugene Klein had bequeathed to his daughter, Dolores Hertz. The Weills regained all four of the blocks (plus a single) in 1968 and 1969, after Mr. B's death, when they bought his entire collection from his estate for some $4 million.

Of all the Jenny blocks, the one that has wandered the most is the left arrow block of four or, to be precise, the two matched horizontal pairs that travel together.

Souren sold the arrow block in 1947 to L.D. White, a New York collector. White sold it in 1949 to the Weills, who sold it the following year to Mr. B. In 1969, after purchasing the Mr. B collection for such a large amount, the Weill brothers moved quickly to recoup some of their costs, and one of the items they resold was the arrow block, to a non-collector buying for investment. It then turned up in the Siegel rarities sale of 1969, going to another anonymous buyer, who submitted his winning $115,000 bid by telephone. Later the Weills obtained it again and sold it in 1970 to "a Western collector, Mr. P." A member of Mr. P's family inherited it in 1971, and the heir sold the block back to the Weills in 1984.

Almost as many transactions are recorded for the handsome, never-hinged center line block. It was sold by Souren to John Stilwell of Yonkers, New York, a vice president of the Consolidated Edison Company and brother of General Joseph W. "Vinegar Joe" Stilwell, American commander in the Far East during World War II. John Stilwell died in 1963, and when his collection was auctioned by Siegel the following year, Roger Weill bought the block for $67,000, a record for a Jenny multiple. "We were actually prepared to go much higher," Roger said afterward.

The Weills sold it to Mr. B; repurchased it from the estate; sold it to "an American collector," and repurchased it from him in 1979. In 1985 the brothers sold the block, along with the lower left corner block, to another "American collector."

That corner block, with the siderographer's initials in the bottom selvage, had been owned by food corporation executive Henry B. Close, who had acquired it directly from Souren. When Eugene Costales sold the Close collection June 23, 1952, the Weills were among the bidders, but lost out to Ezra Cole, who paid $22,000 on behalf of a client who was described in the press as an industrialist whose passion for stamps was a secret even from close friends. Later this closet philatelist was identified as Josiah K. Lilly Jr. of Indianapolis, grandson of the founder of the Eli Lilly pharmaceuticals company. Besides stamps, he had impressive collections of coins, books, jewels, military miniatures and model ships.

Lilly later became a regular customer of the Weills. Every year in January, he would sell a million dollars' worth of common stock and apply the proceeds to his hobbies. On or about January 15 he would meet with Raymond and Roger Weill, give them his budget for the year and pay them for the stamps he had bought the year before. At one point, Lilly strongly urged the brothers to leave their beloved New Orleans and open an office in New York, close to the major auctions. They declined, and he took his business elsewhere, but a few years later he asked them to take him back as a customer.

Lilly died in 1966. Two years later his collection — much of it built by the Weills — was auctioned by Robert Siegel in a series of 10 sales. Among the items the Weill brothers bought was the corner block of Jenny inverts, for which they paid $100,000, the highest price ever fetched by a U.S. philateic item up to then. The block remained in their stock for 17 years. For quick identification, it is still referred to as "the Lilly block."

One of the many other high points of the sales was the 51 lots comprising complete sheets of 19th century plate proofs once owned by Representative Ernest Ackerman; these too went to the Weills, for a surprisingly low $98,000, well below their catalog value.

Altogether, however, the Lilly auctions brought a quite impressive $3,134,127, which was more than double the sum which the 28 Green sales had realized more than two decades earlier.

The fourth Jenny position block was the bottom arrow-plate number block of eight, positions 85-88 and 95-98. Since the upper left stamp, position 85, was detached, this was actually a block of seven. Y. Souren further divided the block on instructions of its owner, Amos Eno. He left intact the four right-hand stamps with the selvage containing the plate number, and Eno kept this block in his collection, along with a single, position 86. Positions 95 and 96 became a horizontal pair with attached selvage showing the arrow.

**Plate number block of the Jenny airmail invert.**

In 1954 Eno sold his collection of U.S. blocks — which included blocks of the 1¢ and 4¢ Pan-American Exposition inverts — through Harmer, Rooke. The Jenny plate block of four was bought by the Weills for $18,250. This price, which amounted to some $4,560 per stamp, seemed to be a rare bargain for a piece with the unique attractiveness of this one, considering that the lower left corner block had been bought for Josiah Lilly nearly two years earlier for $22,000. This time, however, no one with Lilly's buying power and determination was in the auction.

"Mr. Lilly didn't need another block," Raymond Weill explained, "so we didn't have that competition. If you eliminate somebody who would buy something he needed at almost any price, it changes the picture." The Weills sold the plate block to an unnamed Eastern collector who specialized in U.S. errors, and his intention, as expressed to Raymond Weill, was to "die with it."

Of the remaining fragments of that original block of eight, position 85 found its way back into Souren's hands and was sold for $1,800 in the first installment of the dealer's stock to be auctioned after his death. Position 86, kept by Eno, was sold with part of his collection in 1950. The bottom arrow pair, positions 95 and 96, also returned to Souren and was sold for $3,300 in the second sale of his stock, to Lt. Col. Donald L. Harvey of Mobile, Alabama. The pair was described in the Harmer auction catalog as "somewhat creased and left hand stamp (95) thinnings near left margin."

When the Harvey collection was sold in 1955, the arrow pair went to Jack Molesworth, a Boston dealer, for $6,100. Molesworth broke the pair into singles and detached from position 95 the bottom selvage with its half arrow. "Position 95 was described as having a thin and position 96 was sound," he explained later. "Also, I seem to recall that most if not all of the thinning in position 95 was in the sheet margin while the stamp itself had only a gum abrasion and was essentially sound. That is why the sheet margin was removed."

The "Klein-Hertz" block was sold in the 1950s by Dolores Hertz and her husband, Dr. Jay Hertz, for $20,000 to dealer John A. Fox, a family friend. It was Fox who had introduced Dolores and Jay and served as best man at their wedding. Fox advertised the block but failed to sell it, and later resold it to the Hertzes. They then sold it for the same $20,000 price to Robert Siegel, and Siegel sold it to the Weills. "It was just a perfectly centered unhinged block," Raymond Weill enthused.

The brothers in turn sold it to Mr. B, and then regained it, along with his other blocks, in 1968 and 1969. Later they sold the block to an unnamed customer of some 80 years of age who held it for a while and then asked the Weills to break it into singles so his four heirs — three children and a son-in-law — would have no disagreement over the division of his estate. For the same reason, he asked them to break a block of 2¢ Pan-American Exposition inverts, a block of 4¢ Columbian Exposition color errors and other blocks.

"He didn't trust himself to do the actual division," Raymond Weill said. "One perforation torn could cut the value in half. We've separated a lot of blocks, and with great care we separated the (Klein-Hertz) block and the others. We fold them in one direction along the perforations and then fold them in the other direction, and then we repeat the procedure, then we pull them apart.

"Later we bought back all four collections from the heirs, so the blocks need not have been broken."

The Weills have also owned the so-called "Princeton block," which Edgar Palmer's widow gave to her husband's alma mater. Its story will be told in detail in the next chapter.

The final block to be owned by the Weill brothers is the one which Philip Ward sold in 1933 to Ernest Bruechig for "a New York collector." It had not been shown publicly, or even heard of, since then and was considered "lost" to philately. However, early in 1986 the Weills announced that they had bought a collection of rare stamps that included the Ward-Bruechig block, positions 43-44-53-54. The collection had been compiled by the seller's grandfather, a Middle Westerner who was not known as a philatelist, Raymond Weill said. Also included in the purchase was a copy of the prized 10-centavo blue Honduras of 1925 overprinted "Aero Correo 25c" in black.

All six of the surviving blocks of four of the Jenny invert were exhibited at AMERIPEX '86, the great international stamp show held in Chicago from May 22 to June 1, 1986. At the Weill brothers' booth were the left arrow, Ward-Bruechig, center line, Lilly and plate number blocks, the last three on loan from their owners; the Princeton block was shown by its owner, dealer Kenneth Wenger of Fort Lee, New Jersey. Twelve singles were also displayed or offered for sale by various dealers. Never, since Eugene Klein began selling off the specimens not retained by Colonel Green, had so many Jenny inverts been assembled under one roof.

Chapter Fourteen

# The Peak

*"The chart looks tremendous on it."*

**— George Manter**

As inflation, with a great boost from the soaring price of imported oil, tightened its hold on the U.S. economy in the 1970s, people began looking for new ways to shelter their savings. One way was to buy collectibles, including stamps. Prices of quality stamps jumped, and the Jenny invert, which had already experienced a remarkable climb in the 1960s, flew to an unprecedented altitude.

The trend line for U.S. stamp values had been on a steady ascent through the decade, but at the beginning of 1978 it shifted sharply upward. The U.S. Stamp Market Index compiled by *Linn's Stamp News* — a measure of the price movements of selected U.S. stamps, constructed on the same principles as the Consumer Price Index and the Dow Jones Industrial Average — showed the line moving from a base of 100 at the beginning of 1970 to just under 400 in January 1978. At that point it began a series of abrupt jumps, reaching the 900 mark in mid-1980. It held there, tracing a kind of bumpy plateau on the chart, until late 1981.

The Jenny invert's own steep ascent began with a Robert Siegel auction at the American Philatelic Society convention in San Francisco August 27, 1977, where position 69 sold for $62,500, almost double the $33,000 it had brought in 1969. In April 1978, at his annual "rarities" sale, Siegel auctioned position 47 for $72,500; the same stamp, just two years earlier, had brought $47,500.

On November 20, 1978, a Jenny invert reached the $100,000 mark. It was the well-centered position 39, the same specimen that had topped all other singles in the Colonel Green auctions with a price of $3,300. The auctioneer was Sotheby Parke Bernet of New York; the buyer, dealer Stanley Richmond of Boston. The record lasted barely four months, however. At Siegel's April 1979 rarities sale, position 57 went to Irwin Weinberg for $130,000.

The following year Siegel and other major auction houses made a major policy change in an effort to encourage owners of rare stamps to throw them into this blazing seller's market. They cut in half the commission they charged consignors, from 20 to 10 percent, and imposed a 10 percent premium on the buyer, after the fashion of European houses. The buyers were not deterred. Siegel, in his April 1980 rarities sale, sold position 96, a stamp with a "small light thin," for $125,000 plus $12,500. In April 1981 he auctioned position 57 to Harry Hagendorf of Columbian Stamp Company in New Rochelle, New York, for $160,000 plus $16,000.

Finally, at the Siegel rarities auction of April 24, 1982, the ceiling was reached. An anonymous buyer obtained position 77 for a bid price of $180,000 and a total price of $198,000. On the same night, though, a "dark horse" stamp came along and forced the Jenny invert to share the newly set record. In was an inverted-center 15¢ pictorial of 1869, showing Christopher Columbus standing on his head, and it fetched precisely the same $198,000 in combined price and premium.

What was going on? It was part of what the *Wall Street Journal* described as "a boom . . . in some part . . . stimulated by a massive outpouring of investment quackery and flackery, exploiting fear of inflation as well as simple greed . . . (and) based on the theory that financial salvation and the kids' four years at Harvard depended on the accumulation of . . . diamonds, gold coins, baseball cards and lead soldiers, as well as Matisses, Renoirs, Grandma Moseses, Norman Rockwells and phallic deities from New Guinea."

By 1979 the United States Trust Company of New York was recommending that some clients put as much as one-fifth of their total assets into collectibles: Salomon Brothers, investment bankers, tallied the yields on a list of alternative investments over the 1969-1979 decade and reported that stamps had produced a compounded annual rate of return of 15.4 percent, compared to 6.1 percent for bonds and 2.9 percent for stocks. (Chinese ceramics led the list at 18 percent.)

The press helped fan the flames. *Business Week*, *U.S. News & World Report* and *Newsweek* all reported examples of eye-popping profits in stamps, notably the Columbian Exposition commemoratives of 1893, the 1930 Graf Zeppelin airmails — and the Jenny invert.

Individuals billing themselves as stamp investment counselors opened shop, offering to assemble for their clients philatelic "portfolios" with sure-fire profitability. One was Barry Marcus, who in July 1977 founded an organization called Philatelic Growth Corporation of America. For a minimum of $5,000, he said, he could assemble a portfolio that would be immune to price fluctuations and would outperform traditional investments. "There is some degree of risk," he conceded, "but we have made a great deal of money, and it is nothing compared to what we will make in the next five to eight years. We have generally doubled the value of some investments . . . Overall there is a steady, 20 to 40 percent return on our portfolios."

Another consultant was Myron Kaller of Jericho, New York. "Rare stamps have performed admirably during the past five to ten years, and in my opinion price momentum is now on the increase," he said in July 1979. "The fixed (finite) supply of rare stamps, coupled with the growing (infinite) demand . . . has generated the upward price pressure . . . Collectors form a huge base, adding liquidity to the marketplace . . . Collectors are the buyers of last resort; they've been around even during recessions, depressions and economic scare periods. So when investors tire of stamps, or run with their profits elsewhere . . . there's always been the collectors to fill the vacuum . . . Nothing is a sure thing, but we can certainly say that stamps have been a good thing for people who have put their money into rare stamps."

Old-line stamp dealers were more cautious, stressing the importance of the investor making his own studies of stamps and the stamp market before plunging. But even they could not help marveling at what was happening, and pointing out, as Raymond Weill did in 1979, that "for more than 100 years, stamps have only gone one way. They have never gone down."

Into this superheated atmosphere ventured a 28-year-old Florida real estate man eager to make philatelic history. He would do just that before he was through — but it would not be altogether the kind he had anticipated.

* * *

The young realtor was about to acquire one of the six surviving blocks of four of the Jenny invert. It was the "Princeton block," positions 61-62-71-72, which Edgar Palmer's widow had given to Princeton University in 1947. Princeton had put the block away and never displayed it or otherwise publicly proclaimed its ownership of it, and eventually its whereabouts was forgotten by all but serious students of the Jenny.

Then, one day in 1976, Princeton announced it was going to sell the block. Its purpose, it said, was to acquire funds to properly display the remaining stamps in the university's collection — a collection whose existence was news to most people. *

* — Ten years later, the Princeton stamp collection still had not been put on public display.

**Princeton block. Its sale in 1982 epitomized the end of the great stamp boom of the 1970s.**

The block was auctioned by Harmers of New York June 8, 1976. It was not a choice specimen as Jenny invert blocks went. Its vertical centering was poor, with the perforations close to the bottom frame line on each stamp. About three-fourths of the attached left selvage had been trimmed off, by whom or for what purpose no one knew.

The auction catalog described the block as having original gum, but added: "There have been several hinges largely removed, resulting in one small barely visible thin in position 61. A faint natural gum bend — usual with this issue — runs from top right of position 61 through to a portion of position 62." Each stamp, on its back in the lower right corner, bore the imprint of the Economist Stamp Company, which had previously owned the block.

The Weill brothers made the high bid of $170,000 after Irwin Weinberg dropped out at $165,000; the price was the highest ever paid for a U.S. postal item up to then. "The only block we hadn't owned was the Princeton block," Raymond Weill explained. (At the time nobody knew a sixth block existed, the Ward-Bruechig block.) So when the university put the item on the market, Weill said, "in spite of its quality, the fact that it had practically no gum, was poorly centered, there was almost everything wrong with it, we still for vanity's sake bought it because we wanted to be able to say to ourselves, well, now we've owned every block. But we disposed of it perhaps two years afterward because we really weren't too keen about it."

The next buyer, in August 1977, was Myron Kaller, on behalf of a client, a syndicate of nine Florida doctors and a Palm Beach widow. Kaller offered the Weills $210,000, but the brothers, who can be very punctilious, chose to consummate the deal through a third party —

Raymond Weill explained it as their long-standing reluctance to sell stamps for investment portfolios — and they used Harmers' private treaty department for this purpose. Harmers charged a 5 percent commission, so the Weills came away with $200,000, a $30,000 profit on the block in little more than a year.

A much greater profit would soon be made. In the summer of 1979, stamp collectors and investors were startled to read that an unnamed "Florida real estate investor" had bought the Princeton block for $500,000, a world record price for any philatelic item anywhere. The announcement was made by Kaller, who had put the deal together. Kaller quoted his client as predicting that the block might eventually become "the first million dollar single philatelic property in history."

The client was quickly identified as George E. Manter, owner of Venetian Reality Company in Coral Springs, married, father of one, and a man more than willing to talk about his exciting purchase.

**George Manter, when philatelic investments still looked good to him, with stamps and picture of Princeton block.**

To buy the Princeton block, Manter had borrowed an undisclosed sum from the Summit Bank of Tamarac, Florida. It had been necessary to "educate" the bank as to the "upside potential" of the item, he said, by bringing in "some of the top agents in the world . . . This was a brand new field for the bank." He himself had been investing in stamps for only a year, he acknowledged, but he had done "a lot of research" and had "a lot of knowledge." He had concluded that stamps were "one of the best performing vehicles for capital appreciation." He had "charted" rare stamps and found they had never gone back in value. Unlike real estate, a stamp was portable; it was easily stored; the owner didn't have to pay taxes on it or collect rent on it. As with real estate, liquidity could be a problem, but stamps had "collector-based liquidity, 50 million strong" — an echo of Myron Kaller's "buyers of last resort" credo. "There's an auction every day some place in the world."

Why the Jenny block? "It's a real exciting stamp to have. It's the most famous stamp in the world. Everybody knows about it. The chart looks tremendous on it." How long would it take for the block to reach that magic million-dollar sale price? "I can't project . . . Maybe two or three years, maybe a little more. It just depends." He added: "I might try to put together some kind of tax donation with the Smithsonian. I might show it at shows. I just plan to hold on to it and keep it."

In fact, the block went into a safe-deposit box at the Sterling National Bank in midtown Manhattan. It was watched by a Lloyds of London insurance representative, according to Myron Kaller, as it was "dropped into its resting place." And there it stayed, as the stamp market continued to boom, through the balance of 1979 and the first half of 1980.

But early signs of problems for investors in collectibles were visible in the spring of 1981. The inflation rate declined, and rising interest rates began to make the money market and short-term certificates more attractive than tangible assets. High interest also strengthened the dollar, meaning that foreign buyers with their weaker currencies were less capable of bidding up prices of tangibles.

Futhermore, the attractiveness of collectibles as an investment was diminished for some by 1981 tax legislation that specified that such assets as stamps, coins, antiques and art couldn't qualify for favorable tax treatment in a Keogh retirement plan or Individual Retirement Account. Salomon Brothers reported that for the first time in five years, diamonds and Oriental carpets had failed to increase in value in a 12-month period; meanwhile, prosaic common stocks had zoomed. Christie's of New York experienced a disappointing spring with its art auctions, and *Business Week* took note of a "gloom that overhangs many dealerships as the era of spectacular price runups appears to be over."

The stamp boom wasn't wholly over, though. Still to come, in April

1982, were those twin record prices of $198,000 each for outstanding specimens of a Jenny invert and an 1869 invert. Nevertheless, through 1981 the stamp market for the first time saw actual price declines in such blue-chips as U.S. Zeppelins. Salomon Brothers' annual report in July 1982 showed rare stamps as a whole down 3 percent over a one-year period.

And, in midsummer of 1982, something occurred that hadn't happened for years: A specific Jenny invert was resold for less than its purchase price. It was position 6, admittedly a defective copy with its straight-edged top retrofitted with phony perforations by persons unknown. In April 1981 Superior Stamp and Coin Company of Beverly Hills sold it at auction for $75,000. But on August 23, 1982, when Superior sold it again, it fetched only $68,000.

The same thing happened to another invert that fall. The ungummed position 63, which had sold in October 1979 for $70,000 plus 10 percent buyer's fee, went for $50,000 plus fee in October 1982; the beneficiary of this bargain was a Fort Lee, New Jersey, stamp wholesaler named Kenneth R. Wenger.

The lowest price recorded for a Jenny in 1982 was the $47,500 plus buyer's fee which position 24, with a minor thin spot, brought on June 2. Even considering its defects, that was markedly less than comparable Jennies had brought in the past. Rare stamps had never decreased in price, as so many people had been pointing out; but, as others have said with equal accuracy, there is a first time for everything.

In November 1982, in the midst of this deteriorating market, came the wholly unexpected announcement by Harmers that it would auction the Princeton block Monday evening, December 13, at New York's Plaza Hotel. There would be no reserve price, or minimum prescribed by the consignor beneath which the auctioneer would not permit the block to be sold; it would bring precisely what it was worth on the open market. The sale seemed to many to be a masterpiece of bad timing. It was arranged, Harmers said, "by order of Mr. George E. Manter from Florida."

That was not, in fact, exactly the case, although the public would not learn this or other interesting details until later. The loan with which the Princeton block had been purchased, it would turn out, was for $350,000, and it was made to a partnership called Philatelic G.E.M. Associates — the initials were Manter's — in which George Manter and his wife Susan were general partners and unnamed others participated on a limited basis. The balance of the purchase price had come from the partners' other resources. The block was held in its Manhattan safe-deposit box not by Manter but by the Summit Bank.

In due course, after reducing the principal amount to $300,000, the

Manters defaulted on the loan, and the bank went to court to collect. By now it was no longer the Summit Bank, however; that institution's portfolio and assets had been acquired by the Gulfstream National Bank. In the proceedings that followed, the couple signed a stipulation for settlement which provided for a court order directing the sale of the block to reduce their indebtedness.

Gulfstream contacted several leading dealers, including Harmers and the Weills, in an effort to sell the block outright, but was unsuccessful. Back in June 1981 Robert Siegel had offered to buy the block for $330,000 and promised to keep the offer open for a year, but no deal had materialized. Now Keith A. Harmer, president of Harmers of New York, told Gulfstream officials bluntly that they didn't have a chance of covering their $300,000 outlay, let alone the full $500,000 Manter had paid for the Princeton block. The Weills shied away because, Raymond Weill said, they foresaw a question of title arising. Finally the bank returned to Harmers and consigned the stamps for auction.

The sales agreement among the parties specified that the block was being sold by Philatelic G.E.M. Associates and Gulfstream Bank jointly. Though the partnership was the owner of the block, the agreement gave the bank the right to approve all aspects of the sale. As noted, however, Harmers in its advertising named only Manter. Manter, in exercising his rights of joint control over such details as the description of the block and the layout of the auction catalog, retained Myron Kaller as a "philatelic marketing agent-consultant."

As the sale date drew near, philatelists speculated on what the block would bring. Nobody mentioned the phrase "one million dollars." The top prediction was in the $250,000 range. Wrote Michael Laurence, editor of *Linn's Stamp News*: "Being a collector sometimes means selling things for less than what you paid for them. Our guess is that Mr. Manter will shortly savor that experience."

On the evening of December 13, collectors and dealers filled the mirrored Crystal Room of the Plaza Hotel, many of them there to watch rather than bid, and TV cameramen hovered conspicuously. Absent were such frequent Jenny invert buyers as Irwin Weinberg and the Weill brothers, despite what some saw as a clear interest on their part in making sure the Princeton block was bid up to a reasonable price, in order to protect the value of their own holdings. In fact, Myron Kaller reportedly was telling others of a comment he had made to Raymond Weill: "If the Princeton block sells for (only) $200,000, that's your problem."

Earlier that day in the same room Stanley Richmond of Boston's Daniel F. Kelleher Company had auctioned U.S. stamps owned by clients of Kaller. These stamps were originally scheduled to be sold by Harmers that evening, but Kaller and Keith Harmer had disagreed over details, and arrangements were made virtually at the last minute to hold separate sales by two different auction houses.

Harmers' sale consisted of more than 300 lots of U.S. material, including rare 19th century covers and blocks of the Columbian Exposition commemoratives up to the $5 value. However, the overwhelming interest of the crowd and newsmen was centered on Lot 1 — the Princeton block. As George and Susan Manter took front row seats, word of their presence spread through the hall, but few had any idea that Manter was no longer calling the shots for this famous item of philatelic merchandise.

Bernard Harmer, chairman of the firm, took the podium. He announced Lot 1, opened the bidding at $150,000 from the "book" — a bid submitted in advance — and said: "May I have $175,000?"

In the audience were Kenneth R. Wenger and his stepson, Paolo Gianakos, 12. Wenger was the New Jersey dealer who, seven weeks earlier, had bought a Jenny invert for $22,000 less than the seller himself had paid for it. Now he was about to enjoy an even more extraordinary bargain.

**Paolo Gianakos shows how he displayed bidding paddle to register winning bid of $175,000 on Princeton block.**

As for Paolo, it had already been a full day for him, starting that morning with a bomb scare that had emptied the school he attended. Now more excitement lay just ahead. He was holding the bidding paddle, number 300, which was registered to Wenger, and his stepfather told him to hold it up, signifying a bid. Paolo did so and the auctioneer accepted it.

Then, surprisingly, there was no more bidding.

"This is a very disappointing price," Harmer told the crowd.

Still, nothing happened.

A dealer at the rear asked the size of the bidding increments and was told: "The next bid will be $200,000."

But that bid never came, and finally, as TV cameras took it all in, Harmer gaveled the lot sold at $175,000. With the 10 percent house commission added, Kenneth Wenger had obtained George Manter's half-million dollar Princeton block for $192,500.

TV pictures later showed Paolo Gianakos, a young man in a Buster Brown haircut, smiling and slightly self-conscious, holding the paddle that had brought his stepfather the block of Jenny inverts at what seemed to be an extraordinarily low price. TV reporters also sought out George Manter, the investor who had just taken a bath of historic dimensions. He answered their questions with good grace: "I'm obviously very disappointed. I'll cry a little, lick my wounds, then go on to something else."

The next day Kenneth Wenger told reporters he would have been willing to pay at least $250,000 for the block. "Actually," he said, "I thought it would bring at least $300,000."

And the day after that, Manter was still waxing philosophical. He intended to continue to invest in stamps, he said. "This might just be the bottom of the market, the time to get back in," he told an interviewer. As for the auction result, "I'm shell shocked, but I'm not embarrassed or ashamed. This sale will send shock waves around the world, telling people what the stamp market is really all about. Prices can go down as well as up, and timing is as important in stamps as it is in stocks." He was happy to have owned the block, he said: "It opened a lot of doors for me, got me on TV a lot. Owning the Princeton block is probably as close to national media attention as I'll ever get."

There was some second-guessing, most of it focused on the question of the bidding increments set by Harmers. Were the $25,000 jumps the house demanded too high? Some observers thought that lower increments would have stimulated floor action and produced some momentum. Others argued that, given the pre-sale expectation that the block would bring $250,000, increments of $25,000 weren't unreasonable.

Harmers officials and others stressed the relatively poor condition of the goods. Bernard Harmer called the Princeton "a tired block." His son Keith conceded that it had gone "cheap," but pointed out that the total price Wenger paid averaged just under $50,000 per stamp, which is what "seconds" — his term — of the Jenny invert were bringing at the time.

Should the bank have set a reserve price of, say, $200,000? "The bank had asked about reserves," Keith Harmer recalled later. "I said, if you guys set a reserve and don't sell it, if I don't sell it in this sale, what are you going to do with it? You won't have the money . . . and it's so well known that you've got to at least wait two or three years before it comes up again. They said, 'Give us the money' . . . They wanted to pay as much of the loan back as possible." Harmers waived the usual 10 percent seller's fee, so the bank pocketed the full $175,000 bid price.

George Manter had displayed such a stiff upper lip immediately after the sale that the next act in the drama was as surprising as anything that had come before. On February 16, 1983, George and Susan Manter and Philatelic G.E.M. Associates filed suit in the Supreme Court of New York against Harmers, Gulfstream National Bank and "John Doe and Richard Roe," seeking an injunction against the scheduled delivery of the Princeton block to Kenneth Wenger, plus compensatory damages totaling $8 million and punitive damages totaling $12 million. Through this action the stamp world learned for the first time of Manter's default on his loan and the bank's role in the selling of the block.

The plaintiffs' contentions included these:

• That the $25,000 increases demanded by Bernard Harmer were too high, in light of Harmers' own standard policy of moving up the bidding by 5 percent increments, and that the "challenge bid" which was rejected (plaintiffs asserted it would have been for $185,000) might have stimulated additional bidding.

• That Harmers and Gulfstream had conspired to set an opening bid of $150,000, "restraining the trade and commerce of the marketplace."

• That defendants John Doe and Richard Roe represented one or more unknown individuals who "were or are part of a 'ring' whose aim was to stifle competition. Doe and Roe . . . engaged the services of Kenneth Wenger and/or Paolo . . . (who may have been unaware of such a conspiracy) to purchase for their account the Princeton block, and deliberately did not themselves bid on the lot . . . The 'ring' has, or will, subsequently conduct a private auction at which time the Princeton block will be sold to the highest bidder, with the profits shared by the other participants to the ring, and not plaintiff."

• That the auctioneer, in accepting a bid from a minor who was not legally responsible to make good on it, had exposed the seller of the stamps "to the risk of an illusory contract and, thus, its disaffirmance with a concurrent risk of no sale."

• That defendants had damaged George Manter's reputation "in the philatelic and financial planning industry."

Justice Arnold Framen heard the request for an injunction March 7, 1983, and denied it. This released the block to be delivered to Kenneth Wenger, the sale price to be paid to Gulfstream and the $17,500 buyer's fee to be paid to Harmers (which represented "a loss on the whole thing," Keith Harmer said). The court's action also cost George Manter and his co-plaintiffs a $35,000 deposit which the court had required when they filed their petition.

Wenger's happiness was tempered by the fact that he also received a bill from his lawyer, for $8,000. That raised the total cost of the Princeton block to him to just over $200,000, but, as he said, it was still a bargain.

Wenger got a fair amount of promotional mileage out of his purchase. He exhibited the block at the INTERPEX stamp show in New York in March 1984, and for this occasion he had 2,500 souvenir cards printed reproducing the item in color, which he offered for sale at $10 each to help defray the cost of insurance. He also showed it at his booth at AMERIPEX '86, along with four single copies of the Jenny which he owned (these included positions 1 and 100, Alpha and Omega, the two corner copies that had bracketed the original sheet).

Along the way, Wenger said, he turned down an offer of $300,000 for the Princeton block, and he suggested that he might not sell it until it reached the $500,000 price which George Manter paid for it back in the days when it had seemed that the stamp boom would never end.

George Manter chose not to proceed with the rest of his lawsuit, but he didn't specifically withdraw his claim for damages, and so under New York law the suit will remain pending, but inactive, indefinitely.

The case of the Princeton block shocked the stamp market, as Manter had predicted, and activity in Jenny inverts slowed to a crawl. For a long time afterward only a scattered few were offered at auction. One, the attractive position 35, brought only $70,000 plus $7,000 buyer's fee when Harmers put it on the block in October 1983. Robert A. Siegel, who had featured at least one invert in his annual rarities sale every year since 1974, didn't include any in his 1983, 1984 and 1985 sales, and frankly admitted it was because he was afraid they might go at a sacrifice price.

But later in 1985, a steadying stamp market — and the old allure of the stamp — began to bring forth Jenny inverts once more. On June 8 Christie's/Robson Lowe, New York, sold the much-traveled position 78, a copy with minute hinge thins, for $80,000 plus 10 percent. On August 25 the Steve Ivy auction house sold position 48, from the block that Eugene Klein had bequeathed to his daugher, to a West Coast collector who owned two other single copies for $100,000 plus $10,000. On December 7 John Kaufmann of Washington auctioned off the handsome, lightly hinged position 58, the last of the four singles from the Klein block to go under the hammer, for $130,000 plus $13,000. Irwin Weinberg, in a private offering of rare stamps at about the same time, offered the elegant position 59, a stamp with virtually perfect centering and no known flaws, for an audacious $200,000. As of AMERIPEX in the spring of 1986, however, he still owned it.

Chapter Fifteen

# The McCoy Heist

*"Come on, Mr. X, cough it up."*

**— James H. Beal**

Ethel B. Stewart McCoy was a woman of many interests. As the only child of one of the great innovators of American business and the wife of two other successful businessmen, she could afford to indulge them.

**Ethel Stewart McCoy, whose stolen block of inverts was half unaccounted for more than 30 years later.**

Ethel's father, Charles Bergstresser, came to New York City from Pennsylvania in the 1880s to join two fellow fortune seekers, Charles H. Dow and Edward D. Jones, in founding a financial reporting service. Only his willingness to sacrifice vanity to practicality saved the firm from being known, then and now, as Dow Jones Bergstresser & Co.

Her first husband, Bert A. Stewart, was owner of R.A. Stewart and Company, a Manhattan firm that made rubber stamps. Bert died in 1936, leaving an estate of more than three-quarters of a million dollars, and for many years afterward Ethel, his sole beneficiary, continued as an officer of his firm, first as treasurer and later chairman of the board.

She was a patron of the ballet, opera and symphony. She enjoyed poetry and at one time maintained a poetry shelf at the public library in Newton, the rural New Jersey town 50 miles west of Manhattan where she and Bert lived. A prolific producer of needlepoint, she gave away handbags by the score to friends or to benefit one organization or another.

But her greatest love was stamp collecting. She collected Columbian, Trans-Mississippi and Pan-American Exposition commemoratives, including essays and proofs; airmails of the world, and precancels. She helped pioneer what would become a widely popular collecting technique, topical collecting, with her three volumes of stamps showing palm trees.

**The McCoy block of Jenny inverts. The two left-hand stamps, positions 65 and 75, have been recovered.**

Most of all, she prized her block of Jenny inverts, positions 65, 66, 75 and 76, which she had bought in 1936 from Spencer Anderson for $16,000. Besides its philatelic worth, it may have had a sentimental value for her as well; her obituary in the *American Philatelist* declared that the block was a gift to her from Bert Stewart, who, although a coin collector himself, appreciated his wife's love for stamps.

Nevertheless, after Bert's death Ethel candidly told her friends she intended to look for a second husband who would actually share her philatelic interests. She found him in Walter R. McCoy, a retired manufacturer of electrical fixtures. In 1941 the couple went to the altar; he was 61, she 47. McCoy joked afterward that he had married her for her Jenny inverts and she had married him for his "Orangeburg" coil, an extremely rare U.S. 3¢ violet stamp of 1911 named for the New York village where it was distributed.

**Walter McCoy joked that he married Ethel Stewart for her inverts and she married him for his Orangeburg coil.**

McCoy served for several years as librarian of the Collectors Club of New York. He edited its periodical, the *Collectors Club Philatelist*, and in 1951 was elected president of the American Philatelic Congress. He was, in short, the stamp collecting activist Ethel had wanted in a spouse. He died in 1952, and in his memory Ethel established and funded the Walter R. McCoy Award, given annually for the best article in the Congress Book.

For nearly 20 years Ethel exhibited her block of Jenny inverts proudly and often. In the summer of 1937 she took it with her to Washington and met William Robey, who invited her to show it that evening at the Collectors Club of Washington. At her request, Robey autographed the card on which the block was mounted. "Once again I had in my hands part of the original sheet that I had purchased for $24," he wrote. It was the only time he was ever reunited with any of the inverts.

In September 1955, at the request of American Philatelic Society officials, Ethel lent them her block for display at the annual APS convention and exhibition in Norfolk, Virginia. It might have been considered risky; two recent national stamp shows had been marred by the theft of rare stamps, the APS meeting in San Francisco in 1954 and a Society of Philatelic Americans convention in Tampa in 1953. Still, Ethel had exhibited the block many times without mishap, and security at Norfolk seemed adequate. Exhibition Chairman Denwood Kelly put her stamps into a vault in the Bank of Virginia until it was time to take them to the seventh-floor Starlight Room of the Monticello Hotel, where a total of 182 frames were to be shown. Armed guards from the local federal building were stationed in the room. Although their primary job was to guard the Post Office Department's exhibit, the APS had arranged to pay part of their overtime in return for keeping an eye on the rest of the material.

It would prove to be a poor investment.

As always, Ethel's block drew an appreciative audience. Though it was clearly the star of the show, it was not set apart, but was located near the end of a long row of vertical glass-covered display frames, mounted on a small black card held in place by black photographic mounting corners on a page that was marked to show where the block was positioned on the original sheet, and flanked on either side by full sheets of 100 of normal 24¢ Jennies, also from Ethel's collection. Nothing in its write-up hinted at its extraordinary value.

Shortly after 9 a.m. on Friday, September 23, the third day of the show, three local postal supervisors went to the hotel to see the rare stamps. "When we got to the exhibition," one of them, Robert C. Larmore, said later, "dealers had started coming in and were opening up their boxes and talking back and forth. We started down one row of frames, looking at the Confederate exhibit. It might have been as late as 9:30 by the time we got around to where the inverts were supposed to be. I had seen it the day before . . . I noticed that the album page was blank and that the piece of mounting was hanging from the board.

**Top, spectators admire McCoy block at Norfolk show; bottom, Denwood Kelly shows how thief slid back cover and removed block.**

"I checked with Bill Cote (a clerk at the exhibition postal station and a convention committeeman) and asked him what happened to his inverts. He was flabbergasted. But nobody seemed to be down at that end of the hall when we were there."

The only thing immediately clear was that Ethel McCoy's stamps were gone, and there were no suspects. Afterward, APS officers explained that the thief had managed to cut a piece of rope that had bound together two of the display frames. By pulling the invert's frame out of line and sliding back the covering glass a few inches, he was able to pluck the block from its position.

William Allmond, who had been on guard duty until 1 a.m., said Ethel's stamps were still in place when he made his last swing around the room at midnight. Abraham Bonner, who relieved him, said the hotel's night watchman was the only visitor until 7 a.m. Around 8, he said, several stamp dealers appeared, but none went near the area where the invert was located. After 8:30, though, he added, a number of persons were moving around the room. Chairman Kelly said the theft probably took place after 8:30, because maintenance men had swept the entire floor at that hour and would not have missed the pieces of black mounting paper, obviously residue from the grab, which were found on the floor near the looted frame.

Both guards said defensively that they had not been given detailed instructions about guarding the room or told the value of the stamps on display. Still, they must have cringed at the subhead over the story in the next day's *Norfolk Virginian-Pilot:* "Prized Stamps Stolen Under Guard's Noses."

Ethel McCoy, notified in New York of the loss, said — for the record — merely: "It's one of those unpleasant things that happen sometimes." Still, her friends likened the crime to a kidnapping, in view of her great attachment to the stamps. There was, however, no ransom note. The block was insured for $15,000; this was a fair valuation at that time, and proportionate to the $18,250 for which the plate number block of four had sold only the year before, but the sum did not begin to define the magnitude of the loss to Ethel. However, she accepted the amount from the insurance company, with the stipulation, specified in the policy, that if the stamps were recovered she could regain title to them by reimbursing the insurer.

Denwood Kelly speculated that the block would be broken into singles for disposal, and Postal Inspector W.H. Jenkins offered his opinion that the thief might tamper with the perforations in an attempt to obscure the stamps' position on the original sheet. Both looked like prophets when, a little less than three years later, one of the stamps — separated from its mates — turned up.

On July 18, 1958, Louis John Castelli Jr., proprietor of the Ace Coin and Stamp Mart of Chicago, sent the stamp on approval to Raymond and Roger Weill in New Orleans. The Weills received it the next day, routinely checked it against photographs in their files — and concluded that it was position 75, the lower left stamp from the McCoy block. The upper perforations along the right side had been blunted, as if by a combination of trimming and buffing, to remove traces of the vertical guideline that had crossed the block, but other characteristics marked it as the stolen stamp.

The brothers immediately notified the Federal Bureau of Investigation. At the FBI's request, photos of the stamp were made and sent to the agency's Washington laboratory, along with a photo of the McCoy block for comparison. Meanwhile, Castelli was put off with a letter written by a Weill staff member that said both partners were out of town.

The FBI confirmed that the stamp was the real McCoy. However, it also advised the Weills to send it back to Castelli. With reluctance they did so, on July 29, with a terse note saying merely that they couldn't use the item, and were returning it along with the dealer's postage costs. At the same time they urged the FBI to at least question Castelli on how he had acquired the stamp.

Later that year, the press carried stories on the offer of a stolen McCoy stamp to the Weills by an unnamed Chicago dealer; these stories quoted the FBI as saying it was powerless to act because the stamp was valued at only $3,000, and federal laws on the interstate movement of stolen property didn't apply unless the item was worth at least $5,000. The dealer had been questioned, the FBI said, and had asserted that he had owned the stamp before the McCoy block was stolen.

These matters rested until 1970, when the stamp appeared in an October 16-17 auction offering by Simmy's Stamp Company of Boston, its picture gracing the cover of the catalog. Simmy's reported afterward, in its published list of prices realized, that the stamp was sold for $19,000. Who had consigned it, and who bought it, the company says it is unable to say. Somehow, however, it found its way back to Louis Castelli.

Another seven years went by. In September or October of 1977, Peter Robertson, curator of New York's Philatelic Foundation, found himself looking at a Jenny invert that had been brought in to the expertizing agency for a "security clearance." The Foundation's experts, including veteran dealer Ezra Cole, quickly identified the stamp as position 75 — the same stamp from the McCoy block that Louis Castelli had tried to sell the Weills in 1958. Castelli was now offering it to Robert L. Faiman, a Las Vegas hotel owner. Faiman had agreed to buy the stamp at the proffered bargain price of $16,000, providing the Philatelic Foundation certified its authenticity. In November 1977 the Foundation handed it over to the FBI in New York; this time — thanks to the rise in stamp values — the FBI was able to act.

Castelli, questioned once again, said he had obtained the stamp sometime in the 1950s from another Chicago dealer by trading a block of four $5 Columbian Exposition commemoratives for it. He had no documents for the transaction, and the other dealer was now dead. After trying unsuccessfully to sell it to a Florida man and then to the Weills, Castelli said, he put it away until he learned through another dealer of Robert Faiman's interest in buying a Jenny invert. How it got into the Simmy's auction in 1970 wasn't explained.

In January 1979 Ethel McCoy, now 85 years old, in poor health and loath to become involved in a custody contest, assigned all her right, title and interest in her stolen block to the American Philatelic Research Library (APRL) in State College, Pennsylvania. She also authorized the library to take all steps necessary to recover any or all of the stamps from law enforcement agencies, insurance companies or anyone else who might have possession of them. She did this in response to a request by James T. DeVoss, a retired Army colonel who was president of the APRL; the idea had been suggested to him by another collector, Horace W. Harrison of Baltimore.

In January 1980 the Justice Department filed in the U.S. District Court for the Southern District of New York a complaint in interpleader. This was a lawsuit asking the court to settle multiple conflicting claims of ownership by ordering the defendants to "interplead" their claims, and to discharge the plaintiff, the government, from any liability regarding the property. Among the defendants named were the APRL, Faiman, Castelli, the Philatelic Foundation and Ethel McCoy. Also named was one Victor Spilotro who, according to the complaint, had represented himself as the owner of the stamp on May 30, 1971; the Justice Department never identified him beyond that, and his link to the McCoy stamp case could not be determined.

There were also two unknown defendants. One was the "Roe" Insurance Company, so identified because Ethel McCoy had been unable to remember the name of the insurer who had reimbursed her for her block back in 1955, and legal advertisements placed by the federal government had failed to turn up a claimant. The other was "John Doe," representing any other unknown potential claimant.

While the interpleader was pending, Castelli struck a deal with the APRL. He signed a release of his interest in the stamp to the library, similar to the assignment that Mrs. McCoy had executed, in return for the library's agreement not to seek counsel fees and costs from him. That left the APRL and Faiman as the sole claimants to the invert. Faiman's claim was based on nothing more than his contract with Castelli to obtain the stamp at a price which, given the inflation of the preceding three years, was even more of a bargain than ever; no money had changed hands between the two.

The library moved for a summary judgment, relying on affidavits from Philatelic Foundation experts. Faiman opposed the motion, but offered no factual basis for challenging the assertion that the stamp was part of the McCoy block. Instead, he simply argued that expert opinion alone wasn't solid enough grounds on which to determine the stamp's identity, and insisted on his right to cross-examine the Foundation witnesses at a trial.

On January 30, 1981, Judge Robert W. Sweet awarded the stamp to the APRL. "Since it was at Faiman's instance that the Foundation evaluated the stamp," Judge Sweet noted, "Faiman could hardly now attack the Foundation's credentials." A "time-honored rule" holds that title cannot pass through a thief even to a *bona fide* purchaser, the judge said; and there was no dispute that the stamp passed from Mrs. McCoy by simple theft. "Therefore," he concluded, "whatever Faiman's rights to the stamp *vis-a-vis* Castelli may be under the contract assertedly existing between these two, under the facts and the law the stamp still belonged to McCoy" — and now, therefore, to the APRL.

After the waiting period for appeals had elapsed, the APRL's James DeVoss went to the FBI office in New York, where the Jenny invert was turned over to him. He then drove to Washington and placed it in the hands of auctioneer John W. Kaufmann, whom APRL had designated to make the sale.

This sale took place September 25, 1981, in Atlanta, at the American Philatelic Society's annual convention; it was almost 26 years to the day after the McCoy block had vanished from another APS convention. Though along the way the stamp had acquired a small tear and some thin spots, in addition to the shortened perforations, Kaufmann knocked it down for an unexpectedly high $115,000. Perhaps the aura of criminal acts and mysterious dealings which the stamp had acquired gave it an added value that compensated for its physical defects.

Ethel McCoy was not present to see this outcome, however. On Christmas Day 1979 she suffered a massive cerebral hemorrhage in her apartment in New York's Hotel Warwick. A report was published that she had been attacked by an intruder, but this was erroneous. She was taken to Doctor's Hospital, where she remained in a coma for months until her death August 17, 1980, at the age of 87.

Her estate, worth nearly a million dollars, was left to cousins and friends. Most of her stamps had been given to the Collectors Club or sold by the time of her death, but the seven volumes of Trans-Mississippis, two volumes of precancels and three volumes of palm tree topicals remained, and these her executors sold to Robert Siegel for $202,500.

APRL announced it would use the money from the sale of position 75 to create an endowment fund whose income would help support library operations. Though the library expressed its willingness to reimburse the insurance company the $15,000 it had paid Mrs. McCoy in 1955, the company has never identified itself.

Meanwhile, a second McCoy invert had turned up.

It was not immediately identified as such. The stamp was in the collection of Marcel Lutwak, a Chicago businessman and connoisseur of philatelic material. Lutwak had suggested to a well-known philatelic official in the spring of 1981 that he might be willing to donate parts of his collection to the APRL as a tax write-off, beginning with a Jenny invert, and this information was duly relayed to James DeVoss. It was not until 18 months later, however, that DeVoss succeeded in contacting Lutwak personally in order to discuss the proposed gift.

DeVoss had reason to think the invert might be a McCoy, but he delicately avoided mentioning the possibility for fear it would chill the deal. After some negotiating by phone and mail — Lutwak wanted to be certain, for instance, that APRL was an educational organization to which donations were tax deductible — the two men met at New York's Plaza Hotel November 19, 1982, and Lutwak gave the invert to DeVoss. DeVoss took a taxi to the 60th Street branch post office and mailed the stamp to himself at his home address in State College, in a registered envelope he had carefully prepared in advance. Before posting the invert, however, he gave it a quick examination, compared it to a photograph of the McCoy block which he had brought with him, and concluded that it was position 65.

The next day, Saturday, DeVoss encountered an old friend, James Beal, at the American Stamp Dealers' Association convention and briefed him on developments. Beal was chairman of the American Philatelic Society's Stamp Theft Committee and had been a major participant in the continuing search for the McCoy stamps. He had worked closely with FBI agents on this project, just as he routinely did in all stolen-stamp cases. Now he and DeVoss — two pillars of the philatelic community — fell into a vigorous argument over what the ex-Army colonel had done. Beal (who described himself afterward as "getting the flu and with a plane to catch") asserted that if the stamp was a McCoy, it was a hot property, should not have been accepted by the APRL — and should now be turned over to the FBI, forthwith. DeVoss replied that one way or another the stamp belonged to APRL. If it was part of the stolen block it was now the library's by virtue of Ethel McCoy's assignment, and if by some chance it was another invert it was APRL's by virtue of a *bona fide* gift transaction. His first concern as an authorized representative of APRL, DeVoss said, was to acquire possession and worry about details later, and he argued that it would be a mistake to give up the stamp, not knowing when and how it would be recovered.

Nevertheless, Beal declared that he intended to notify the FBI as soon as he returned to his home in Warren, Ohio. On Monday, he phoned DeVoss in State College to say he had spoken to Earl Sumner, an FBI agent in Akron with a special expertise in stamp-theft cases, and that Sumner wanted DeVoss to call him. DeVoss complied, and the agent asked him to deliver or mail the stamp to Beal. Before doing so, however, Sumner added, DeVoss should photograph it, make a thorough examination and then write a report giving his opinion on whether it came from the McCoy block.

That afternoon DeVoss went to the State College post office and picked up the registered mail he had sent to himself the preceding Friday. He took it to a lawyer's office, where it was opened in the presence of witnesses and a photocopy of envelope and stamp made for the record. He then took the invert home, photographed it in color and black and white, sent the film to a local photo shop for processing, and arranged for the APRL's insurance agent to write a $150,000 policy on the stamp.

DeVoss was still unhappy, however, with the prospect of giving up possession to the FBI of a stamp which he felt the APRL had every right to keep—its ownership confirmed by a U.S. District Court in the interpleader judgment on position 75. Pursuing that case had cost the APRL several thousand dollars, and DeVoss was understandably reluctant to face another court action, especially when, this time, no other party was claiming title to the stamp. He consulted the local lawyer, and also called the American Philatelic Society's attorney in Yakima, Washington, for advice.

The APS lawyer, after a round of phone calls, arranged for DeVoss to meet with Beal and agent Sumner the following Wednesday, December 1, at noon at the Gold Eagle Restaurant in Brookville, a town just off Interstate 80 in northwest Pennsylvania, roughly halfway between State College and Beal's home in Warren. DeVoss should bring the stamp and his report on its identification, the lawyer told him.

DeVoss kept the appointment, accompanied by Richard L. Sine, editor of the *American Philatelist,* and after an intense discussion around the restaurant table the APRL president reluctantly agreed to relinquish custody of the invert. Beal and Sumner took it back to the FBI's Cleveland, Ohio, office, where it went into a vault while the Bureau studied DeVoss's report.

In Chicago, agents questioned Marcel Lutwak. He asserted that he had bought the stamp before 1974 from a seller whom he knew only by first name. The FBI had no reason to charge him with anything, and in fact, no one connected with the case has suggested that Lutwak's role was other than an innocent one. Of the Chicago collector — who has since died — Earl Sumner said: "We believed him to be an innocent purchaser of stolen goods." Said James DeVoss: "From my very first telephone call with Mr. Lutwak . . . through subsequent telephone conversations and our personal meeting in New York on November 19, I had the distinct feeling that he was honest and sincere in his dealing with me . . . My feeling was that any person who knowingly purchased stolen property would never have offered to donate it to the APRL who already had legal title to the item. Such a person would probably have destroyed the item and disposed of the evidence, thus the APRL would be the big loser."

The report DeVoss brought to the Gold Eagle Restaurant, dated November 24, definitely identified the invert as position 65, the upper left stamp from the McCoy block. DeVoss, a former chairman of the American Philatelic Society's Expertizing Committee, reached this conclusion after examining the stamp under a Zeiss stereo microscope capable of magnification of up to 80 times and comparing it with an enlarged illustration of the McCoy block appearing in Henry Goodkind's monograph. As with the first recovered stamp, the right-hand perforations had apparently been blunted to remove any trace of the red vertical guideline; in addition, the upper left corner perf had been altered to slightly change the stamp's appearance.

DeVoss's report offers a revealing look at how experts "plate" Jenny inverts (the numbers refer to the arrows which DeVoss affixed to the accompanying photograph):

**The arrows point to the identifying characteristics on the stolen McCoy 24¢ Jenny airmail invert (see text).**

"The paper inclusion (1) in the top margin below the space between the fifth and sixth perforations is clearly visible on both references" — meaning the stamp and the Goodkind photograph;

"The paper inclusion (2) in the top margin almost touching the eighth perforation is another distinct point of similarity;

"On the right frame line (3) just above the third perforation from the bottom is a dark dot immediately under the red frame line;

"In the bottom margin (4) under the right '2' of '24' is a thin wavy line of red ink;

"The perforations at the left of the stamp reveal several points identical with those of the stamp illustrated in Goodkind's handbook — the slant (5) on the corner perforation at the bottom and the unusual angle (6) of the separation between the fourth and fifth perforation from the top;

"The position of the inverted airplane with relationship to the frame is identical . . . The various margins between the frame lines and the perforations are identical;

"Most important of all is the fact that by extending both frame lines at each corner (total of eight extensions) the lines intersect the perforation holes in exactly the same relationship as position No. 65 of the illustration of the McCoy block of four. Because of the typical characteristics of line perforations as opposed to comb or harrow perforations, no two stamps could possibly exist with all eight extensions intersecting in the perforations exactly the same."

The stamp had original gum with only a very light hinge mark, DeVoss reported. He noted a slight separation of paper fibers in the left margin and extending through the outer and inner frame lines, starting at the fourth perforation from the bottom.

He found no evidence of a penciled position number on the gum during his initial one-hour examination of the stamp on November 23. However, in additional examination, using a variety of lighting situations, DeVoss discovered "definite evidence" of such a mark. "The notation has been partially removed but by turning the stamp at the right angle I can distinguish the number '6' and a portion of the vertical stroke of the number '5,'" he wrote.

During his second look at the invert, the expert also detected a blue position dot (7) covered by the red ink of the bottom of the frame line immediately below the E of CENTS.

The FBI, convinced by DeVoss's studies and its own comparison of stamp and photographs that the stamp was a McCoy, duly returned it to the APRL, setting the ex-colonel's fears at rest. As of this writing the library still has the stamp, with no immediate plans to sell it. At the American Philatelic Society's annual conventions in 1985 and 1986, the society exhibited the invert as part of an ingenious "real McCoy" contest for showgoers. Along with another genuine Jenny — position 22, loaned by the society's executive director, Keith Wagner — it was shown beside a faked invert. Spectators who were able to correctly identify the McCoy copy were eligible for a random drawing for a cash prize.

Meanwhile, two McCoy stamps — positions 66 and 76 — remained undiscovered. The FBI considers the case still open and is keeping its attention focused, understandably, on the Chicago area. James Beal neatly summed up the situation in a report in the *American Philatelist*:

"Their current possessor (but not owner) would do well to arrange their return to the proper owner, the APRL. This would be a simple matter — just call the local office of the FBI or the Stamp Theft Committee. The end of a long period of frustration would be at hand — the frustration of having a valuable piece of stolen property, and knowing that an effort to market it will result in immediate and serious problems.

"Come on, Mr. X, cough it up. Who really wants the Mona Lisa in his closet?"

Chapter Sixteen

# The Miller Heist

*"With your nose in our books, you may not see the crooks*
*"Whose records of purse-snatching mount.*
*"If you're robbed by these thieves, while the Library grieves*
*"It cannot be held to account!"*

**— Sign posted in New York Public Library, 1977**

Security guard Martin Ambrose could hear the burglar alarm jangling in the dark when he let himself into the New York Public Library on the morning of Monday, May 9, 1977, and he doubtless knew it was going to be a long day. The sound was echoing off the marble walls of the big lobby just inside the main entrance on Fifth Avenue, in an area that contained some treasures well worth stealing. And stealing, Ambrose soon discovered, was exactly what had happened.

On either side of the information desk at the back of the lobby, ten of a set of 100 vertical golden-oak display frames had been pulled out

**After burglary, plywood covered space occupied by frames that housed New York Public Library's Miller collection.**

of their recessed cabinets. Their transparent plastic coverings had been pried loose or burned with a blowtorch to get at the contents. Gone from the frames were 153 items from the Miller stamp collection, one of the finest holdings in the country of 19th and early 20th century U.S. issues and one that had been seen by tens of thousands of people over more than half a century.

The police dusted for fingerprints and interviewed Ambrose and other employees while library officials took a hasty inventory. Nobody on the staff, it turned out, had a good working knowledge of the collection, but they did come up with a rough preliminary estimate of $250,000 to $500,000 for the value of the missing stamps.

One of these stamps was the Jenny invert which Benjamin Kurtz Miller had bought from Eugene Klein for $250 in the first wave of sales of singles and blocks from Colonel Green's sheet. Gone with it were two plate number blocks of 12 of the normal 24¢ Jenny that were mounted on the same album page: one, from the brief second printing, with the single word "TOP" in blue in the upper selvage; the other, from the third printing, with the word twice, in red and blue.

With an optimism that in retrospect would prove ironic, Lieutenant Harold Smith of the Manhattan Burglary Squad suggested that the invert would be "hard to trade." "It is famous," Smith explained. "Any amateur collector will know it's stolen."

Other missing items included:

• Two invert errors from the 1869 pictorial series, the 15¢ and 30¢. (A 24¢ 1869 invert wasn't taken.)

• Four blocks of four of the extremely rare 1908 Washington series on bluish experimental paper, including the rarest of all, the 4¢ and 8¢ values.

• Two large blocks of the 5¢ New York City postmaster's provisional of 1845, which predated the first U.S. stamps by two years. These were a bottom margin block of 10 of the stamp, and a proof block of nine of the 1862 reprint on blue bond paper.

• A vertical block of six of the U.S. 10¢ stamp of 1847, used.

• A 30¢ Franklin stamp of 1867 with full grill (a pattern of tiny squares cut into the fibers of the paper), of which only six are known.

Curiously, the burglar had passed up a number of riches, including the only known set of imperforate Columbian Exposition stamps (in horizontal pairs), a 4¢ Columbian printed by mistake in blue instead of ultramarine, three Pan-American Exposition inverts in singles and a block, and several full sheets of 19th century classic issues, painstakingly reconstructed.

How could this burglary have happened? Gerald Gold, the library's business manager, explained to newsmen that budget cuts had forced a layoff of nearly half the guards, with only a maintenance man on duty during the night on weekends. The Sunday night man, Donald Welch, said he had checked the lobby around 2 a.m. and found everything in order. When the burglar alarm connected to the stamp cases went off, he was in another part of the two-block-wide building and hadn't heard it; it was an audible alarm only, unconnected to police headquarters or guard station.

Detectives, finding no sign of forced entry, suggested the burglar might have hidden in the library since the 6 p.m. closing Saturday, emerged to do his work early Sunday, hid again with his loot and then walked out as a member of the public after the 10 a.m. Monday opening. (There was apparently no search of the building before the public was let in.) Whether the alarm was set off when the theft began, or whether the

**The stone lion guarding the New York Public Library was of no help protecting the library's rare stamps.**

intruder somehow bypassed it only to trip it later, was unclear.

The effect of the experience on the library was immediate and long-lasting. The library already was sensitive to criticism voiced over the years that its stewardship of the Miller collection had been too casual. Now, although the great bulk of the collection was still intact, the library stashed it all away. Years after the burglary it was still unavailable to casual viewer and serious student alike.

That development was in clear violation of the articles of agreement under which Benjamin Miller on February 6, 1925, turned his great collection over to the library. "The party of the second part (the library) accepts said collection," the articles declared, ". . . and agrees with said party of the first part (Miller), and with his personal representatives, to take care of such collection, house the same, and exhibit it to the public." Affixed to the document were the signatures of Miller, his two attorneys, and the president and secretary of the New York Public Library.

Benjamin Miller was born in Milwaukee, educated at Pennsylvania College in Gettysburg, lived in later years in Minneapolis, and loved New York. He retired from a successful law practice in 1906 at the age of 49 and devoted his time to travel, big game hunting, and the care and development of his stamp collection.

His purpose in giving "his entire collection of United States postage stamps, and the albums containing them" to the library was, again in the words of the articles of agreement, to have it "exhibited to the public for purposes of instruction and pleasure." Here, he believed, the collection would benefit a wide range of people, from average collectors who would otherwise never see such stamps to specialists who could examine his reconstructed sheets and learn the location thereon of various major and minor plate varieties.

Until he died three years later, Miller continued to add to the collection as if it were still his own. Once he wrote to the library: "It may interest you to know that of the 3-cent 1851 stamps necessary to make complete plates of the 13 states of these plates — 2,600 stamps — you have all but 31 and I am in hopes of getting these before very long."

The library hired Elliott Perry, the New Jersey dealer who had tried to buy an option on William Robey's Jenny invert sheet back in 1918, to mount and annotate the collection. But in time it came to view the gift as a mixed blessing. There was never enough money available to properly arrange and display everything; and over the years some of the items disappeared — sold or stolen. In the summer of 1934, for instance, a thief cut the glass of one of the frames and made off with a block of four of the 4¢ Pan-American Exposition inverts.

George Sloane complained in 1946 that this "really extraordinary collection" was "treated as an unwanted stepchild." "It is definitely known that a large part of it was quietly sold at a New York auction a few years ago," Sloane wrote. "If there was any other reason for this sale, beyond a wish to get rid of some of it, it was never made known. The sale brought thousands of dollars and included numerous entire mint sheets of stamps, with Omahas and other commemoratives in abundance, sheets of the bluish papers, and many other fine things . . . Some of the rarities even were robbed from the exhibition frames a few years ago through lack of proper supervision and it has never been reported that they were ever recovered . . .

"There should be a lesson to all philatelists in the consideration that was shown to the B.K. Miller collection by a large public institution, for it is evident that few, if any, such institutions have reached the stage where they know how properly to care for a valuable stamp collection."

Even when the display area was moved from an upper floor to the main lobby and enlarged, reports of neglect continued. Stamp writer Ernest A. Kehr once spent a long period of time examining the displays when he suddenly realized that nobody had passed him, no guard had walked by, since he began. Kehr thought, "This is a hell of a way to leave this material."

The library's performance after the burglary was consistent with its earlier treatment of the collection. The FBI soon launched an investigation, aided by an old ally in such matters, the Stamp Theft Committee of the American Philatelic Society. But their efforts were hampered by the inability of the library to produce any usable photographs of the stolen material. The best it could come up with were photocopies several times reproduced, on which perforations were partly or completely invisible, which severely limited their use in identification.

* * *

For 40 years Lambert W. Gerber operated a stamp and auction business in Tamaqua, Pennsylvania, a pleasant little mountain community between Allentown and Hazleton. He had a particular interest in U.S. essays and proofs, and many of his catalogs carried large sections devoted to this specialty. He was official convention auctioneer for the American Philatelic Society and later for the Society of Philatelic Americans, and held occasional auction sales in New York.

Beginning in 1978 Gerber began to advertise for sale some stamps of unusually high quality.

A full-page ad in *Stamps* magazine for April of that year invited readers to send $1 for a copy of Volume 5 of Gerber's Gems and Rarities price list. Both the ad and the price list illustrated three specimens of the Jenny invert. One of them, priced at $38,500, was a copy that had never been seen before in a sales offering.

The stamp seemed to be from the top row of the original sheet, for it had a straight edge at the top. Late in 1978 dealer John W. Kaufmann of Washington bought it for a reported $32,000 and took it to the offices of the Philatelic Foundation on Madison Avenue in New York for an opinion. Though Kaufmann and Foundation officials later gave conflicting versions of just who said what that day, Kaufmann emerged apparently satisfied that the stamp was position 9 — the only top-row

Jenny invert of which no picture was available. (The real position 9, the "locket copy" which Colonel Green had encased and given to his wife Mabel, had not yet been found and photographed.)

Whatever the nature was of the assurance Kaufmann received, it was purely verbal; he didn't ask for a written opinion in the form of a Philatelic Foundation certificate. His explanation later was that the Foundation had a six-month backlog of certification applications, and under the terms of his purchase of the stamp he couldn't wait that long.

In any event, the stamp next appeared in an illustration in Kaufmann's catalog for his auction of May 5, 1979, identified as position 9.

The illustration attracted the attention of a handful of students of the Jenny invert, whose first reaction, whenever they see a picture of the stamp, is to ask themselves "What position is it?"

One of those students was Clifford C. Cole Jr. of Atlanta, whose fascination with the Jenny inverts goes back decades. On April 29, 1966, while visiting the New York Public Library, he had made a sketch of the Miller invert, using the blank inside cover of a Harmer, Rooke & Company auction catalog. His purpose was to try to identify the position of the stamp in the original sheet, since the library had no such information. In his drawing he concentrated on the most common points of identification — the corner perforations, any teeth that were longer or shorter than normal, the centering of the design, the location of the aircraft inside its frame. From these clues he concluded that the library stamp was position 18, a stamp which, like position 9, had never appeared in a public sale.

Now both Cole and Calvet M. Hahn of New York, a stamp writer with a long-time interest in the invert, studied the Kaufmann illustration and independently theorized that the stamp being offered at auction wasn't position 9 at all but rather the stolen library stamp with its top perforations cut off to disguise it. As Hahn pointed out, the position of the plane inside the frame was not that of a stamp from the top row of the sheet. Hahn mentioned his theory to Philatelic Foundation officials and was told it would be passed along to the FBI.

A third Jenny invert expert, Daniel M. Bagby of Scarsdale, New York, had noticed another detail during several close examinations he had made of the stamp at the library during the five years before the burglary. The "2" of the left "24" had a small brown paper speck, visible to the naked eye. Now, in April 1979, Bagby went to the Biltmore Hotel in New York, where Kaufmann was displaying stamps from his forthcoming auction, examined the invert and noted the spot in the same location.

However, he didn't then connect the straight-edged stamp before him with the fully perforated copy he had seen at the library.

That light didn't dawn until one day, early in 1981, while he was working on his pet project, a chart of the Jenny invert which photographically re-created the original sheet through auction-catalog pictures of the various positions arranged in the proper order.

**New York Public Library's Jenny invert, position 18, after top perforations had been removed to disguise stamp.**

Suddenly Bagby noticed that the teeth on Kaufmann's "position 9" didn't match those on pictures of positions 8 and 10. If, however, he moved the Kaufmann stamp picture down into position 18 — a position for which he had no prior photograph — it lined up with positions 17 and 28. Then he remembered the brown spot in the "2," and concluded that this was the stolen Miller stamp.

Meanwhile, Kaufmann had held his auction and sold the invert to Lawrence A. Bustillo of Suburban Stamp Inc., Springfield, Massachusetts, for $47,000 plus the 10 percent buyer's fee, a total of $51,700. Suburban, in turn, sold it in an auction of its own October 11, 1980, describing it as having a "natural straight edge." An unnamed Florida collector bought it for $105,000.

Bagby encountered both Kaufmann and Bustillo at the INTERPEX '81 stamp show in New York's Madison Square Garden in March 1981 and told them he was convinced the stamp they had each bought and sold was the stolen library copy. This could not have been welcome news to either dealer.

To return to the Lambert Gerber advertisements: They aroused the suspicions of Philip T. Wall, a North Carolina lawyer and collector who specialized in the 5¢ New York postmaster's provisional. Wall compared photos of the two large Miller blocks of the provisional which had been published in old auction catalogs with pictures of smaller blocks in Gerber price lists and catalogs of 1979 and 1980. His conclusion: The Gerber multiples had been cut from the Miller blocks.

* * *

Lambert W. Gerber died August 8, 1981, at the age of 66. After his death, additional interesting details about this veteran dealer came to light. One was that he had practiced what might be termed creative advertising — and that at least twice his creativity involved Jenny inverts.

In the same full-page ad in *Stamps* for April 1978 in which the mutilated Jenny position 18 was pictured — and in the Gerber price list which the ad promoted — were also illustrated two other inverted Jennies. Though not identified by position number, they were in fact positions 25 and 3. It is almost certain that Gerber owned neither one; they seem to have been included simply to draw attention to the copy he did have in stock, position 18.

Position 3 had undergone a remarkable transformation since the last time it had been pictured in a price list (also Gerber's), in 1976. That list, entitled "Philatelic Gems and Rarities of the United States," put a price of $29,000 on the stamp. Two illustrations, one in color on the cover, the other in black and white inside, showed it just as it had come from the Bureau of Engraving and Printing, with a straight edge at the top.

Gerber's 1978 ad and catalog, however, displayed a "new look" position 3 — one with a handsome row of perforations where the lowly straight edge had been. The stamp, now much more socially acceptable, was priced accordingly higher, at $59,000. Phony perforating? Yes — but in the picture, not the stamp. When position 3 was next illustrated in a sales offering — this time in the catalog for a John Kaufmann auction December 5, 1981 — its original straight edge had been miraculously restored, and it looked just the way it did in Gerber's 1976 advertisement.

A reasonable guess can be made as to the purpose of this pictorial hocus-pocus. If the 1978 ad had turned up a buyer for the stamp, Gerber could not possibly have produced it as illustrated, unless he were to have performed a fast perforating job, which he didn't. Most likely he would have apologized and explained that he no longer had that particular copy, and then called the customer's attention to the Jenny he really did have available — position 18, masquerading with its straight edge as a top-row copy, and cheaper by $20,500.

As for position 25 — to which Gerber appended a price tag of $69,000 — the illustration was made not from a new photograph but from a halftone, obviously from one of the several auction catalogs that had listed the stamp since it first reached the market in Green sale XIX in February 1945. (Though this picture seemed to be still more bait for a bait-and-switch operation, it's theoretically possible that Gerber could have delivered position 25 if pressed to do so. He would have had to track down the real owner, however, and persuaded him to sell it.)

Gerber's most ingenious bit of Jenny invert advertising, however, had appeared many years earlier. The October 15, 1960 issue of *Stamps* carried a Gerber ad urging readers to apply for the free catalogs issued for his "philatelic gem auctions" held at three-week intervals. The ad illustrated 14 different U.S. stamps. Most of them were 19th century

**"Non-existent" invert illustrated in a Gerber ad in *Stamps* in 1960.**

classics, but one was a poorly centered Jenny invert with a straight edge at the right. Experts who studied the picture in perplexity and compared it to photos of known positions finally concluded that it was a fabrication — that no such position existed.

They were proved correct after Gerber's death when his widow contributed to the American Philatelic Society's reference collection several items which he had used in his advertising. The "non-Jenny" pictured in the 1960 ad turned out to be what one expert called a "schoolboy fake," made by scraping off the airplane vignette from a normal Jenny stamp and pasting on an inverted one in its place. (The American Philatelic Society later would display this phony copy alongside two genuine Jenny inverts in its "real McCoy" contest mentioned in the last chapter.)

A letter which Gerber wrote to a customer a month after the ad with the phony Jenny appeared opened with the straight-faced statement: "The s.e. (straight edge) is gone." However, Gerber went on, "I attach a copy of the forthcoming catalog with the other copy."

The catalog was for a Gerber auction scheduled for December 29 and 30, 1960. It pictured on the cover another Jenny invert, which was described inside as having "usual faint gum creases and centered a trifle to R; a fine OG (original gum) copy of one of the most popular of all rarities." The stamp pictured was position 6, which at some stage of its career had had false perforations added to its original straight edge at the top. The catalog made no mention of this "improvement." Whether Gerber sold the stamp at his auction is unknown.

Mrs. Gerber's gifts to the American Philatelic Society after her husband's death also shed some light on how that 1978 advertisement in *Stamps* was created. One of the items in the assortment was a cut-out and carefully perforated colored illustration of position 25, lithographed on thin paper and with an orange stamp of Morocco on its reverse. It was this facsimile that was used to represent position 25 in the 1978 ad.

* * *

In the May 1982 issue of the quarterly *Chronicle* of the U.S. Philatelic Classics Society, Philip Wall published his findings on the whereabouts of the 5¢ New York provisionals stolen from the library. Wall didn't name the dealer who had offered the stamps, but *Linn's Stamp News* soon afterward identified him as Lambert Gerber.

After that, things began to happen.

In November a small delegation visited Dr. Vartan Gregorian, who in 1981 had been made president of the New York Public Library, and expressed frustration over the failure of his staff to find any useful photographs of the stolen material. The visitors included Leo Farrell, special agent for the Brooklyn-Queens Division of the FBI, and James Beal, chairman of the APS Stamp Theft Committee. Gregorian promised cooperation, and miraculously, while the group was still in his office, an aide produced a full set of photostatic reproductions of the Miller collection, far superior to anything that had been shown up to then, that had somehow been overlooked in the library's files. Now, for the first time, more than five years after the burglary, the FBI and Stamp Theft Committee were in a position to make some identifications that would stick.

Results came quickly. The library's photograph of the Jenny invert was compared with pictures of the Kaufmann/Bustillo copy, and, except for the ersatz straight edge on the latter, the two matched. The FBI then asked Bustillo to retrieve the invert he had sold to his Florida customer. Bustillo did so, convinced by written point-by-point arguments from the Stamp Theft Committee that the stamp was the library copy, and on December 22 he turned it over to an FBI agent in New York City.

Finally, in January 1983, a federal grand jury was empaneled in New

York to investigate the library burglary. It was reportedly the first time a grand jury had ever been convened for the specific purpose of dealing with a theft of stamps.

The FBI, which had been following the leads provided by the Gerber advertisements but had been frustrated by witnesses who claimed dealer-client privilege, served notice it would ask the grand jury through the U.S. attorney's office to follow the trail of stolen stamps back to their source. "We're now expecting full cooperation from the philatelic community," said Leo Farrell. "If we don't get voluntary cooperation, then the powers of the grand jury are quite sufficient to force it."

In fact, the publicity itself flushed out yet another stolen item. *Linn's Stamp News*, in its story on the grand jury, ran a picture of the block of six of the U.S. 1847 10¢ which Philip Wall had dug out of an old auction catalog. A lawyer and stamp collector from Cleveland, Oklahoma, named William R. Grimm saw the photo and thought something about it looked familiar.

When he compared the pictured block with a horizontal pair of the stamp he had bought at a New York auction a few years earlier, he realized that his pair had been cut from the bottom of the stolen block. An edge had been trimmed and parts of a cancel added to further disguise it, but the stamps could still be identified.

Grimm notified both the FBI and the Stamp Theft Committee, and after lengthy discussions turned the pair over to federal lawmen. In return he received an official declaration that his stamps were stolen, and with it he received a full refund from the auction house.

Meanwhile, U.S. District Judge Whitman Knapp had imposed Rule 6-E of the Federal Rules of Criminal Procedure, the so-called "gag rule," which prevented any witness, the FBI or the Stamp Theft Committee from commenting publicly on the case. The rule remained in force for some time after the grand jury concluded its investigation, and was finally lifted October 10, 1984.

Six days after that, the FBI announced that a total of 81 of the stolen Miller stamps had been recovered and were in the hands of the U.S. attorney in New York. All of them, the FBI said, could be traced back to Lambert W. Gerber.

Sixty-nine of the recovered items had been found in Tamaqua in the stock of stamps that was part of Gerber's estate. Seven additional stamps were obtained from collectors, and five from dealers. All 12 had been sold by Gerber, and in some cases the items had changed hands several times since.

(An 82nd stamp that had been subpoenaed by the grand jury was determined to be not a library stamp and was returned to the Gerber estate at the conclusion of the case. It was a 2¢ dark brown Andrew Jackson portrait from the special printings of 1873.)

Besides Lawrence Bustillo's Jenny invert and William Grimm's 10¢ 1847s, the recovered stamps included the rest of the block of six from which Grimm's pair had come; the 30¢ full-grill Franklin of 1867; all but three of the 19 New York postmaster's provisionals; and portions of the 1908 Washington bluish-paper blocks, including two each of the 4¢ and 8¢ values. One of the two plate blocks of 12 of the normal 24¢ Jenny stamp that had shared a frame with the invert was recovered, but not the other.

Some of the stolen material had been offered by Gerber in price lists and auction catalogs but wasn't found in his estate and had probably been sold. Other still-missing items — including the two used 1869 inverts — were never publicly advertised by the Tamaqua dealer and may never have been in his stock.

Even though Gerber's records and bank statements were subpoenaed, the FBI was unable to learn how he had come to possess the stolen stamps. The statute of limitations on the burglary expired in 1982, and sadly, once again — as in the case of the theft and mutilation of the McCoy block — a major stamp heist involving the Jenny invert led to no indictments or arrests.

In May 1984 the Justice Department, finding itself with the recovered Miller stamps on its hands, had filed a complaint in interpleader asking for determination of ownership. The court was the same U.S. District Court for the Southern District of New York where the interpleader action on Ethel McCoy's Jenny invert had been initiated four years earlier. The defendants included the library and three insurance companies that had paid to it a total of $237,500 after the burglary. Several stamp dealers and collectors who had possessed some of the stolen material at one time or another also were named, as was Grace Gerber, Lambert's widow and executrix of his estate.

The suit touched off a flurry of answers, counterclaims, cross-claims and interrogatories, and sent an assembly of lawyers periodically trooping into Judge Knapp's courtroom at 1 St. Andrew's Plaza in Manhattan to schedule motions and otherwise defend their clients' interests. The library, as part of its response to the interpleader, filed suit against eight "conversion defendants," including William Grimm, John Kaufmann and Lawrence Bustillo, claiming that they collectively or individually "injured and damaged all or some of the stolen postage stamps," thus diminishing the value of the library's property.

There was more than a touch of irony in the library's assertions in view of its long-time failure to produce usable photographs of the stolen material that would have allowed the stamps to be intercepted before they had passed through so many hands. That point was raised explicitly in a cross-claim in the interpleader action by Kaufmann and Bustillo. These two dealers contended that the library had forfeited its rights to the stolen Jenny invert because it "failed or refused to provide" a description of the stamp to the Philatelic Foundation after Kaufmann had gone there with the invert.

"If the library had provided copies or photographs," they said, "the fact that the stamp in question was one which had been or might have been stolen from the library would have been uncovered. By their failure, refusal or lack of cooperation and/or interest, the library prevented the Foundation, and defendant Kaufmann, from making a determination as to the possibility of theft . . . The actions of the library amount to an abandonment of any interest in the stamp."

In the end, Kaufmann and Bustillo waived their claim; in fact, they were ordered by the court to pay the library $833.72 for costs stemming from "undue delay" they had engendered "without justification in concluding this action." Their withdrawal and that of other parties left the field to the library and its three insurers, St. Paul Fire and Marine, Commercial Union and Royal Exchange Assurance of America.

Over a period of many months the lawyers worked out an agreement by which the library would reimburse the insurance companies $180,000 for the claims they had paid on the recovered material. Judge Knapp signed a judgment to this effect June 10, 1986, and Assistant U.S. Attorney Franklin H. Stone opened the safe in her office on July 8 and turned over to library representatives the 81 stamps — including Jenny invert position 18 — that had vanished from the Miller collection more than nine years earlier.

Without the alertness, expertise and efforts of individual stamp collectors and the Stamp Theft Committee, it never would have happened. The library's own contribution to the recovery — the discovery of the usable pictures — came very late in the game, and only after a change of leadership at the top. Now the library, as if chastened by the experience and dismayed by the bad press it had received, announced its intention to henceforth give the Miller collection the care it deserved. The stamps would be remounted and re-annotated with the help of philatelic experts. The recently restored Edna Barnes Salomon room on the third floor would be their new display area, where six panels at a time would be shown, in slant-type display cases, on a rotating basis.

Thus the Jenny invert, like the other star attractions, would not always be on public view. However, stamps not on display would always be available in the manuscript room to be consulted by "serious scholars." The entire collection would be rephotographed and a catalog published, if funds could be found for this purpose. The library hoped to have its new-look stamp collection ready for the public by early 1987.

As for the 72 stolen stamps still unrecovered, the library promised to pursue any that might turn up. As had been the case with the others, however, a spokesman said, "We have to rely on the good will and help of the philatelic community in spotting and identifying them when they appear on the market."

Chapter Seventeen

# The Proofs

*"It was believed that a die-proof would be of marked interest. . ."*

— **W. Irving Glover**

As we have seen, the U.S. Post Office Department resisted any temptation it might have felt to deliberately create additional Jenny inverts for its own collection, as it had done with the 4¢ Pan-American Exposition invert in 1901. It did, however, print some die proofs of the error, in the original colors, for exhibition and record purposes.

W. Irving Glover, third assistant postmaster general, formally requisitioned two error proofs from the Bureau of Engraving and Printing May 3, 1922, and Bureau Director A.W. Hill sent them over May 31. One, number 1158557, was passed along to "Miss Kate" Manning at the Smithsonian Institution to round out the Post Office Department's exhibit of die proofs that was being prepared for the Brazilian International Centennial Exposition that would open later in the year in Rio de Janeiro. The other, number 1158558, was placed in the album of die proofs kept as part of the official record by the Division of Stamps.

A news account of the creation of the proofs was published in an unspecified foreign stamp periodical that came to the attention of Eugene Klein, the original dealer in Jenny inverts. The author had his facts askew, however. He reported that the Post Office Department had "brought upon itself doubtful renown by specially manufacturing to complete the exhibit of U.S.A. stamps, two 'reprints' of the rarest of all aeroplane adhesives — the 24-cent red and blue of May, 1918, with centre inverted — a stamp with a '150-pound look.' One of these has been sent to Rio and the other deposited in the archives at Washington. Presumably the ultimate destination of the former is the National Collection in the Smithsonian Institute."

Klein, no doubt shaken by the news that the government was reprinting rarities in which he had invested considerable money and reputation, dashed off a letter to the third assistant postmaster general asking for "a verification of this story if true." "Kindly also let me know, if true," he added, "whether two sheets were printed or only two stamps. If two stamps, were they printed from single dies? Also whether the stamps were finished in every way with regard to perforation and gum."

On October 2 he received this reassurance from Glover:

"You are informed that the Department authorized the Director of the Bureau of Engraving and Printing to prepare two die-proofs of the 24-cent red and blue issue of May, 1918, with the center inverted. This was done in order that the collection of die-proofs sent to the Brazilian International Centennial Exposition . . . could be as complete as possible.

"In view of the interest manifested in this inverted stamp, it was believed that a die-proof would be of marked interest. No stamps were reprinted and no stamps will be authorized to be reprinted. The inverted die-proofs on exposition (sic) are printed on India paper with no gum and no perforations, and it is the intention of the Department that one die-proof will be retained in the exhibition cabinet for future expositions and the other will be part of the official record in die-proof album of the Division of Stamps of this Department."

In 1923 the other die proof — the one that didn't go to Brazil — was shown at the International Stamp Exhibition in London.

Since then, several other Jenny invert die proofs have been made. At least three were reported to exist in the 1930s, of which two were kept on exhibit at the old Post Office Department headquarters on 14th Street in Washington, and the other traveled to stamp exhibitions and fairs like the 1936 Texas Centennial Exposition and the 1937 Texas and Pan American Exposition.

Bureau records show that the Post Office ordered invert die proofs on at least three later occasions:

• On July 25, 1957, to include in a 32-page stamp exhibit for TABIL, the international philatelic show at Tel Aviv, Israel. The Bureau printed the invert (number 209578B) August 20, along with a proof of the normal stamp and separate proofs of the red frame and blue vignette, all of which the Post Office had also ordered.

• On February 25, 1960, for the International Philatelic Congress in Barcelona, Spain. The invert and a normal die proof were made February 29.

• On July 11, 1960, "as part of the collection for the philatelic museum" — plans for which the Post Office later abandoned. The invert was delivered July 14, along with another set of separate frame and vignette proofs.

Why it was necessary to requisition new proofs each time isn't known.

Nor can all the specimens created over the years be located. As of this writing, the Bureau and the U.S. Postal Service can account for four invert proofs, all of them in the custody of the USPS, which made them available for inspection to the author.

Three of the four are on small, square pieces of India paper, with no identification markings. Of these, one is permanently displayed in the Hall of Stamps at the USPS headquarters in Washington's L'Enfant Plaza. Like the other rare stamps and proofs in the Hall, it is in a neat glass-covered wall recess illuminated by approach-activated lights. The other two are kept in the USPS vault and occasionally are brought out for loan to philatelic exhibitions.

The fourth USPS proof is the only one that can be identified as to date and purpose. The paper on which it is printed is about 2½ inches square, mounted in the die-sunk center of a piece of cardboard. The cardboard bears two identification numbers (33120C, 33122C) which, when matched against Bureau records, show that it is the "Barcelona" proof, made February 29, 1960. It has been subjected to very rough handling. The proof itself is intact, but the left side of the cardboard has been torn away, and what remains is torn in three places.

In 1957, one Jenny invert die proof is known to have escaped from official custody. It turned up in Miami, Florida, in the hands of a former Bureau of Engraving and Printing employee, Edward R. Frisbie of Poland Spring, Maine, who was trying to sell it.

Frisbie, then in his 70s, had become a "prover" in the Bureau's Engraving Division in 1908. Scores of the proofs of full stamp plates now owned by the Smithsonian Institution carry his name stamped on the back, including several that were made in May 1918 when the 24¢ Jenny stamp was produced. (The plate proofs of the Jenny frame and vignette were made, however, by another prover, George T. Jones.)

No one knows which of the Jenny invert die proofs Frisbie had in 1957, or how he got it. Possibly, as a veteran hand at the Bureau, he had been able to obtain the original dies and make it himself. He also had die proofs of 10 U.S. stamps made in the 19th century by private printing firms for the Post Office Department, before the Bureau got into the stamp business. These included the very first government adhesives, the 5¢ Franklin and 10¢ Washington of 1847, and five high-value Columbian Exposition commemoratives of 1893.

Somehow Franklin R. Bruns Jr., curator of the Smithsonian philatelic collection, learned of Frisbie's attempt to sell the Jenny proof and notified the Secret Service. The proofs were impounded by U.S. District Judge George Whitehurst in Miami while the government brought suit to recover them. Eventually Frisbie agreed to return the proofs.

On January 29, 1958, Bruns, who by now had switched jobs and become director of the Post Office Department's newly created Division of Philately, wrote to L. Rohe Walter, special assistant to the postmaster general, asking for the proof on the Smithsonian's behalf.

"It is my understanding that such a transfer is now possible," Bruns wrote. "In view of the fact that our (the Post Office's) Philatelic Exhibition Room has such a die proof and also in view of the fact that we can have one prepared at any time we choose, I suggest I be given authority to advise both the Secret Service and the Bureau of Engraving and Printing that the Post Office Department has no objection to such a transfer."

The communication was initialed "OK (Walter) 1-30-58."

Bruns, while at the Smithsonian, had been eager to get a Jenny invert for the museum's collection, and only one month earlier he had finally obtained one as a gift from the Raymond H. Weill Company. But his letters show that he still hoped to obtain a die proof for the Smithsonian as well.

On February 10, 1958, he wrote to Henry J. Holtzclaw, director of the Bureau of Engraving and Printing. "I have discussed the matter with Mr. L. Rohe Walter . . . and have recommended that he approve such a transfer or deposit if in accord with governmental procedures," Bruns wrote. "He has given such approval . . . "

All that effort should have been crowned with success. It wasn't. There is no record at the Smithsonian that it ever received a Jenny invert proof. Over at the Bureau, a memo is on file indicating that the Secret Service in November 1957 returned to officials there the 11 proofs — including the Jenny — which they had taken from Frisbie in Miami. A notation on it says: "Please hold this material until Holtzclaw gives instructions as to their ultimate disposal." Holtzclaw has since died, and the Bureau now cannot say what those instructions were, or if any were ever given, or, indeed, what became of Frisbie's proofs.

Chapter Eighteen

# The Next Invert

*"The Post Office Department isn't running a jackpot operation."*
**— Postmaster General J. Edward Day**

When William Robey bought a sheet of stamps with inverted centers and wouldn't give them back, the Post Office Department swallowed its embarrassment, such as it was, and went on to other things.

More than 40 years later, another stamp slipped out to the public with one of its colors inverted. But this time the governmental response was different. In a swift, extraordinary and totally unexpected reaction, the Post Office undertook to destroy the value of the errors to their finders by reprinting them by the millions. This time there was no windfall for anyone, no dispersal of a handful of rarities whose changing ownership could be followed down through the decades. It was almost as if the new inverts had awakened some deep institutional memory in the Post Office and stirred a bizarre and disproportionate response.

The principal victim was Leonard Sherman of Irvington, New Jersey. Sherman was a struggling 38-year-old jewelry salesman with a wife, five children, a dog and an old Ford with a door that wouldn't stay closed. He was also a stamp collector — not just a collector, but a stampaholic. "I used to buy stamps like crazy, full pads at a time, and keep the plate blocks," he recalled. "I had file cabinets full of stamps."

On October 24, 1962, he went to the post office in New Brunswick, New Jersey, to buy a few panes of 50 of the new 4¢ three-color commemoratives honoring Dag Hammarskjold, the late secretary-general of the United Nations. The next day he bought some more in Newark. Back home, he noticed something odd about one sheet. Closer examination showed that the yellow background color was printed upside down.

It wasn't nearly as spectacular as a wheels-up airplane. In fact, the error was very difficult to detect. Still, it was the first U.S. color invert

**Normal copy of 4¢ Dag Hammarskjold stamp issued by the United States Post Office in 1962 to honor the former U.N. secretary-general.**

**Dag Hammarskjold stamp with yellow background color inverted. The inverted color is most noticeable in the shading at left in this illustration.**

since the Jenny. The Bureau of Engraving and Printing now had new rotary presses from Germany called Gioris that could print multiple colors in one pass, producing sheets of 200 that were then quartered into panes for post office distribution.

It had opted for two separate passes for the Hammarskjold stamp, however, so that the brown and black vignette could be superimposed on the yellow background. One press applied the yellow to a stack of blank, pregummed sheets, which were then put on a skid and moved into position facing a second press, where a gripper picked them up one at a time and fed them through to receive the vignette. Murphy's Law struck again, and at least two sheets got turned around between passes.

**Leonard Sherman, 20 years after losing battle with Post Office Department, and photo of his sheet of inverts.**

Sherman's heart, unlike William Robey's, did not "stand still" when he realized what he had. He stayed calm until he read a wire-service story in the *Newark News* November 11 about some collectors in Ohio who had 19 stamps like his that could be worth "up to $200,000." (The reporter may have arrived at that figure by using the going rate for the Jenny invert.)

Gerald P. Clark of Cuyahoga Falls, a pharmaceutical salesman, had bought a pane of Hammarskjolds in his hometown post office, but didn't realize they were errors until he had used 33 of them on letters. Then a friend, William Throop, spotted the anomaly in the 17 mint specimens remaining.The two men and Russell Ferguson, who shared a part-time stamp business with them, went looking for more inverts, but found none. They did, however, retrieve two canceled copies which Clark had used on letters to his wife and daughter.

Sherman phoned the *News* to say that he had a full sheet of the inverts. The story went out on the wires, and the next day the jewelry

**Gerald P. Clark of Cuyahoga Falls, Ohio, displays some of his 4¢ Dag Hammarskjold inverts.**

salesman was a celebrity. Reporters and TV people flocked to his house. Hugh Downs invited him on the "Today" show, where he announced happily that he would sell the sheet and set up funds to put his sons through college — and oh, yes (shades of William Robey!), buy a new car.

Officialdom was taking note of all this, however. Postal inspectors were dispatched to examine the Sherman and Clark stamps — unlike Robey, these finders had no reason to be wary, and they let them do it —and verify that they were errors. They turned out to be from two different sets of plates, meaning that at least 300 more error stamps — six more panes of 50 — were out there somewhere. As it had done with the Jennies in 1918, the Post Office suspended sale of Hammarskjolds until all stocks had been checked.

Then, on November 13, the department dropped the bomb that blew away the dreams of Leonard Sherman and the Ohio collectors.

James F. Kelleher, special assistant for public information to Postmaster General J. Edward Day, announced that the department would deliberately print more Hammarskjold stamps with the yellow inverted and sell them at face value "in unlimited quantities . . . to satisfy collectors' demands" and destroy the "artificially inflated value" of the Ohio and New Jersey errors. "Now every boy in the country can have one if he wants it," Kelleher said. Added Day: "The Post Office Department isn't running a jackpot operation."

**Postmaster General Day. Ordered errors reprinted because Post Office wasn't "running a jackpot operation."**

Len and Roslyn Sherman were stunned. The government's plan made no sense. There had been no demand from collectors for duplicates; in fact, collectors, who all secretly dream of making a William Robey-like find, were angry. One Greensburg, Pennsylvania, man sent this ironic telegram to Kelleher:

"In view reprint of Hammarskjold commemorative misprint request reprint of 1918 American 24-cent carmine rose and blue with inverted center which is not available to any but wealthiest philatelists please advise availability date return wire collect."

(Kelleher, with no sign of amusement, wrote back: "This administration has no jurisdiction over stamps issued or errors which might have occurred prior to 1961. Such stamps as the 24-cent inverted airmail stamp will not be reprinted.")

The *Newark News* declared editorially that the Post Office was "in the grotesque position of trying to correct a small error by committing 400,000 errors." The *Nation* headlined its report on the episode "Murder of Santa Claus," and *Newsweek* said: "The blow was a cruel one for American stamp collectors — perhaps the cruelest in the 100-odd years they have been following their hobby." Columnist Inez Robb called Sherman "a knight in shining armor" who was "fighting for the right of all us to dream." She added: "The government, the big bully, ought to be ashamed of trying to deprive us ever of this inalienable right."

James Kelleher, who was believed to have been the instigator of the reprint operation, was a successful young public relations man from Indiana who had toiled diligently in John F. Kennedy's 1960 presidential campaign. At the Post Office he was considered innovative, even brilliant. His greatest coup was to conceive and carry out the hush-hush production of the Project Mercury stamp, which appeared unannounced at stamp windows across the nation simultaneously with John Glenn's pioneering orbital flight.

Sherman's theory afterward was that Kelleher, proud of the accolades he had received for Project Mercury, couldn't stand the thought of an error marring his record — and the record of the Post Office, with which he identified himself. Indeed, a defensive note was obvious in the press release that announced the plan to reprint the errors. It noted that since the 1918 Jennies, the Bureau had produced "one trillion, 100 billion American postage stamps without a comparable error reaching the public," and also that "more than one billion stamps requiring two press runs have been printed on present equipment without error."

One close associate of Kelleher believed, however, that the cause lay deeper. Kelleher, the associate said, suffered from a chronic disease of the nervous system, and this could have affected his judgment and contributed to a temporary flight from reality after the Hammarskjold inverts surfaced.

Whatever the reason, Kelleher told Sherman in a heated telephone conversation that the Post Office couldn't worry about "speculating collectors." Sherman tried to call President Kennedy. Finally he hired a lawyer, who sought a restraining order against the Post Office. On November 15 a U.S. district judge in Newark scheduled a show-cause hearing — but declined to issue a temporary restraint. That turned out to be fatal for Sherman's hopes.

The Post Office, moving fast, announced that the reprinted misprints would go on sale next morning in Washington. Working against time, Sherman's attorney appealed, and at 10:30 a.m. November 16 an appellate judge granted the restraining order. The lawyer hopped the train to the capital to serve the papers.

It was too late. The Post Office, knowing the injunction was coming, used its four hours of lead time to sell some 375,000 of the deliberate inverts. Leonard Sherman's case was moot. Twenty years later his lawyer, Richard Amster, couldn't talk about it without getting angry again.

"It was a petulant act by the Postmaster General," he said. "We wired Day as soon as the order was signed. In 33 years of law practice I have never seen a more outrageous act by government."

As if to rub it in, Kelleher sought out Sherman in person at the American Stamp Dealers Association show in New York's Armory two days later, chatted with him for a few minutes about the reprinting of the inverts, then introduced himself as "the man who was responsible for it."

Sherman was flabbergasted. "You took the find of the century away from me," he told Kelleher. "You have put me through hell for a whole week. This has never been done before. I bought a beautiful error — every stamp collector in the world is looking for something like this, and you took it away from me."

"What did you buy?" Kelleher countered. "I'll tell you what. You bought $2 worth of United States Government stamps. And that's what you got, $2 worth of stamps."

A crowd gathered, and, according to stamp dealer Leo August, sided with Sherman. "Kelleher was white as a sheet," August recalled. "The whole stamp exhibition was on his back. The police had to come and escort him out."

Sherman may have won that skirmish, but Kelleher had already won the war. On November 20 Sherman withdrew his suit, and in return the government gave him an affidavit saying that what he owned was the "discovery" sheet. He and Kelleher shook hands, and just to show there were no hard feelings, the one who had just deprived the other of many thousands of dollars gave him the 1961 edition of *Postage Stamps of the U. S.*, a Post Office paperback, inscribed: "To my recent antagonist and fellow preoccupier of the Dag Hammarskjold invert, J. Kelleher." At 4 p.m. that day the sale of the inverts was resumed in Washington.

The Post Office announced it would reprint 10 million of the errors, two million each by the original error plate combinations, yellow 27275 and black 27266 (Sherman's pane) and yellow 27282 and black 27279 (the Ohio pane). Inverts would also be printed on the other six plate combinations used for the Hammarskjolds. This was because of the heavy demand, the department said, but many thought the real purpose was to "Shermanize" any collectors who might have found additional panes of inverts and were lying low. Ultimately, 40,270,000 stamps were printed.

Both Sherman and Gerald Clark had taken steps themselves to establish their stamps as genuine error specimens. Sherman had persuaded 10 leading philatelists at the American Stamp Dealers Association show to sign and date his sheet on the selvage to certify that it was the original. And Clark, at the urging of *Linn's Stamp News* columnist Bob Jones, put some of his inverts on covers, got them postmarked with a November 14 Cuyahoga Falls machine cancel to prove that they predated the reprinting, and then had them notarized.

**Gerald Clark obtained the November 14, 1962 Cuyahoga Falls cancel on this cover to prove that the invert it bore predated the reprinting.**

About this time it was disclosed that a third pane of errors had been bought in mid-November at a Joliet, Illinois, post office. The owner, George Grant, was photographed with his stamps by the *Chicago Tribune*, but the stamps were cropped out of the photo that was published in the November 16 early editions, leaving Grant with no proof afterward that his pane was authentic.

Better luck befell Carlo Stabile, a coal miner and cover collector from Luzerne Mines, Pennsylvania. Four months after the reprinted inverts went on sale, he reported that among the first day covers of the original Hammarskjold stamp which he had ordered from the New York post office were some 22 covers bearing inverts, neatly tied to the envelopes with the October 23, 1962, "First Day of Issue" cancellation.

No affidavits, signatures or dated postmarks, however, could salvage more than a fraction of the value the original inverts would have had if the government had left things alone. What that value would have been is speculative; some experts guess $250,000 for a pane of 50. Sherman, for one, never tried to test the market for his autographed pane, and at this writing was planning to donate it, along with his scrapbooks and other related material, to the American Philatelic Research Library. Clark, retired and living in Florida in 1980, declined to talk about the status of his Hammarskjold inverts except to say that he still owned them.

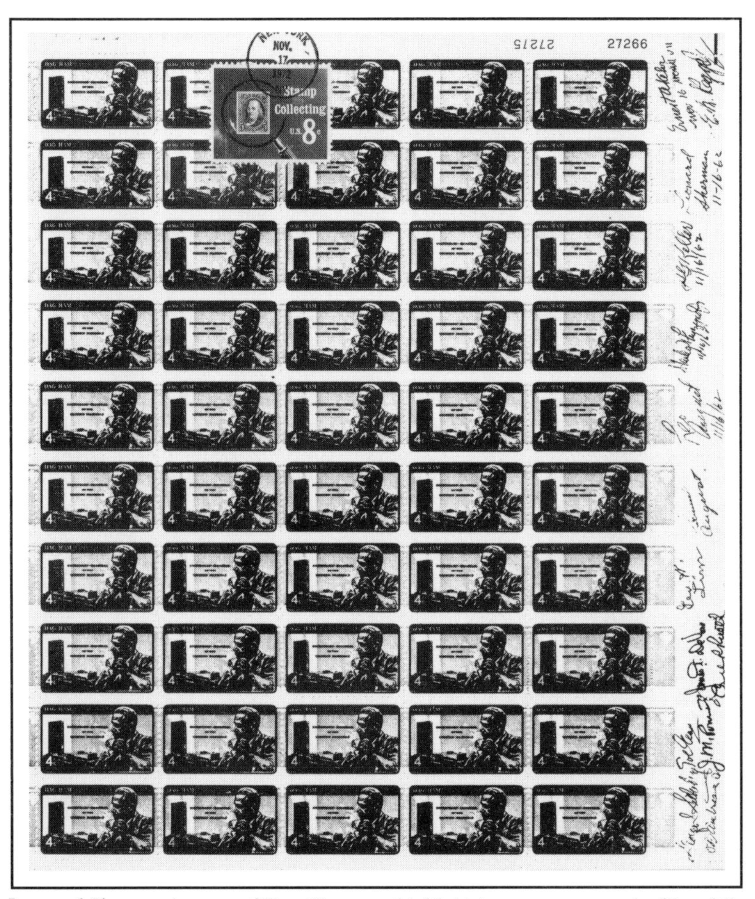


**Leonard Sherman's pane of Dag Hammarskjold 4¢ inverts, autographed by philatelic bigwigs to certify that it was the "discovery sheet."**

* * *

The Bureau of Engraving and Printing made some changes, as it had done after the Jenny inverts were found, to try to prevent any more inverted colors on stamps that required a second press run. It began making a diagonal corner cut on each sheet and scanning the sheets with an electric eye. Any uncut corner, meaning a reversed sheet, would stop the press.

Since then, the Bureau has greatly diminished the risk of producing color inverts by converting most of its stamp production to advanced equipment that prints stamps in multicolor intaglio, or intaglio-offset or intaglio-gravure combination, on a continuous web with no need for separate passes through the press.

Even so, one further example of an invert has since turned up. It was the $1 value of the Americana definitive series, first issued in 1979, showing an antique rush lamp and candle holder. In 1986 a pane of 100 stamps on which the red and yellow offset-printed candle flame was at the bottom of each stamp, instead of being superimposed over the engraved candle where it belonged, was purchased for use by a Washington-area office. Fourteen stamps had been sent out on letters before someone noticed the error and salvaged the remaining 86 specimens; one of these mint copies was auctioned at AMERIPEX May 26, 1986, for $5,000. Chances are, however, because of the Bureau's technological improvements, that this will be the last of the color inverts.

But it is even more clear that whatever types of stamp error may appear in the future, the finders will be able to announce and capitalize on their discoveries, safe from the danger that the federal government will do to them what it did to citizen Leonard Sherman. And this, ironically, is because somebody else won a court fight exactly like the one Sherman lost.

The stamp at the center of the fight was a 4¢ Canal Zone commemorative issued October 12, 1962 — 11 days before the original Hammarskjold stamp went on sale — to mark the opening of the Thatcher Ferry Bridge across the Panama Canal. It was black with a bridge superimposed in silver. Like the Hammarskjold issue, (a) it was produced by the Bureau of Engraving and Printing by a two-stage process on the Giori press and (b) something went wrong. One sheet of 200 went through the second press stuck to the sheet above it and missed getting the silver imprint.

Three of the four 50-stamp panes from the defective sheet were discovered by inspectors and set aside, but the fourth escaped and was found by employees of H.E. Harris and Company, a Boston stamp firm, among 60 panes ordered from the Canal Zone Philatelic Agency. Harris announced its find a few days before the Hammarskjold inverts came to light. On November 13, when the Post Office decided to reprint the Hammarskjolds, James Kelleher notified Canal Zone officials of that decision so they could decide whether to do the same thing.

Taking the clear hint, Zone Governor Robert J. Fleming announced

**Normal copy of the Canal Zone 1962 commemorative featuring the Thatcher Ferry Bridge uniting the continents.**

**A block of the Canal Zone "missing bridge" stamps.**

the next day that 100,000 of the bridgeless bridge stamps would be printed and sold to deflate the value of the Harris find. The Harris company quickly put the high-powered Washington law firm of Arnold, Fortas & Porter to work getting a preliminary and permanent injunction. In this effort Harris had a couple of advantages which Sherman lacked.

The Bureau had scheduled its Gioris to capacity with the new Christmas stamps, being issued that year for the first time; a new Winslow Homer commemorative issue; and now the rush job to duplicate the Hammarskjold errors. It was unable to get to another assignment right away. More significant, the defendants in Harris' suit were officials of the Canal Zone and the U.S. Treasury Department, not James Kelleher and the Post Office Department hard-liners, and they agreed to await a court's ruling before going ahead.

The suit dragged on for nearly three years. Harris's lawyers argued that the Canal Zone had no statutory authorization to issue flawed stamps merely to lower the price of philatelic rarities, and that to deliberately destroy the value of a person's property amounted to taking it without compensation and denying him equal protection of the laws.

Judge George L. Hart agreed. In March 1965 he granted Harris his motion for summary judgment, forbade the reprinting and told the Canal Zone never to distribute the three remaining error panes in its possession.

But by now the government had lost its appetite for reprinting errors. The new postmaster general, John A. Gronouski, said he had no intention of doing any such thing. Under the terms of a consent agreement, one of the remaining bridgeless panes was given to the Smithsonian Institution — today it occupies a display case right next to the Smithsonian's Jenny invert — and another went to the Canal Zone Museum; the third was destroyed. Plans to appeal Judge Hart's decision were dropped. Thus the government in effect conceded it couldn't legally reprint the Canal Zone errors — and that the Hammarskjold operation had been illegal too.

That didn't help Len Sherman. Happily, however, other things broke right for Sherman in the ensuing years. He became the owner of four jewelry stores, which his sons managed for him. He acquired a nice home, an art collection, a Mercedes. He and Roslyn traveled extensively. He became quite philosophical about his experience with the government.

Of James Kelleher, who died of a heart attack in 1970, leaving a wife and four children, Sherman said: "It was a sad thing, and I bear him no malice." Sherman did change his political allegiance, though. "The Democratic Party was always for the little guy, the working guy," he said. "Well, that's what I was, and they let me get shafted. I've been a Republican ever since." But he no longer mourned his lost riches.

"I made some good friends, I was on TV and got a lot of attention, I was mentioned in the Encyclopedia Britannica yearbook," he said. "Maybe things happened for the best. It was the thrill of a lifetime, actually."

Without realizing it, Len Sherman had used virtually the same words William Robey once employed to describe his own find — a find that Robey, unlike Sherman, had been permitted to convert to profit.

Chapter Nineteen

# Jenny Miscellany

## Those "Other Sheets"

Among the most common of the apocryphal tales about the Jenny invert is the one about the "other sheet" — or sheets — that escaped from the Bureau of Engraving and Printing and fell into collectors' hands.

These stories seem to have begun almost immediately after news of Robey's discovery was reported. During this period in 1918 it was a regular occurrence, or so Henry M. Goodkind was told, for someone to rush to a stamp dealer's shop with a report like this:

"Did you hear that another sheet with the airplane upside down has been found in a post office out west? It was bought for $500! It's true. I just heard it from someone who was in Scott's office."

More than two decades later, such stories were still being broadcast — only by now they had names and places attached.

In 1941 Philip H. Ward Jr., who had been writing about the invert from the beginning, passed along a "most interesting" story told by a Mr. A.P. Rasin of the Internal Revenue Service. It seems that in 1918 Rasin, then a bank president in Chestertown, Maryland, had bought a sheet of 24¢ Jennies at his post office one day and noticed that the centers were inverted. The accommodating Rasin, unlike William Robey, called the clerk's attention to the error before the deal was completed, after which "the sheet was quickly withdrawn and Mr. Rasin was told that instructions from Washington prevented him from selling the sheet."

In 1946 the Larkspur-Madeira (California) *News* published a front-page story about a local man, one T.C. Reindollar, who recalled that when he was a boy stamp collector in 1918 Mrs. Hattie Henry, the long-time stamp clerk at the San Rafael post office, had told him: "We had to send one sheet of the two-color 24-cent airmails back to

Washington to be destroyed" because the airplanes were upside down. Added the *News* proudly: "The postal lady is still unaware of the fabulous fortune in stamps which might have been hers, the boy's or the philatelic world's had not a sense of duty and honesty impelled her, according to post office regulations, to return them to Washington."

Such stories, of course, are beyond proving or disproving. We know, however, as reported in Chapter Four, that the director of the Bureau asserted in January 1919 that his inspectors had flagged eight invert sheets that were still on the premises; he said nothing of any that had been returned from the field by postal employees.

## The Other Heist

At least one other Jenny invert besides the ones owned by Ethel McCoy and the New York Public Library was the object of a burglary. It was part of a stock of stamps stolen in 1959 while awaiting sale at auction near Dublin, Ireland. The heist touched off a chain of consequences, starting with the collapse of the auction house — a house that had grown in only five years to become one of the biggest and best-publicized international stamp businesses in the world. That was followed by two long trials that ended with the acquittal of the firm's guiding genius on fraud charges.

The stolen Jenny was position 21, an attractive single with the left-hand selvage attached. It had been owned by an unnamed Philadelphia collector, was sold at auction in New York in 1954, was auctioned in England in 1958 for 1,450 pounds ($4,060), and thence found its way to the stock of Shanahans Stamp Auctions Ltd. Shanahans reported the stamp sold in its auction of February 7, 1959, but that was apparently a phony transaction, for the item was listed again in Auction No. 100, scheduled for May 23 of the same year.

Shanahans' managing director, 47-year-old Paul Singer, was a man of great magnetism and striking appearance. He weighed in at 260 pounds or more and had a black beard and piercing blue eyes, one of which continually winked from a facial tic. A doctor of political and social science from the University of Lausanne, he chose to be called "Dr. Singer."

After the stamp business had brough wealth to him and his wife Irma, the couple bought a mansion on a 13-acre estate, furnished it with antiques and decorated it with costly paintings. Here they threw parties for which they imported world-class entertainers from London and the continent and flew in epicurean food from various parts of the globe. When Singer would return from one of his frequent trips abroad to buy stamp collections or seek consignors of auction lots, he liked to be greeted at Dublin's airport by claques from his 90-member staff singing from the balconies: "For he's a jolly good fellow."

Singer's father in 1930 had foreseen the coming of the Nazis and taken his family from Austria to London to avoid persecution for their Jewish faith. The son studied law, married, and in 1954 moved to Ireland. Here he persuaded Jerome Shanahan and his son Desmond, owners of a modest auction house in Dun Laoghaire specializing in furniture and antiques, to join him in a stamp auction business. Singer had an amateur collector's knowledge of stamps and a born hustler's genius for promotion. In a short time the business was flourishing and had its own newsletter-catalog (*"Green ISLE Philately"*), edited by Singer and sent worldwide to every name on every mailing list he could get his hands on.

Singer solicited investments in the collections he was buying abroad for resale. As little as 10 pounds ($28) was accepted, and repayment without loss was guaranteed in four months, with assured profits of 20 to 100 percent. In fact, initial investors earned around 25 percent in the first four months, and fresh money poured in.

As time went by Singer seemed well on his way to becoming the world's biggest stamp dealer, to the chagrin of long-established dealers in London and on the continent. His illustrated auction catalogs grew to 80 or more pages each, listing up to 2,000 lots. His greatest coup came at the very end, when for approximately a million dollars he bought part of the world-famous Maurice Burrus collection that had been eagerly sought by many dealers, with an option to buy the rest for $4.6 million.

A few days later, on the night of Saturday, May 9, 1959, the Singers celebrated the fifth anniversary of Shanahans with a lavish party. The host, drunk, lurched through the halls, insulting women and making impromptu roaring speeches. The event was a last hurrah, however. Early that morning, Shanahans had been broken into by a burglar or burglars who removed steel bars from a ground floor window, drilled open the locks of four metal cabinets and got away with a large number of stamps awaiting auction — including the Jenny invert. The stamps, which Singer said were worth about $1.2 million, turned out not to have been insured.

News of the burglary alarmed investors, who began clamoring for their money back. Singer quickly scheduled an auction of Burrus stamps to try to restore confidence, but it was no use. On May 24 he had to summon the directors to vote the firm into liquidation, subject to court approval. The liquidator, a Dublin accountant, in time would be confronted with claims totaling almost $5.6 million from nearly 9,000 creditor-investors.

Harsher action was to come. On June 1 the four directors — Singer, his wife Irma, and Jerome and Desmond Shanahan — were charged with conspiring to defraud. The state in time would accuse them of running a huge Ponzi scheme in which they paid dividends to investors out of money from new investors, while faking many of the stamp auction sales that were ostensibly generating the profits. Meanwhile, Singer was transferring more than $2 million to his credit in banks in Switzerland and elsewhere, supposedly for stamp purchases.

A court later dismissed charges against Jerome Shanahan, a disabled World War I veteran who apparently was little more than an errand boy for the enterprise. Desmond Shanahan was found guilty on some counts, however, and sentenced to 15 months in prison, though even the judge acknowledged that he had been largely a pawn of Paul Singer.

It was Singer who was a big fish in the attorney general's net. The charges against him resulted in a series of marathon court sessions over a two-year period, in which Singer handled the bulk of his own defense. Unable to find the independent bailsman the court demanded, he spent the time in Mountjoy Prison, where officials obligingly let him convert a cell into a library housing several hundred law books.

His preliminary hearing lasted 62 days. A 40-day trial followed, ending with a jury verdict of guilty of "fraudulent conversion" (of new investors' money into old investors' profits) and a sentence of 14 years in prison.

However, Singer had only begun to fight. In a 26-day-long appeal hearing he made the surprise revelation that the jury foreman was an investor in Shanahans and an associate of the liquidator. He was granted a new trial. This one lasted 46 days and ended with a directed verdict of not guilty, on a technical failure of the prosecution to prove specific instances of conversion. The day the trial ended was Singer's 262nd day in court. It had been the longest legal battle ever fought in Ireland.

The courts still had need of Singer's presence for the bankruptcy proceedings. Here he would have had to explain those overseas deposits and discuss other interesting details. And Irma was free on $28,000 bail awaiting her own trial. But the two Singers had had enough of Ireland. They slipped out of the country, probably on the night of his acquittal, and vanished. Nearly 25 years later, they still have not reappeared.

Meanwhile, some of the stolen stamps were recovered, including an estimated $14,400 worth which a municipal garbage collector found in a suitcase in an alley near the auction house. The liquidator issued an elaborate illustrated catalog of the remaining material, which was widely circulated.

More than two years later, in October 1961, Swiss and Italian authorities announced the recovery of an additional $850,000 worth of Shanahans stamps. A Greek who had worked at Shanahans as a stamp describer was arrested in Geneva and charged with possession of stolen property — indicating strongly that the burglary was an inside job. The actual burglar, however, was never arrested, which points up a dismal record alluded to earlier: That although at least six Jenny inverts have been stolen in three separate episodes, no individual has ever been so much as charged with any of the thefts.

The Shanahans Jenny, like the other stamps from the company, was eventually sold on behalf of the liquidator by Robson Lowe International Ltd. of London. It was purchased by Robert Lehman of New York. The Jenny was auctioned by Robson Lowe in Geneva in 1976, bringing 90,000 Swiss francs ($39,600).

**Caught in the Blitz**

Some time in the 1930s a Jenny invert, position 63, was acquired by a British nobleman, John Crichton-Stuart, the fourth Marquess of Bute. Where he obtained it isn't recorded, but the marquess was a frequent customer of London's H.R. Harmer and Company, and it's possible his Jenny was one of the two which Harmers cited in its 1932-1933 resume as having been "secured for English collectors."

The marquess could well afford the stamp. Though his title was named for an island in Scotland's Firth of Clyde, he owned tens of thousands of acres all over Great Britain. His forebears had developed the city of Cardiff in Wales out of a seaside village, and in 1938 Lord Bute sold approximately half the city, including houses, shops, pubs, cinemas, docks and farmlands, for a reported 20 million pounds in the biggest real estate deal in British history.

He kept his Jenny and other stamps in the vault of the Chancery Lane Safe Deposit in London. On the night of September 24, 1940, Luftwaffe bombers set much of central London afire in one of the heaviest raids of the Battle of Britain. Afterward, three feet of water stood in the Chancery Lane storage room, immersing the albums on the lower shelves. When the room was finally entered a month later, the collection was taken for drying and inspection to Cardiff Castle, an old Norman castle which the third marquess had rebuilt beginning in the 1860s. The Jenny invert had lost its gum, of course, but was otherwise unharmed.

The fourth marquess died in 1947. His son, the fifth marquess, who inherited the stamp collection, died in 1956 and the invert was sold at auction three years later for 1,050 pounds ($2,950). It has had several owners since.

**High and Dry**

Three other Jenny inverts came within hours of damage or destruction by flood when the Susquehanna River broke through a dike on June 24, 1972, and inundated downtown Wilkes-Barre, Pennsylvania.

The Jennies were among an estimated million dollars or more worth of stamps owned by Irwin Weinberg and his investors' syndicate and kept in a vault in the basement of the Wilkes-Barre bank building where Weinberg's offices were located.

**Irwin Weinberg in his Wilkes-Barre office, where he brought his inverts only hours ahead of a devastating flood.**

Weinberg was in New York as tropical storm Agnes was moving up the East Coast, bringing torrential rain with her. "I became very nervous about conditions at home," he recalled, "so I cut my visit short and flew to Wilkes-Barre the next morning. Because of the storm our plane could barely land at the airport.

"I sat around my office all day getting more and more concerned, and finally I called the bank to ask about the safety of the vault. I was told they had contacted Civil Defense, which said that if the dikes along the river didn't hold and the pumps broke down, anything could happen.

"Shortly before the bank closed at 3 I went downstairs, determined to get the contents of my safe deposit box and move them upstairs to my own safe on the seventh floor. The girl at the vault had gone home early, leaving the master key locked in her desk. Very apologetically I sought out the manager, who agreed to open the desk, get the lock-box key and let me in. I took the box, while apologizing again for the inconvenience and promising to bring it back the next morning.

"There was no 'next morning.' The Susquehanna broke through, putting downtown Wilkes-Barre and the bank vault under water. That vault was not opened again for at least 30 days. Most everything in it was a soggy mess when the doors finally were unjammed by locksmiths. The stamps would have been ruined and insurance would not have covered them."

Soon after the news of the flood had gone out over the wires, Weinberg received a cablegram from the British Broadcasting Corporation asking whether the 1¢ magenta British Guiana, which he and his syndicate then owned, was safe.

"BBC didn't know," Weinberg said, "that unlike our other stamps, that one had been high and dry in New York all along."

## The Cuban Connection

Cuban stamp collectors, more so than any others in Latin America, have had an affinity for the Jenny invert. At least four prominent Cubans owned copies at one time or another.

The best-known was Dr. Andres Domingo y Morales del Castillo, who was presidential secretary to Cuban dictator Fulgencio Batista and at one time served as interim president himself. Morales del Castillo specialized in airmail stamps and owned several rarities, including a block of four of Mexico's 1935 Amelia Earhart overprints, used, on cover. Reportedly, his Jenny invert was given to him as a birthday present by a group of friends, including Dr. Carlos Nunez, a banker. No doubt they considered it a good investment, given Morales del Castillo's proximity to the seat of power.

The stamp was obtained for the fortunate recipient from Havana dealer Julio Asseo for $3,500 some time in the 1950s. Asseo, writing years later from Miami, recalled that he had gotten it from Gordon Harmer of Harmer, Rooke in a private sale, but didn't know the stamp's position number.

When Fidel Castro seized power January 1, 1959, Morales del Castillo fled the country with Batista and other government leaders. He left most of his valuable stamps behind, but took the Jenny invert with him, according to Richard Milian, a past president of the Cuban Philatelic Club. When U.S. dealer John Fox visited Havana in the early 1960s at the invitation of the Castro government to appraise the Morales del Castillo collection, which the government had confiscated, he found the Mexican Earhart stamps and other choice specimens, but no Jenny. Morales del Castillo died in Miami in 1979; what became of his airmail invert is unknown.

Richard Milian himself owned a Jenny invert, which he bought in

1948 from a Cuban dealer named Cano and sold in 1951 through Harmer, Rooke in New York, where he and his bride had gone on their honeymoon. This may have been position 37, which Harmer, Rooke sold at auction in October 1951.

Alberto Perez, owner of several match factories in Cuba, had Jenny position 28 in his collection in the 1940s; it was sold in New York with the other Perez stamps in 1947 by Fred W. Kessler.

And Rafael Oriol, a representative of the DuPont Company in Cuba and the only foreign national ever to serve as president of the American Air Mail Society, once owned position 100. His invert was sold at auction in 1961, also by Kessler, a personal friend. Oriol, who also had fled the Castro revolution, died in 1977 in Caracas, Venezuela.

Reports that the Cuban Postal Museum owned a Jenny invert were checked out through correspondence by the American Philatelic Society Stamp Theft Committee in 1982 and found to be incorrect. Wrote Richard Milian in 1986: "I can assure you that at the present time there are not any inverted Jennies in Cuba."

**Institutional Jennies**

Three Jenny inverts are known to be owned by public institutions—by coincidence, one in each of the cities served by the original airmail. However, as of this writing only one can be viewed by the general public. This is position 70, owned by the Smithsonian Institution's National Philatelic Collection.

The Smithsonian's Jenny was donated by the Raymond H. Weill Company December 23, 1957. It has a straight edge at the right and, like several other straight-edge Jennies from Colonel Green's collection, is without gum. Along with other selected gems from the Smithsonian's collection it is on display in the "Philatelic Rarities" alcove off the main stamp exhibition area on the third floor of the National Museum of American History. The lights over the horizontal display cases automatically switch on as a visitor approaches, then turn off after a brief interval, to retard fading.

The Franklin Institute in Philadelphia also owns a straight-edge Jenny invert, position 2. The stamp was part of a major U.S. collection, heavy in 19th century classics, bequeathed to the Institute by Harry L. Jefferys of Ardmore, Pennsylvania, who died April 1, 1948. Jefferys had bought the Jenny at Green Sale XIV February 24, 1944, for $1,030. It was available for public inspection until early in 1986, when the Institute's rare stamp gallery was closed for remodeling. An Institute official said the gallery would be reopened "possibly early in 1987."

When the author last saw the invert, in September 1984, it was mounted on an album page, displayed horizontally under glass on a waist-level stand under continuous but indirect light. Its blue color appeared good, but the red, which is more sensitive to light, seemed slightly faded. However, other rarities from the Jefferys collection on exhibit in the same section of the museum had faded badly, especially the red pigments in the 2¢ Pan-American Exposition invert, the 1869 30¢ invert and the $4 Columbian Exposition commemorative.

The third institutional Jenny is, of course, the New York Public Library's Miller copy (see Chapter 16).

Princeton University's nearly 30-year ownership of a block of four Jennies was of little benefit to the public, as was reported in Chapter 14; the university never exhibited the item. Another American institution of higher learning did much better by its gift of a Jenny.

In 1967 Ellen Douglas Williamson, Quaker Oats heiress, author and trustee of Coe College in Cedar Rapids, Iowa, gave her airmail stamp collection of some 75 volumes to Coe. It included a Jenny invert single, position 93. The stamp was hardly a choice copy; it had had several owners beginning with Dr. Philip G. Cole of Tarrytown, New York, and it was creased, thinned and regummed. Still, it was a Jenny, and it never ceased to draw viewers when the college exhibited it, as Coe did frequently during the decade it owned the Williamson collection. Eventually the trustees decided to sell the stamps and add the proceeds to one of the endowment funds set up by Mrs. Williamson, and this was done through a Robert Siegel auction January 7, 1977. The invert brought $23,000. In its most recent resale, in January 1985, it fetched $52,000 plus the 10 percent buyer's fee.

## Jenny on Other Stamps

On May 15, 1968, the Post Office Department issued a 10¢ airmail stamp to mark the 50th anniversary of the first airmail flights. The stamp was of the large commemorative size, arranged horizontally, and was designed by Hordur Karlsson of the graphic arts staff of the International Monetary Fund in Washington. Karlsson reproduced in somewhat larger dimensions the image of Jenny 38262 (number and all) that had appeared on the first airmail stamp. So faithful was his copy that even the wavy lines in the background that represented sky and clouds were engraved to conform to those on the original.

The stamp, like its predecessor 50 years earlier, was printed in two steps. A blue background and blue and red trim on the plane's vertical stabilizer were applied by lithography, and the vignette and lettering were then printed from plates produced in intaglio. The Post Office did not carry tradition to extremes, however; this time it created no inverted specimens.

Torrey Webb, who as a young first lieutenant had carried the mail from New York to Philadelphia on May 15, 1918, in Jenny No. 38278, expressed regret in a 50th anniversary interview that the commemo-

**Jenny 38262 flies again — on the 10¢ 50th Anniversary commemorative issued by the United States May 15, 1968.**

rative stamp didn't picture his plane. After all, said Webb — a retired vice president of Texaco — 38278 was the first airmail plane to reach its destination; 38262, flown out of Washington by Lieutenant George Boyle, had gone astray and never got to Philadelphia.

**Lieutenant Torrey Webb's Jenny — the first mailplane to complete its mission — shown on a 1975 U.S. stamp.**

Perhaps in response to Webb's altogether reasonable complaint, the U.S. Postal Service did put his plane on a stamp a few years later. It was a 10¢ multicolor commemorative issued August 24, 1975, as part of a block of four different designs to mark the 200th anniversary of the U.S. Post Office. The stamp also pictures a Boeing 747 jetliner, added by designer James L. Womer to contrast old and new methods of mail transportation. The Jenny is on the ground, and its last three digits, 278, are visible behind a man in a dark blue suit who is handing up a bag of mail to a brown-clad helmeted pilot in the cockpit. One may infer that the pilot is Lieutenant Webb, although he is not so identified (to conform to U.S. law which forbids the portrayal of living persons on stamps. Webb in fact died in November 1975 at the age of 82, three months after the stamp was issued.)

**This Jenny postal card was designed by Keith Ferris, who painted murals for the National Air and Space Museum.**

Another Curtiss JN4H, in flight and with Army insignia on the wings, is pictured in a view from in front and above on a 21¢ multicolor international airmail postal card issued September 16, 1978. The designer was Keith Ferris of Morris Plains, New Jersey, who was one of three aerospace artists commissioned to paint murals for the National Air and Space Museum in Washington.

Jenny has been featured on foreign stamps as well. China's first airmails, a five-value set issued July 1, 1921, shows a Jenny in flight over the Great Wall, with the bars of the Republic's flag painted on its tail. In 1976 Nicaragua issued a set of seven regular stamps and five airmails depicting "*estampillas raras y famosas*" in their natural colors. The 5-centavo value reproduced a U.S. Jenny invert.

**Jenny on Souvenir Cards**

In 1973 two official souvenir cards were issued reproducing the 24¢ Jenny stamp, one normal, one inverted.

The U.S. Postal Service produced a card in compliment to the 50th anniversary of the Aero Philatelic Club of London and its international airmail exhibition July 4-7 at Manchester, APEX 73. On it were reproduced, in natural colors but slightly larger than life size, three famous airmail stamp rarities: the Newfoundland De Pinedo of 1927,

**Nicaragua reproduced a Jenny invert in a 1978 series picturing rare and famous stamps from around the world.**

the 1925 Black Honduras overprint and, in the middle, the 24¢ Jenny invert. (The descriptive text misspelled "Curtiss," using only one S.)

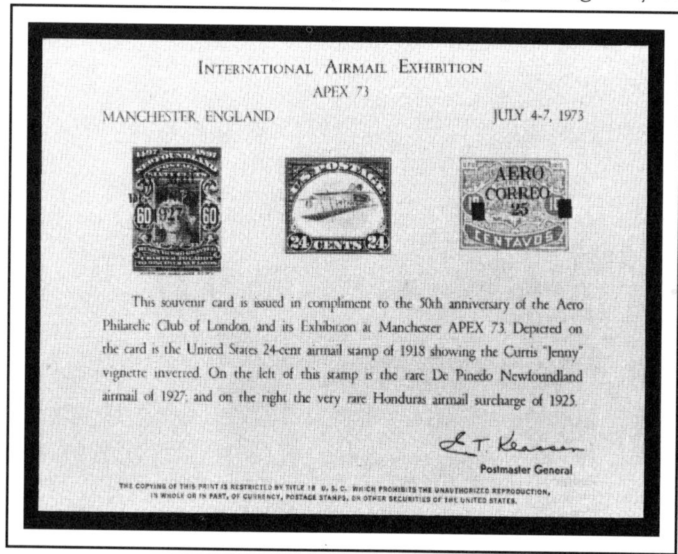

INTERNATIONAL AIRMAIL EXHIBITION
APEX 73

MANCHESTER, ENGLAND — JULY 4-7, 1973

This souvenir card is issued in compliment to the 50th anniversary of the Aero Philatelic Club of London, and its Exhibition at Manchester APEX 73. Depicted on the card is the United States 24-cent airmail stamp of 1918 showing the Curtis "Jenny" vignette inverted. On the left of this stamp is the rare De Pinedo Newfoundland airmail of 1927; and on the right the very rare Honduras airmail surcharge of 1925.

E. T. Klassen
Postmaster General

THE COPYING OF THIS PRINT IS RESTRICTED BY TITLE 18 U.S.C. WHICH PROHIBITS THE UNAUTHORIZED REPRODUCTION, IN WHOLE OR IN PART, OF CURRENCY, POSTAGE STAMPS, OR OTHER SECURITIES OF THE UNITED STATES.

**This souvenir sheet issued by the United States Postal Service in 1973 reproduced a copy of the Jenny airmail invert.**

Later that year, the Bureau of Engraving and Printing issued a souvenir card for NAPEX '73 in Washington September 14-16, marking the 50th anniversary of the American Air Mail Society. The Bureau used the original stamp dies to reproduce a block of four of the normal 24¢ Jenny, with plane right side up, but with denomination and lettering removed, as is customary with Bureau-issued souvenir cards.

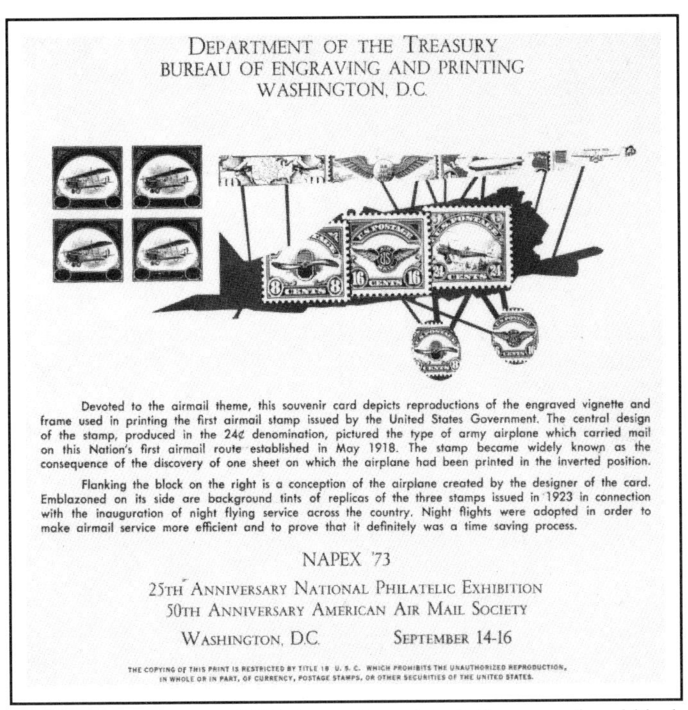


**Bureau of Engraving and Printing, using original dies, reproduced block of normal Jenny stamps on 1973 souvenir card.**

On October 1, 1982, the Postal Service again produced a souvenir card depicting a larger-than-life Jenny invert. This time no other stamp reproductions were included. The occasion was National Stamp Collecting Month, which USPS sponsored in cooperation with the Council of Philatelic Organizations. "Curtiss" was correctly spelled.

## By the Numbers

Most American stamp collectors, when they are being formal about it, refer to the Jenny invert as "C3a." This is its designation in the U.S. section of Scott's *Standard Postage Stamp Catalogue*, the reference book most used by U.S. philatelists. In Scott practice, an "a" after a catalog number denotes a major variety of the normal stamp. "C3" is the number assigned to the normal 24¢ Jenny.

That wasn't always its Scott designation. The stamp, both normal and inverted versions, was first listed in the 1919 edition of Scott's. It was included with the regular postage stamps. Explained the catalog:

"Though this stamp was intended primarily to pay the postage on letters sent by aerial post, it is not restricted to special use, is available for ordinary postage and forms part of the general issue."

The stamp was assigned the number 432 and priced at 34¢ unused

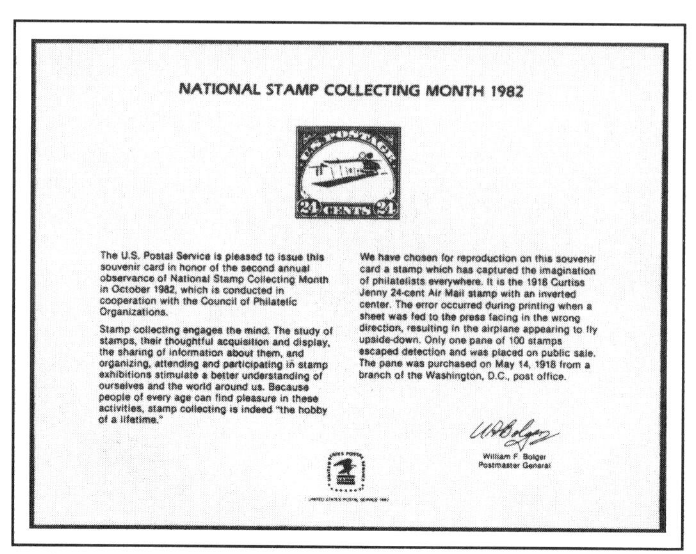

NATIONAL STAMP COLLECTING MONTH 1982

The U.S. Postal Service is pleased to issue this souvenir card in honor of the second annual observance of National Stamp Collecting Month in October 1982, which is conducted in cooperation with the Council of Philatelic Organizations.

Stamp collecting engages the mind. The study of stamps, their thoughtful acquisition and display, the sharing of information about them, and organizing, attending and participating in stamp exhibitions stimulate a better understanding of ourselves and the world around us. Because people of every age can find pleasure in these activities, stamp collecting is indeed "the hobby of a lifetime."

We have chosen for reproduction on this souvenir card a stamp which has captured the imagination of philatelists everywhere. It is the 1918 Curtiss Jenny 24-cent Air Mail stamp with an inverted center. The error occurred during printing when a sheet was fed to the press facing in the wrong direction, resulting in the airplane appearing to fly upside-down. Only one pane of 100 stamps escaped detection and was placed on public sale. The pane was purchased on May 14, 1918 from a branch of the Washington, D.C., post office.

William F. Bolger
Postmaster General

**Another souvenir card depicting a Jenny airmail invert was issued to celebrate National Stamp Collecting Month in 1982.**

(it was still available at face value at some post offices then) and 10¢ used. As for 432a ("centre inverted"), it was unpriced. No picture accompanied the listing, of course, because of the law forbidding illustration of U.S. stamps.

In the 1920 edition, No. 432 was joined by No. 430, the 6¢ orange Jenny stamp, and No. 431, the 16¢ green. The catalog editors had reversed the chronological order in which the stamps were issued in favor of numbering them in ascending face value. No. 432a, the invert, remained unpriced until the 1922 catalog, when it was assigned a value of $750.

In 1930, Scott's for the first time segregated airmail stamps from regular postage, giving the airmails numbers at the 1300 level. The Jenny invert thus became No. 1302a, valued at $2,000. Ten years later, with new issues proliferating and the numerical gaps narrowing between the distinctive stamp categories, Scott shifted to another numbering system. Airmail stamps were assigned the prefix "C," and the inverted Jenny became C3a, which it has been ever since.

Scott's originally described the color of the stamp's frame as "carmine" and later changed it to "carmine rose," but the Post Office, in its official descriptions, has always used the more prosaic "red."

The *New Worldwide Postage Stamp Catalog*, first issued by Minkus Publications in the 1950s, lists the first three U.S. airmail stamps as Scott does, in order of denomination. The 6¢ Jenny is A1, the 16¢ A2 and the 24¢ A3, with the invert designated A3a. The *Standard*

*Catalogue of Air Post Stamps*, first published during the 1930s by dealer and aerophilatelist Nicholas Sanabria, originally listed the 24¢ Jenny No. 3 and the invert 3a. But in 1950 the editors changed the 24¢ to No. 1, explaining that it was the "first stamp produced expressly for airmail purposes," and deserved the leading spot.

On the other hand the *American Air Mail Catalogue*, an official publication of the American Air Mail Society, has listed the 24¢ Jenny as No. 1 ever since its first edition in 1940. (The invert is noted, but given no separate listing or sub-listing.)

Stanley Gibbons' catalog, the major British reference work, like Scott's originally placed airmails with regular stamps and later separated them and designated the 24¢ Jenny A3. As of this writing it again lists airmails with regular stamps, but gives them an "A" prefix, and the Jenny has become A548.

**The Counterfeits**

From time to time enterprising rascals have tried to counterfeit the Jenny invert.

The usual *modus operandi* involves some careful shaving and splicing of two normal copies of the 24¢ airmail stamp. However, the Philatelic Foundation has been asked to certify at least one specimen of a Jenny invert that was cut from a souvenir card issued by the U.S. Postal Service. Aside from the other obvious signs that this item was a fake, the souvenir card replica of the Jenny stamp was perceptibly larger than the original.

And in August 1950 the press carried reports that Secret Service agents had arrested two Burbank, California, men in a shack outside North Hollywood with printing equipment and color proofs that indicated they planned to counterfeit the Jenny invert. The engraving work was described in the news stories as "exceptionally good," but the suspects had been unable to match the colors of the original. Unfortunately, no further information on the case can be found.

Generally, efforts to market skin-and-paste counterfeits have been unsuccessful. The fakery readily shows up when the stamp is dipped in the benzine or carbon tetrachloride which collectors use to reveal watermarks as well as hidden thin spots and repaired tears. Even without this type of verification, experts who know the characteristics of all 100 genuine Jennies can quickly expose a phony. One such two-piece invert was hawked unsuccessfully around New York in the late 1930s with an asking price of $3,000. *Stamps* obtained and published a photo of it as a warning to the unwary.

It has been reported that once, however, an innocent party was stung by a Jenny counterfeit that was made by removing the center of a normal copy, replacing it upside down in its frame, then rebacking it and regumming the stamp. The source of the report was Henry M. Goodkind, and he gave it this way in his 1956 monograph:

"About 20 years or so ago, a man walked into a stamp dealer's office and offered for sale a copy of the 24-cent air mail invert. The dealer, not wanting to buy this for his stock, told this party that he would like to retain this stamp on consignment for a short time because he thought he had a prospective buyer. This was agreed upon. The dealer gave this man a written receipt for a 24-cent air mail invert at the asking price.

"The dealer at once wrote to his prospective customer. But between the time after the owner departed and the prospect replied, someone in the dealer's office inspected the copy left on consignment more thoroughly. Only then was it discovered to be a fake, made from cutting out the center from a normal copy as described above.

"When the owner of this copy returned to learn if the dealer had been able to sell it to his customer, he informed the seller of the status of his copy. But its return was refused. The man maintained that he had delivered a genuine 24-cent airmail with an inverted center and had a written receipt for such a copy, not a faked one. The case went to court and a verdict was rendered against the stamp dealer. The court ruled that the written evidence showed a receipt for a genuine copy of this valuable error and the dealer had to make good."

Goodkind admitted he had not troubled to consult the "court records" (he also did not include such helpful information as to what court it was) and for that reason, he said, "accuracy will be somewhat sacrificed," but "nevertheless, the story . . . is believed to be generally factual." The reader, then, is left with a take-it-or-leave-it choice. This author asked several veteran philatelic writers, including Herman Herst Jr. and Ernest A. Kehr, about the story, but they were unable to recall any specifics. At this point in time the chances that it can be verified seem most unlikely.

* * *

The story of the Jenny invert is one that can never be completely told. Count on it: strange and remarkable things will continue to befall these stamps.

And questions will remain. Some may in time find answers, but others will take their place.

For example: where are the missing copies? Who stole the McCoy, the Library, the Shanahans stamp? Where is the designer's original artwork? Most basic of all: *How were the Jenny inverts created?*

We have a wealth of knowledge about these great pieces of Americana. What we don't know makes it more appealing still—and guarantees that the appeal will endure.

# Appendix

What follows is a brief history of each of the 96 Jenny inverts that have figured in recorded transactions since the breakup of the original sheet acquired by Col. Edward H.R. Green.

In attempting to establish as complete a provenance as possible for each stamp, I received invaluable aid from several long-time specialists in the invert. I am also indebted to many dealers who were more than generous with their time and with access to their records. All these individuals are named elsewhere, in my list of acknowledgements. In addition, I have searched through hundreds of auction and private treaty catalogs and scores of periodicals for descriptions of individual stamps offered for sale.

I believe the result is the most complete summary ever published of the sales and ownerships of individual copies of the Jenny invert. Still, no listing of this nature can ever be complete. Many sales of the stamp have been private ones. For some of the public sales during the early years, records have been lost. Even where records exist of those early sales, no notation was made of the stamp's position number. And in the majority of the Jenny invert sales, early and late, the seller has kept confidential the name of the buyer at the latter's request.

The prices listed, in most cases, were furnished by the auction houses themselves. It has not been unknown in the past for an occasional stamp auctioneer, like brokers of other commodities, to inflate an announced price now and then, or even report a sale that did not in fact take place. Still, the great majority of the auction houses that have dealt in Jenny inverts have been firms of high reputation, whose statements of prices realized have been widely accepted by the philatelic community.

Abbreviations: SE, straight edge; OG, original gum; NH, never hinged; NG, no gum; HR, hinge remnant; PFC, Philatelic Foundation Certificate.

1. The upper left corner stamp, with full sheet selvage at left, SE at

top. Centered slightly to left. Perforations close at bottom but clear of design. Sold October 20, 1942, in Green Sale IV by Irwin Heiman, New York, for $860. Described as NG. Offered at auction September 20, 1943, by Nicholas Sanabria, New York. Described as "1 on the sheet, very fine, sheet margin at left, unique $2,500+." (Not illustrated.) Sold January 18, 1985, by Steve Ivy Philatelic Auctions Inc., Dallas, to Kenneth Wenger, dealer, Fort Lee, New Jersey, for $56,000 plus $5,600 buyer's premium.

2. SE at top. Centered very slightly to left; at bottom, perforations just miss the frame line. Sold February 24, 1944, in Green Sale XIV, by Edson J. Fifield, New York, for $1,030, presumably to Harry L. Jefferys, Ardmore, Pennsylvania. Bequeathed in 1948 by Jefferys to the Franklin Institute, Philadelphia, where it is on public exhibit.

3. SE at top. Perforations close at bottom. Part OG (per PFC 106461). Offered at auction May 20, 1974, by J.&H. Stolow, New York. Described as having "light suggestion of a hinge." Advertised for sale in 1976 by Lambert W. Gerber, Tamaqua, Pennsylvania, for $29,000. Advertised for sale in *Stamps* magazine April 8, 1978, by Gerber for $59,000, accompanied by an altered photograph showing perforations at top. Sold at auction December 5, 1981, by John W. Kaufmann, Washington, to a West Coast collector. Catalog photograph showed natural SE at top. Stamp described as "position 3 as noted in pencil on the back before the sheet was broken, full OG, very lightly hinged." Stamp later returned to Kaufmann by buyer in partial payment for position 58 (which see). Offered at auction by Kaufmann March 26, 1986. Described as having "full OG, very lightly hinged."

4. SE at top, but unnaturally close to frame, as if someone attempted to perforate the natural SE, spoiled the job and trimmed it. Near-perfect centering at sides. Sold in 1971 or 1972 by estate of a Mr. Hudson, New Jersey, to Greg Manning Company, South Orange, New Jersey. Pictured in *Linn's Stamp News* October 16, 1972, and identified as part of the Manning stock. Sold by Manning to an unnamed collector. Offered at auction January 30, 1976, by Daniel F. Kelleher Company, Boston. Described as "OG . . . perfs (sic) clipped at top."

5. Originally had SE at top. Centered slightly to right, close at bottom. Sold September 23, 1942, in Green Sale I, by Hugh C. Barr, New York, for $1,750 to unidentified Baltimore collector. Described as mint. Sold at auction February 3, 1949, by Harmer, Rooke & Company, New York, for $1,450. Described as "mint and NH. Brilliant copy and probably the finest of the SE copies." At some point, stamp was given false perforations at top (per PFC 105292). Sold at auction April 5, 1980, by Robert A. Siegel, New York, for $70,000 plus $7,000 to Irwin Weinberg, Wilkes-Barre, Pennsylvania. Described as "very

lightly hinged, reperfed at top." Offered in May 1986 at AMERIPEX by Steve Ivy; not sold. Sold at auction August 22, 1986, at STAMPSHOW '86 by Ivy for $53,000 plus $5,300 to Gary Posner, dealer, Leonia, New Jersey.

6. Originally had SE at top. Centered to right with perfs touching frame. Vertical red sheet guideline shows on tips of perfs at left. Sold October 5, 1942, in Green Sale II, by Laurence & Stryker, New York, for $1,350. Described as having "light 16 mm. corner crease. Thin trace in bottom right corner perforation. OG." At some point, stamp was given false perforations at top (per PFC 73742). Sold at auction July 6, 1951, by Sylvester Colby, New York, for $1,800. Reperf not mentioned. Offered at auction December 29-30, 1960, by Lambert W. Gerber. Described as having "usual faint gum creases . . . OG." Reperf not mentioned. Sold by Century Stamp Company, Los Angeles, to Steve Markoff, Hollywood. Offered for rent by Markoff in advertisement in *Linn's Stamp News* January 17, 1972. Offered for sale by Markoff in advertisement in *Linn's* October 30, 1972, for $28,950 as "full gum, unhinged, original." Sold by Markoff to Superior Stamp and Coin Company, Beverly Hills. Offered at auction November 15, 1977, by Superior. Described as having "light creases . . . insignificant." Sold at auction April 6, 1981, by Superior for $75,000. Described as having "defects." Sold at auction August 23, 1982, by Superior to a woman "celebrity" for $68,000. Again described as defective. Sold at auction October 29, 1984, by Superior to a local TV personality for $70,000 plus $7,000. Offered in May 1986 at AMERIPEX by Superior.

7. SE at top. Centered to right and bottom but perfs clear of design. Extra wide margin at left. Sold October 17, 1942, in Green Sale III, by Daniel F. Kelleher for $1,025. Described as having "faint gum breaker crease" (although flat plate stamps had no gum breakers) and "full OG." Sold at auction November 14, 1973, by Robert A. Siegel as part of collection of Miss Katharine Matthies for $20,000. Described as "lightly hinged, normal light natural gum bends."

8. Originally had SE at top. Centered to right and bottom but perfs clear of design. Has tiny spot in "S" of "U.S." Sold December 1, 1942, in Green Sale VII, by J.C. Morgenthau & Company, subsidiary of Scott Stamp & Coin Company, New York, for $1,350. Described as "a good OG copy with . . . tiny spot in paper." At some point, stamp was given false perforations at top, regummed and cleaned (per PFC 1455). Sold at auction April 3, 1951, by Harmer, Rooke for $1,500. Described as "hinge removed and gum disturbed. U.L. corner perf weak. Faint, barely visible crease." Reperf not mentioned. Sold June 2, 1964, by Irwin Heiman for $7,000. Described as "part OG, reperfed at top, tiny paper speck." Sold at auction May 25, 1986, at AMERIPEX by

Robert A. Siegel with the "Isleham collection" for $55,000 plus $5,500. Described as "disturbed OG, hinge remnant, natural inclusion in 'S' of 'U.S.', reperfed at top."

9. SE at top. Perfs close at right, almost touching at bottom. Condition of back cannot be determined. Encased in round glass locket, back to back with a normal 24¢ Jenny stamp, and given by Colonel Edward H.R. Green to his wife Mabel. Bequeathed by Mabel Green in 1950 to a Long Island woman. Stamp was photographed for the first time December 26, 1984, at the Bank of New York, Fifth Avenue and 44th Street, New York.

10. The upper right corner stamp, with SE at top and right. Centered to right and bottom with SE at right very close to frame. Sold as part of a vertical pair with position 20 October 25, 1943, in Green Sale X, by Irwin Heiman for $1,500 to Paul Wise, New York dealer. Described as NG. Offered as singles or a pair, depending on the higher bid. Wrongly described as "the only known pair of this rare variety" (vertical pairs later sold in Green Sales XXIII and XXVII). At some point thereafter, pair was separated. Position 10 was offered at auction December 1, 1947, by F.W. Kessler, New York, as part of airmail collection of Milton J. Harris. (From the same collection Kessler also offered position 30, also from the right-hand vertical row. In both cases catalog wrongly reported that all top-row and right-row copies were without gum.) Position 10 was offered July 8, 1955, by Lee Gilbert. Sold at auction June 28, 1968, by Earl P.L. Apfelbaum for $9,100. Described as "the choicest position on the sheet . . . NG." Last reported owned by a Texas collector.

11. Perfs touching at bottom, extra wide margin at top. "Some wrinkling and a small thin spot at right" (per PFC 43109). At one time this stamp with position 12 comprised a horizontal pair, with left sheet selvage attached, owned by Joseph A. Steinmetz, Philadelphia. Position 11 was sold at auction March 21, 1929, by Eugene Klein as part of Steinmetz collection for $1,060. Described as "a little off at bottom, as most of them come, adhering marginal strip at left, OG." Offered at auction April 2, 1947, by Cosmos Stamp Company. Left selvage was no longer attached. Described as OG. Sold May 11, 1965, by H.R. Harmer, New York, as part of collection of late Ellwood R. Burdsall, Great Barrington, Massachusetts, for $8,000. Described as "OG . . . negligible gum wrinkles and tiny thin." Sold at auction January 29, 1977, by Jacques Schiff Jr., New York, for $36,000. Described as having "HR, tiny thin, slight wrinkles."

12. See 11. Perfect centering at sides, perfs touch at bottom, wide margin at top. Creased and with small thin spots (per PFC 24594). Sold by Joseph A. Steinmetz circa 1928 to J. Insley Blair, banker,

Tuxedo Park, New York. Sold at auction April 19, 1943, by Harmer, Rooke for the Blair estate. Described as having "tiny insignificant thinning . . . OG." Sold at auction November 17, 1966, by Robert A. Siegel for $8,500. Described as having "small ungummed area at L.L., very light gum bend, almost invisible pinpoint thin speck." Sold at auction September 29, 1967, by Simmy's Stamp Company, Boston, for $13,500. Described as "OG . . . invisible slight natural paper bends (not creases), insignificant minute thin specks."

13. No record.

14. Near-perfect centering at sides, perfs close at bottom. Sold March 19, 1945, in Green Sale XXI, by Irwin Heiman for $2,100. Described as "full OG." Sold privately by Harmer, Rooke around 1961 to a New Jersey collector for $9,000. Sold February 1, 1974, by Daniel F. Kelleher as part of collection of Charles A. Schafer, Atlanta, for $29,000. Described as OG. Offered at auction November 14, 1978, by Scott Auction Galleries, in association with Harmer, Rooke. Described as "full OG." Sold at auction July 14, 1982, by Robert A. Siegel for $95,000 plus $9,500. Described as lightly hinged, with Sanabria handstamp guarantee on back. Has PFC 76268.

15. Centered to bottom and slightly to right. Has distinctive long perforation tooth midway across top. Purchased with collection of John H. Clapp by Spencer Anderson, New York dealer, and advertised for sale for $2,500 in *Stamps* June 27, 1942. Described as full OG. Sold by Anderson to Mrs. Louise F. Hoffman, New York. Sold March 1, 1966, as part of Mrs. Hoffman's airmail collection by H.R. Harmer to Robert A. Siegel for $9,000. Described as "OG . . . a small circle of gum removed in the center resulting in a tiny thin." Sold at auction May 2, 1973, by Siegel as part of collection of Dr. Drew B. Meilstrup for $27,000. Sold at auction July 17, 1980, by Siegel for $65,000 plus $6,500. Described as having "trivial insignificant thin speck" and Spencer Anderson handstamp guarantee on back.

16. Perfs touching at right, centered slightly to bottom. Vertical red sheet guideline shows on tips of perfs at left. Mostly OG (per PFC 16312). Sold by Metta Heathcote in 1954 or 1955 to Raymond H. Weill Company, New Orleans. Sold by Weill to Bruce Daniels, Boston. Sold June 10, 1955, by Daniels for about $2,500. Acquired by Weill for stock and later sold to Harmer, Rooke. Sold at auction April 3, 1957, by Harmer, Rooke for $2,100. Described as having "diagonal gum crease and tiny black paper spot . . . OG."

17. Centered to right and bottom. Has light diagonal crease (per PFC 44922). Sold at auction December 3, 1948, by Pollitz and Paige, Boston, for estate of the Rev. Thatcher R. Kimball, Hyde Park (died 1927) for $1,700. Described as "OG . . . diagonal crease not showing on face."

18. Originally perforated all around. Centered to right and bottom. Has small visible spot in "2" of left "24." Sold by Eugene Klein to Benjamin Kurtz Miller, Milwaukee, for $250. Given by Miller with his collection to the New York Public Library February 6, 1925. Sketched at the library by Clifford C. Cole Jr. April 29, 1966. Stolen from the library May 9, 1977. At some point thereafter top perforations were trimmed off to disguise stamp. Advertised by Lambert W. Gerber for $38,500 in Volume 5 of "Gems and Rarities" price list, 1978. Purchased in 1978 by John W. Kaufmann for reported $32,000. Sold at auction by Kaufmann May 5, 1979, to Lawrence A. Bustillo of Suburban Stamp Inc., Springfield, Massachusetts, for $47,000 plus $4,700. Described as "SE at top (pos. 9 in sheet), OG, HR (faintest trace of hinge thin mentioned only for the sake of accuracy)." Sold at auction by Bustillo October 11, 1980, to a Florida collector for $105,000. Described as having "natural SE." Recovered from collector by Bustillo and turned over to FBI December 22, 1982. Returned to New York Public Library July 8, 1986, under terms of order signed June 10, 1986, by Judge Whitman Knapp, U.S. District Court for the Southern District of New York.

19. Centered to right and bottom. Once owned by Sir Lindsay Everard, Great Britain. Exhibited at the British Philatelic Exhibition, South Kensington, December 28, 1946, to January 4, 1947. Not included in Everard U.S. airmail collection sold at auction in 1953. Later owned by Bernhard D. Forster, vice president of the Manhattan Company, now Chase Manhattan Bank (died November 27, 1964). Stamp sold at auction October 1, 1965, by Harmer, Rooke of London for 4,500 pounds ($12,600). Described as "full OG." Sold privately in 1984 by Christie's (Italy) to Andrew Holtz, Toronto, dealer. Illustration of back of stamp showed Forster signature and signatures of G. Bolaffi '65, A. Diena and Enzo Diena (1983). Sold by Holtz to a collector. Has tiny thins (per PFC 120259).

20. See 10. As a single, offered at auction March 25, 1972, by Peter Kenedi, Sherman Oaks, California. Described as OG (when part of a pair, it was described as NG). Offered in May 1986 at AMERIPEX by Chandler's of Evanston, Illinois, on behalf of a Midwestern collector. Asking price $60,000. Not sold. Described as NG.

21. Centered to left and bottom, with full left sheet selvage attached. Offered at auction June 3, 1954, by J.&H. Stolow as part of "a celebrated collection from the estate of a prominent Philadelphia collector." Described as "in never hinged mint condition . . . full OG." Sold at auction November 17, 1958, by H.R. Harmer Ltd., London, for 1,450 pounds ($4,060). Described as "brilliant mint." Offered at auction February 7, 1959, by Shanahans Stamp Auctions Ltd., Dun

Laoghaire, Ireland. Reported sold for $3,650 plus $365, but then listed by Shanahans in auction scheduled for May 23, 1959. Reported stolen from the Shanahans office the night of May 8-9, 1959. Recovered, date and circumstances unknown. Sold by Robson Lowe International Ltd. on behalf of the liquidator of Shanahans to Robert Lehman, New York. Sold at auction in Geneva, Switzerland, April 30, 1976, by Robson Lowe for Lehman estate for 90,000 Swiss francs ($39,600) to collector in Spain. Described as "a superb mounted mint example."

22. Centered to bottom. Sold at auction June 1, 1939, as part of air-mail collection of Mrs. Anson McCleverty, by Harmer, Rooke & Co. Ltd., London, for 475 pounds ($2,360). Described as "a superb mint example." Sold at auction September 23, 1952, by Harmer, Rooke & Co., New York, to Keith A. Wagner, later executive director of the American Philatelic Society, for $2,500. Described as having "small paper spot on back near center . . . OG."

23. Centered to bottom. Has "tiny spot covered by gum" (per PFC 108068). Offered in February 1941 by Spencer Anderson for $3,500. Described as "mint." Offered in ad in *Stamps* December 20, 1941, by Anderson for $3,000. Sold at auction June 19, 1942, by Hugh C. Barr, New York, for $2,100. Described as full OG. Sold April 26, 1943, by Philip H. Ward Jr., Philadelphia, as part of collection of William West, investment banker, Philadelphia, for $1,910. Buyer believed to be Carl E. Pelander, New York. Catalog wrongly reported that "there are no singles in the Green collection perforated on all sides." Sold at auction October 4, 1982, by Harmers of New York for an English collector for $52,000 plus $5,200. Described as having "trace of tiny thin spot . . . full OG."

24. Centered to bottom. Sold May 23, 1950, by Harmer, Rooke, New York, as part of Frank B. Allen collection, for $2,600. Described as having "tiny, insignificant thin . . . OG." Sold June 2, 1982, by Harmers of New York for $47,500 plus $4,750. Described as "large part OG . . . has a few gum spots, trace of tiny thin next to hinge." Offered at auction April 15, 1983, by David Feldman at Zurich, Switzerland. Described as OG with "cert. Sorani." Sold at auction April 7, 1984, by Steve Ivy Philatelic Auctions for $80,000 plus $8,000 to James O. Hewitt, San Diego. Described as "OG . . . free of any faults." Sold at auction May 26, 1986, at AMERIPEX '86 by Steve Ivy for Hewitt for $75,000 plus $7,500 to a Midwest collector (who also owned position 93). Has PFC 120294.

25. Centered somewhat to bottom. Sold February 19, 1945, in Green Sale XIX by Eugene N. Costales, New York, for $2,450. Described as OG. Sold February 5, 1975, by H.R. Harmer for $28,000. Described as having trace of minute hinge thin "hardly worth mentioning." Sold

by private treaty by H.R. Harmer at INTERPHIL, Philadelphia, 1976, for $40,000 (misidentified in brochure as position 23). Described as OG. Offered at auction April 8, 1977, by Paramount Philatelics, Englewood, Ohio. Sold at auction November 21, 1977, by Sotheby Parke Bernet, New York, for $47,500. Sold in April 1986 by Harmers of New York to a Midwest collector for $80,000.

26. Centered to right with perfs touching frame, and to bottom. Vertical red sheet guideline shows on tips of perfs at left. Sold March 5, 1945, in Green Sale XX by Laurence and Stryker for $1,150. Described as OG.

27. Centered to right and bottom. Sold May 22, 1945, by Irwin Heiman as part of Carlton Smith collection for $2,100. Sold November 7, 1957, by Heiman as part of Caroline Cromwell collection for $3,900.

28. Centered to right and bottom. Has position dot under "N" of "CENTS." Sold at auction June 18, 1940, by Harmer, Rooke, New York, for George R.M. Ewing, New York, for $2,750. Described as "exceptionally fresh and brilliant copy with full OG." Sold with collection of Alberto Perez, Havana, Cuba, February 3, 1947, by F.W. Kessler, New York, for $3,550. Described as "full OG." Sold at auction February 3, 1949, by Harmer, Rooke for $2,700. Described as OG. Sold at auction November 29, 1950, by Harmer, Rooke as part of collection of E.E. Kistner, Elizabeth, New Jersey, for $2,600. Described as OG. Has PFC 2923.

29. Centered to bottom, well centered at sides. Has paper speck above "G" of "POSTAGE." Sold October 15, 1945, in Green Sale XXIII, by Hugh C. Barr, New York, for $3,000. Described as mint. Sold by Walter Emerson, Chicago dealer, to a Southern physician. Sold in 1965 by the physician to Raymond H. Weill Company. Sold by Weill to a Southern collector. Sold in 1969 by the Southern collector with his collection to Weill. Sold August 28, 1969, by Weill to Hermann Schnabel, Hamburg, West Germany. Described by buyer as NH. Has PFC 31292.

30. SE at right, very close to design. Centered to bottom. Sold February 1, 1944, in Green Sale XIII, by Laurence & Stryker for $1,000. Described as NG. Offered at auction April 22, 1944, and November 8, 1945, by Laurence & Stryker. Sold at auction July 18, 1946, by Laurence & Stryker for $1,005. Offered at auction December 1, 1947, with Milton J. Harris collection by F.W. Kessler. (See position 10.) Sold at auction October 26, 1967, by Robert A. Siegel for $8,250. Described as having light crease. Offered at auction August 28, 1981, by Steve Ivy Philatelic Auctions. Offered at auction December 10, 1981 by Jacques C. Schiff Jr., Ridgefield Park, New Jersey. Described as NG. Sold at auction October 2, 1982, by Steve Ivy for $56,000 plus $5,600.

Offered in May 1986 at AMERIPEX by Andrew Levitt, Danbury, Connecticut.

31. Originally had left sheet selvage attached. Selvage has been removed. Centered very slightly to left and bottom. Disturbed OG, minutely thinned, especially in L.R. corner perforation (per PFC 29200). Sold at auction October 8, 1968, by "Uncommon Market" (Robson Lowe Ltd. and Urs Peter Kaufmann) in Basel, Switzerland for 90,000 Swiss francs plus 9,000 SF buyer's fee ($20,853 plus $2,085). Gum described as "a little roughened and missing in two small spots." Offered at auction March 26, 1970, by Robson Lcwe, London, but not sold. Same description as above. Sold in private sale in Europe to Louis Grunin, Spring Valley, New York. Sold at auction December 1, 1971, with Grunin collection by Robert A. Siegel for $23,000. Described as "part original gum, suspicion of tiny thin speck." Sold at auction September 20, 1972, by Harmer, Rooke for $24,000. Described as "OG, somewhat disturbed. Tiny thin." Has Royal Philatelic Society certificate.

32. No record. Illustration of stamp with characteristics matching those of position 32, centered slightly to left and bottom, appeared in the 1932-1933 Resume of H.R. Harmer Ltd., London, with this notation: "Two copies of the rare U.S.A. airmail 'invert,' the highest price air stamp in existence, were secured for English collectors . . ." Same stamp is illustrated in the book *Stamps of Fame* by L.N. and M. Williams (London, Blandford Press, 1949).

33. Centered slightly to bottom. Offered at auction March 23, 1939, by Harmer, Rooke, London, with collection of F. King-Wainwright, Philadelphia. Price realized believed to have been $2,500. Described as "mint . . . with original gum." Offered at auction April 1, 1940, by Nicholas Sanabria. Described as "mint . . . the best centered copy we have ever seen." Sold at auction April 12, 1943, by J.C. Morgenthau as part of the collection of the late Philip B. Philipp, New York, for $3,050 to Clifford C. Cole Jr., Atlanta.

34. Centered very slightly to bottom. Some perfs blunted. Small thin spot (per PFC 70886; also had PFC 803). Sold at auction March 7, 1941, by H.A. Robinette, Washington, with collection of Mrs. William Deyo for $2,550. Offered March 1, 1945, by Robinette with collection of Charles Rubel, Chevy Chase, Maryland. Described as having "tiny spot of gum off." Sold at auction October 16, 1947, by Harmer, Rooke for $2,050. Described as having "slight thin, possibly only a gum disturbance. OG." Sold at auction March 23, 1977, by Robert A. Siegel for $35,000 to Kenneth Wenger. Described as having "tiny natural paper inclusion speck, tiny faint thin spot." Sold at auction September 24, 1978, at American Philatelic Society STAMPSHOW, Indianapolis, by Jacques C. Schiff Jr. for Wenger to Robert L. Faiman, Las Vegas,

Nevada., for $62,500. Described as having "HR, tiny natural paper speck, faint thin."

35. Well centered, slightly to bottom. Sold at auction October 30, 1937, by Nicholas Sanabria, New York, with airmail collection of Roger Steffan to Emil Bruechig, New York, for $3,900. Described as OG. Sold at auction June 30, 1938, by Harmer, Rooke Ltd., London, for "a prominent New York collector" for 725 pounds ($3,603). Described as "full OG." Sold at auction September 29, 1939, by Sanabria for $2,750. Described as "mint." Sold at auction February 24, 1966, by Robert A. Siegel to Raymond H. Weill for $18,000. Described as "full OG." Sold at auction March 25, 1969, by Siegel to Ezra D. Cole for $27,000. Described as "nearly full OG." Sold at auction October 27, 1983, by Harmers of New York to West Coast buyer for $70,000 plus $7,000. Described as OG. Has PFC 30393.

36. Centered to right, with perfs almost touching, and to bottom. Sold at auction November 5, 1976, for widow of Sidney A. Hessel by Harmers of New York to Kenneth Wenger for $32,500. Described as LH. Advertised for sale in *Stamps* November 19, 1977, *et. seq.* by White, Kirsh and Co., Fort Lee, New Jersey, for $59,000. Offered at auction April 1, 1978, for Kenneth Wenger by Jacques Schiff. Withdrawn when it failed to realize $46,000 reserve price. Described as LH. Offered in May 1986 at AMERIPEX by Wenger. Not sold. Has PFC 67000.

37. Centered to right and bottom. Sold at auction June 23, 1948, by Harmer, Rooke for $2,800. Described as having "tiny, insignificant thin under one perf . . . full OG (never hinged)." Sold at auction October 23, 1951, by Harmer, Rooke for $2,200. Described as having "slight gum crease, couple of perfs tiny thin . . . OG." Sold at auction February 3, 1954, by Harmer, Rooke for $3,500. Same description as above.

38. Centered slightly to right. Sold at auction November 3, 1939, with collection of the late Stephen D. Brown, Glens Falls, New York, by Harmer, Rooke Ltd. to the Economist Stamp Company for $4,100. Described as "full OG." Sold at auction June 11, 1957, by Harmer, Rooke with collection of the late Oscar R. Lichtenstein for $4,100. Described as "full OG." Offered at auction February 3, 1978, by Daniel F. Kelleher Company. Described as OG. Sold at auction April 17, 1979, by Sotheby Parke Bernet as part of a specialized collection of special delivery stamps for $100,000. Described as OG. Has PFC 66743.

39. Extremely well centered, slightly to bottom. Owned by J.K. Storrow of Washington and sold to Col. E.H.R. Green with the Storrow collection by the Economist Stamp Company. Sold May 26, 1943, in Green Sale VIII, by Harmer, Rooke for $3,300. Described as full OG. Sold at auction June 25, 1952, by Eugene N. Costales with

Henry B. Close collection for $4,100 to Raymond H. Weill. Described as having "almost invisible tiny natural paper fault visible in benzine that does not detract in the least from the appearance . . . OG." Sold at auction March 24, 1970, by Robert A. Siegel for $34,000 to Irwin Weinberg. Offered by Weinberg in 1973 private treaty catalog for $42,000. Described as "one of the finest known copies." Sold at auction November 20, 1978, by Sotheby Parke Bernet for $100,000 to Daniel F. Kelleher Company. Described as OG. Sold by Kelleher to a collector now deceased. Has PFC 33198.

40. SE at right, almost touching frame. Otherwise well centered. Sold March 27, 1944, in Green Sale XV, by Hugh C. Barr for $885. Described as NG. Offered at auction January 27, 1966, by Irwin Heiman as part of collection of the late Max L. Simon, Passaic, New Jersey. Described as having "slight thin, repaired tear at top and slight scrape." Sold at auction August 29, 1981, by Steve Ivy to a Midwest collector for $58,000 plus $5,800. Described as "NG . . . mended 16 mm. tear at top and thinned . . . Signed Sanabria." Has PFCs 7092, 3348.

41. This stamp, with positions 42, 51 and 52, comprises the left arrow block of four. The block is separated along the guideline into two horizontal pairs. Each pair has full selvage, with half-arrow, attached. Stamps are well centered at sides, centered slightly to bottom, so that horizontal guideline appears only on upper perfs of lower pair. Reconstructed block sold March 25, 1946, in Green Sale XXVI, by Harmer, Rooke to Y. Souren, New York, for $13,750. It had been offered as two horizontal pairs or a block, whichever brought highest total bid. Position 42 described as having "tiny, insignificant gum thin." Pair 51-52 described as having "part gum." Souren sold block April 5, 1947, to L.D. White, a New York collector. Sold by White October 5, 1949, to Raymond H. Weill. Sold by Weill November 2, 1950, to an "Eastern collector, Mr. B." Sold by estate of Mr. B to Weill December 2, 1968. Sold by Weill to anonymous collector. Sold at auction March 25, 1969, by Robert A. Siegel to anonymous (telephone) bidder for $115,000, after offering option of buying it in two pairs. Top pair described as "most OG." Position 42 described as having "insignificant pin point gum thin." Bottom pair described as "most OG." Sold by Weill January 29, 1970, to a "Western collector, Mr. P." Inherited by a member of Mr. P's family February 17, 1971. Sold by heir to Weill March 26, 1984. Exhibited by Weill in May 1986 at AMERIPEX.

42. See 41.

43. This stamp, with positions 44, 53, and 54, comprises a block. Red guideline runs along horizontal perforations. Centering nearly perfect. Sold by Philip H. Ward Jr. February 15, 1933, as agent for a New York bank to settle estate of a Western collector, for $12,000

to Emil Bruechig, New York. Sold by Bruechig for $15,000 to a New York collector. Pictured in the *Philadelphia Bulletin* February 16, 1933. Sold in 1985 by grandchild and heir of long-time owner (not a New Yorker) with balance of late owner's collection to Raymond H. Weill. Described as lightly hinged. Exhibited by Weill in May 1986 at AMERIPEX.

44. See 43.

45. This stamp, with positions 46, 55 and 56, comprises the center line block of four. Stamps are well centered at top and bottom, with perfs close on right side of two right-hand stamps. Sold January 8, 1946, in Green Sale XXIV by Irwin Heiman to Y. Souren for $22,000. Described in catalog as "outstanding and spectacular show piece . . . the gem of the . . . Green collection as well as that of both the United States and airpost sections of philately." Sold by Souren to John Stilwell. Sold at auction February 27, 1964, by Robert A. Siegel on behalf of Stilwell to Raymond H. Weill for $67,000. Described as OG. Sold by Weill to "Mr. B," who also had owned left arrow block. Sold by Mr. B estate to Weill in 1968-1969. Sold in April 1971 by Weill to anonymous collector for "approximately $150,000." Sold by same collector to Weill in 1979. Sold by Weill in 1985 to another anonymous collector. Exhibited by Weill in May 1986 at AMERIPEX.

46. See 45.

47. This stamp, with positions 48, 57 and 58, at one time comprised a block with horizontal guide line owned by Eugene Klein. The block was almost perfectly centered. It was inherited some time after Klein's death in 1944 by his daughter, Dolores Hertz. Sold by Mrs. Hertz for $20,000 to dealer John A. Fox, Floral Park, New York. Offered by Fox in advertisement in *Stamps* April 23, 1955, price on request. Later sold by Fox back to Mrs. Hertz. Sold by Mrs. Hertz to Robert A. Siegel for $20,000. Sold by Siegel to Raymond H. Weill. Sold by Weill to "Mr. B." Sold by estate of Mr. B to Weill in 1968-1969. Sold by Weill to anonymous collector who later asked Weill to divide block into singles. As a block, stamps had PFC 10000 ("genuine in all respects"). As a single, position 47 is centered slightly to right. Horizontal red sheet guideline shows on tips of perfs at bottom. Sold by one of the collector's heirs to Weill. Sold at auction by Robert A. Siegel October 10, 1974, for $42,000. Described as "full OG, bare trace of light hinging." Sold at auction March 31, 1976, by Siegel for $47,500. Sold at auction April 11, 1978, by Siegel for $72,500. Described as "full OG, barest trace of light hinging." Offered at auction April 5, 1986, by Siegel on behalf of a physician from Eastern U.S. Withdrawn when it failed to realize $135,000 reserve price.

48. See 47. Centered slightly to right. Horizontal red sheet guideline

shows on tips of perfs at bottom. Sold by an heir of owner of one-time block 47-48-57-58 to Raymond H. Weill. Sold at auction March 25, 1975, by Robert A. Siegel to a dealer for $28,000. Described as having "couple tiny negligible thin specks." Sold soon afterward to a collector. Sold at auction August 25, 1985, by Steve Ivy to a West Coast collector who owned two other single copies for $100,000 plus $10,000. Described as having OG "that has been hinged lightly a couple of times . . . free of the typical gum bends and skips." Has PFC 52965.

49. No record.

50. SE at right, close to design. Well centered top and bottom. This stamp was part of a vertical pair with position 60, with red horizontal guideline between, that was sold April 23, 1946, in Green Sale XXVII, by Edson J. Fifield, New York, for $2,300. Pair described as having "very tiny bit of gum missing along extreme right edge of bottom stamp (position 60), never hinged, OG." Pair was acquired by Warren Colson, dealer of Proctorville, Vermont, and sold for him in December 1960 by Daniel F. Kelleher to Stanley J. Richmond, Boston, for $12,000. Pair sold by Richmond to Robert A. Siegel.

51. See 41.

52. See 41.

53. See 43.

54. See 43.

55. See 45.

56. See 45.

57. See 47. Centered slightly to right. Horizontal guideline visible on perf tips at top. Sold by an heir of the owner of one-time block 47-48-57-58 to Raymond H. Weill. Sold at auction March 27, 1974, by Robert A. Siegel for $41,000. Described as having "bare trace of a single hinging." Sold at auction April 4, 1979, by Siegel for $130,000 to Irwin Weinberg. Same description as above. Sold at auction April 29, 1981, by Robert A. Siegel for $160,000 plus $16,000 to Harry Hagendorf, president of Columbian Stamp Company, New Rochelle, New York. Same description as above. Sold by Columbian to anonymous buyer.

58. See 47. Centered slightly to bottom. Sold by an heir of the owner of one-time block 47-48-57-58 to Raymond H. Weill. Sold in 1975 by Weill to a Mr. Hoover of Georgia for $48,000. Described as lightly hinged. Sold at auction December 7, 1985, by John W. Kaufmann for Hoover for $130,000 plus $13,000 to a West Coast collector who gave position 3 in partial payment. Described as "full OG, lightly hinged." Has PFC 151843.

59. Virtually perfect centering. Horizontal guideline visible on perf tips at top. Offered for sale in 1942 in price list of Economist Stamp

Company. Sold at auction November 13, 1946, as part of the airmail collection of W.E. Pollock, retired manufacturer of Miami Beach, Florida, by F.W. Kessler to Raymond H. Weill buying on behalf of a Texas collector for $4,050. Described as having full OG. Offered by Irwin Weinberg in 1975 private treaty catalog for $52,500. Described as "extra fine in all respects." Offered by Weinberg in 1985 private treaty catalog for $200,000. Described as "OG . . . probably the finest known example." Offered by Weinberg in May 1986 at AMERIPEX. Has PFC 29562.

60. See 50. As single stamp, horizontal guideline is visible on perf tips at top. Sold March 28, 1968, by Robert A. Siegel for $20,000. Sold April 23, 1970, by Siegel as part of collection of W.T. Seymour of Texas for $20,000 to Greg Manning, dealer of South Orange, New Jersey. Sold by Manning to Ray Lundgren and Sam Frudakis, California dealers, for $23,000. Offered at auction April 28, 1972, by Corinphila at Zurich, Switzerland. Described as OG. Offered at auction June 22, 1972, by Simmy's. Described as having "light hinge trace." Sold at auction October 10, 1974, by Robert A. Siegel for $25,000. Has PFCs 27999, 41106.

61. This stamp, with positions 62, 71 and 72, comprises the "Princeton block." Its stamps are well centered at the sides, with perfs close at the bottom of each stamp. Position 72 is missing first perforation tooth at bottom. Left sheet selvage is attached, but about three-fourths of its width has been trimmed off. Each stamp, on its back in the lower right corner, bears the imprint of the Economist Stamp Company. The block was owned by Edgar Palmer and was presented to Princeton University in 1947 by his widow. Block was sold June 8, 1976, for the university by Harmers of New York to Raymond H. Weill for $170,000. Block was exhibited beforehand by Harmers at INTERPHIL '76. Catalog description was as follows: "Bright fresh colors . . . on the face there is a barely noticeable natural brown paper speck in the bottom right corner of position 72 . . . The block is with original gum. There have been several hinges largely removed, resulting in one small barely visible thin in position 61. A faint natural gum bend — usual with this issue — runs from top right of position 61 through to a portion of position 62. This is not visible on the face. There are no perforation separations." Sold in 1977 by Weill through Harmers' private treaty department for $210,000 to Myron Kaller, Jericho, New York, buying on behalf of a syndicate of nine Florida doctors and a Palm Beach, Florida, widow. Sold in July 1979 by syndicate through Kaller to George Manter, Coral Springs, Florida, for $500,000, with $350,000 loan from Summit Bank, Tamarac, Florida. Sold December 13, 1982, by Harmers of New York on behalf of Gulfstream National Bank, successor to

Summit Bank, to Kenneth Wenger for $175,000 plus $17,500. Has PFC 64046 ("genuine with tiny thin spot in top left stamp and a natural gum bend diagonally across top two stamps"). Exhibited in May 1986 at AMERIPEX by Wenger.

62. See 61.

63. Centered to bottom and slightly to left. Blind (unpunched) perforation on right side. Stamp was in collection of John Crichton-Stuart, fourth Marquess of Bute, and lost its gum when the vault of Chancery Lane Safe Deposit, London, was flooded after a German air raid September 24, 1940. Inherited in 1947 by the fifth Marquess of Bute. After his death in 1956 stamp was sold at auction March 25, 1959, by Robson Lowe Ltd., London, to an Eastern U.S. dealer for 1,050 pounds ($2,940). Described as "without gum and centered to foot." Sold at auction March 25, 1964, by Robert A. Siegel for $7,800. Described as having "almost invisible pinpoint thin speck." Sold at auction March 25, 1978, by John W. Kaufmann for $39,000. Described as having "barest trace at (sic) minute shallow thin." Auction catalog reported erroneously that stamp had "never before been offered at public auction" and that it was sold by Eugene Klein "to a collector in the Caribbean Islands who removed the gum as he was afraid the stamp might be stained by the gum while in the tropics." Sold at auction October 24, 1979, by Richard Wolffers, San Francisco, for $70,000 plus $7,000. Described as "NG, tiny trivial thin spot." Offered at auction February 2, 1982, by Daniel F. Kelleher company. Described as "NG, trivial tiny thin spot barely shows only in fluid; this stamp survived the London Blitz, during which the gum was removed." Sold at auction October 26, 1982, by J.&H. Stolow for $50,000 plus $5,000 to Kenneth Wenger. Described as having "minute trivial thin spot and NG." Offered in May 1986 at AMERIPEX by Wenger. Has PFCs 10854, 18937 and 76345A.

64. Centered to bottom and slightly to left. Has blind perf on left corresponding to same on position 63. Sold February 14, 1945, by H.R. Harmer Inc. as part of collection of Mrs. Haydon of Minneapolis for $2,350 to Col. E. Albert Aisenstadt. Described as OG. Sold at auction October 19, 1982, by Butterfield and Butterfield, San Francisco, for $85,000 plus $8,500. Described as having small hinge remnant, with original pencil marking (64) on back.

65. This stamp, with positions 66, 75 and 76, comprised the "McCoy block." Its stamps were well centered at sides, centered toward bottom. The block had a vertical red guideline between right and left stamps. It is believed to be the block owned by Arthur Hind of Utica, New York, and sold at auction November 22, 1933, by Charles J. Phillips and William C. Kennett for Hind estate to Hugh M. Clark for the

Scott Stamp and Coin Company for $12,100. Sold in 1936 by Spencer Anderson, New York, to Ethel B. Stewart (later Ethel McCoy) for $16,000. Block was stolen from Mrs. McCoy September 23, 1955, while it was on display at the American Philatelic Society convention, Norfolk, Virginia. Mrs. McCoy was reimbursed $15,000 by the block's insurer. Rights to block assigned January 12, 1979, by Mrs. McCoy to the American Philatelic Research Library (APRL), State College, Pennsylvania. Position 65 as a single stamp was given by Marcel Lutwak, Chicago, to James T. DeVoss, on behalf of APRL, in New York November 19, 1982. Stamp was later turned over to FBI and subsequently returned to APRL. Stamp described by DeVoss as having OG with very light hinge mark; "on the right frame line just above the third perforation from the bottom is a dark dot immediately under the red frame line; in the bottom margin under the right '2' of '24' is a thin wavy line of red ink." No trace of red vertical guideline on right-hand perforations. Penciled notation "65" on gum partly removed, but "definite evidence" remains.

66. See 65. Stamp not recovered as of this writing.

67. Centered to bottom and slightly to right. Once owned by Philip H. Ward Jr. Sold at auction October 6, 1964, by Robert A. Siegel for a Texas collector to Ezra Cole for $10,500. Described as "lightly hinged once." Sold by Cole to Herbert Klee, Highland Park, Illinois, dealer. Resold by Klee to Cole and sold by Cole to Henry M. Goodkind, New York. Sold May 6, 1971, by H.R. Harmer as part of Goodkind airpost collection for Goodkind estate to Irwin Weinberg for $31,000. Described as lightly hinged. Misidentified in auction catalog as position 27. Offered by Weinberg in 1973 private treaty catalog for $42,500 and in 1975 private treaty catalog for $49,000. Described as "extra fine in all respects." Has PFC 36279.

68. Centered to bottom. Sold at auction December 11, 1959, by Robert A. Siegel as part of collection of Theodore A. Stevens, Columbus, Ohio, for $6,400. Described as never hinged.

69. Centered to bottom, slightly to left. Sold at auction November 26, 1969, by Robert A. Siegel to Irwin Weinberg for $33,000. Offered by Weinberg in 1975 private treaty catalog for $47,000 and in 1976 private treaty catalog for $52,500. Described as "extra fine in all respects." Sold at auction August 27, 1977, at American Philatelic Society convention by Robert A. Siegel for $62,500. Has PFC 32184.

70. SE at right, centered slightly to right and bottom. Sold January 18, 1944, in Green Sale XII, by J.C. Morgenthau and Co. for $1,000. Described as NG. Sold at auction July 6, 1951, by Sylvester Colby, New York, for $1,075. Described as NG. Sold by Earl Lowe, Birmingham, Michigan, to Raymond H. Weill for $3,800. Donated

December 23, 1957, by the Weill company to the Smithsonian Institution, where it is on display. Has PFC 6452.

71. See 61.

72. See 61.

73. Centered slightly to left and bottom. Sold at auction May 7, 1976, by Robert A. Siegel to Andrew Levitt for $28,000. Described as having "tiny barely noticeable pinhead thin speck." Sold by Levitt to a Dr. Whitbridge. Sold at auction September 22, 1983, by Siegel for Whitbridge estate for $60,000 plus $6,000. Described as having "hinge remnant, minute pinpoint gum thin speck, truly insignificant." Offered by private treaty in October 1983 by Irwin Weinberg. Has PFC 55645.

74. Centered slightly to left and bottom. Sold at auction December 14, 1932, by George B. Sloane for former U.S. Senator Joseph S. Frelinghuysen, Morristown, New Jersey, for $2,750 to Mrs. Peter H.B. Frelinghuysen, Morristown. Described as "full OG, NH." Transferred shortly afterward to anonymous collector who still owned the stamp in 1986.

75. See 65. Stamp has had right perfs blunted to remove traces of vertical guideline. Has small tear just into design and thinning (per PFC 105495). Offered for sale by Louis J. Castelli Jr., Chicago, in 1958. Sold at auction October 16-17, 1970, by Simmy's for $19,000. Described as "OG . . . U. R. cor. & left side thin, & tiny thin at top, nat. diag gum crease, still a lovely copy of this rare issue." Offered for sale by Castelli in 1977 for $16,000. Confiscated by FBI. Awarded to American Philatelic Research Library (APRL) in January 1981 by U.S. District Court for the Southern District of New York as result of complaint in interpleader filed by U.S. Justice Department to determine ownership. Sold at auction September 25, 1981, at American Philatelic Society convention, Atlanta, by John W. Kaufmann on behalf of APRL for $115,000 plus $11,500. Described as "OG . . . but has been thinned and has a small tear just into design."

76. See 65. Stamp not recovered as of this writing.

77. Centered slightly to right and bottom. Owned by Frederick H. Douglas, Rumson, New Jersey. Sold at auction July 30, 1959, for Douglas estate by John A. Fox to Raymond H. Weill on behalf of a Southern physician for $6,100. Described as NH. Sold at auction April 24, 1982, by Robert A. Siegel for $180,000 plus $18,000, a record for a single U.S. stamp. Described as NH. Exhibited at AMERIPEX by Weill.

78. Centered slightly to left and bottom. Offered at auction June 13, 1942, as part of collection of Hugh M. Southgate, Chevy Chase, Maryland, by H.A. Robinette, Washington. Described as "mint." Sold

at auction December 15, 1953, by Irwin Heiman for "prominent Southern philatelist" for $2,800. Described as having "faint natural gum crease." Offered at auction March 30, 1954, by F.W. Kessler. Described as "full OG." Sold by Raymond H. Weill to Robert S. Fisher, Keokuk, Iowa. Sold at auction February 15, 1957, by Herman Herst Jr. for Fisher for $4,055. Described as "OG . . . bare trace of hinges." Sold at auction April 28, 1966, as part of the "Ambassador" collection, so called because it was mounted in Ambassador albums, owner anonymous, by Robert A. Siegel for $18,500. Sold at auction March 23, 1971, by Siegel for $36,000. Sold at auction January 9, 1973, by Siegel for $37,000. Sold June 21, 1973, by Raymond H. Weill to Hermann Schnabel, Hamburg, West Germany, for $39,000. Offered at auction October 15, 1973, by Edgar Mohrmann and Company, Hamburg, West Germany, for Schnabel and purchased by consignor for DM 100,000 ($31,380). Sold at auction June 18, 1985, by Christie's/Robson Lowe, New York, for Schnabel for $80,000 plus $8,000. Offered in May 1986 at AMERIPEX by Robert A. Siegel. Has PFCs 41612 and 0146582. Described in latter as "with tiny thins due to hinge removal."

79. No record.

80. SE at right. Centered slightly to bottom. Sold November 29, 1943, in Green Sale XI, by Harmer, Rooke for $875. Described as NG. Sold at auction December 8, 1970, by Robert A. Siegel for $12,000. Described as NG. Has PFC 35140.

81. With positions 82, 91 and 92, this comprises the lower left corner block with full sheet selvage at left and bottom and partial siderographer's initials (S. DeB.) in selvage below position 91. Individual stamps centered very slightly to left and bottom. Position 82 missing first perforation tooth at top. (Inexplicably, the corresponding perforation tooth is also missing at bottom of adjacent stamp in sheet, position 72.) Block sold February 18, 1946, in Green Sale XXV, by Eugene N. Costales to Y. Souren for $17,000. Described as OG. Sold by Souren to Henry B. Close. Sold by Costales June 25, 1952, for Close estate to Ezra Cole for Josiah K. Lilly, Indianapolis, for $22,000. Described as having "slight gum disturbance on the right hand stamps, mentioned merely for the sake of accuracy." Sold February 8, 1968, by Robert A. Siegel for Lilly estate to Raymond H. Weill for $100,000. Described as "lightly hinged." Sold in 1985 by Weill to "an American collector." Exhibited in May 1986 at AMERIPEX by Weill.

82. See 81.

83. Centered slightly to left and bottom. Sold at auction February 25, 1957, by John A. Fox for estate of Dr. Charles C. Lieb, professor

of pharmacology at Columbia University, for $2,500. Described as having "tiny thin, faint crease, OG."

84. Centered very slightly to left. Sold at auction January 14, 1950, by Daniel F. Kelleher to Bruce G. Daniels, Boston dealer, for $2,650. Described as NH. Sold in 1954 by Daniels to Jack Dick for $3,500. Sold at auction May 26, 1955, as part of Dick collection by Robert A. Siegel. Sold at auction November 4, 1964, by H.R. Harmer as part of collection of Thomas A. Matthews, Springfield, Ohio, to Raymond H. Weill for $15,500. Described as NH. Sold at auction May 28, 1969, by H.R. Harmer by order of the United States Trust Company, New York, to Myron Kaller for $31,000. Described as NH. Sold at auction May 30, 1974, by Harmers of New York for $47,000. Described as NH. Has PFC 31163.

85. This stamp, with positions 86, 87, 88, 95, 96, 97 and 98, comprised the block of eight with attached selvage containing bottom arrow and inverted partial plate number 8493. The block was sold November 13, 1944, in Green Sale XVII, by Harmer, Rooke to Y. Souren for $27,000, buying on behalf of Amos Eno, Princeton, New Jersey. The description: "The upper left copy (position 85) has been removed and lightly replaced and the two left stamps (positions 85 and 95) are slightly thin. Few unimportant gum creases . . . A spectacular and gorgeous block, beyond a doubt the greatest show piece in all philately." Position 85 was sold separately February 27, 1951, by H.R. Harmer as part of the dealer stock of Y. Souren for $1,800. Stamp is centered to left, with trace of vertical guideline on right perfs. Described as "OG... two small thin spots at T and TL resp., also a light diagonal gum crease extending from RB and in no way visible on face." Sold in 1952 by Milton Heitman, Marengo, Iowa, to William O. Bilden, Minneapolis dealer. Sold in 1952 or 1953 by Bilden to Wilber H. Schilling Jr., Minneapolis. Given by Schilling to his son, Wilber H. Schilling III.

86. See 85. Centered very slightly to right. Trace of vertical guideline of left perfs. Sold at auction by Harmer, Rooke February 7, 1950, as part of the Amos Eno collection, to "Speigel" for $3,000. Described as having diagonal gum crease, OG. Has "minor diagonal crease and mount glazed OG" (per PFC 104000).

87. See 85. With positions 88, 97 and 98, now comprises the plate number block of four. This block was retained by Amos Eno after the four stamps on the left side of the original block of eight were detached. Sold May 18, 1954, by Harmer, Rooke as part of Eno collection of U.S. blocks to Raymond H. Weill for $18,250. Block described as having "slight gum creases. U.R. stamp has small spot." Sold by Weill to "Mr. B." Sold by estate of Mr. B to Weill in 1968-1969. Sold in 1971 by Weill for $150,000 to Eastern collector who specialized in

U.S. errors. Block exhibited at ANPHILEX '71, by Weill at INTERPHIL '76, and again by Weill in May 1986 at AMERIPEX.

88. See 85, 87.

89. Large margins. Centered slightly to left. Sold November 9, 1954, by Harmer, Rooke for estate of William Fitts, Moravia, New York, for $2,800. Described as having "tiny thin . . . OG." Sold at auction February 24, 1965, by Robert A. Siegel to Raymond H. Weill for $12,500. Sold at auction February 18, 1970, by H.R. Harmer for $23,000. Described as "OG somewhat disturbed, there is a tiny thin and corner bend." Sold at auction April 24, 1982, by Siegel for $75,000 plus $7,500. Described as "gum disturbed & small thin spot." Sold at auction June 16, 1983, by Siegel for $65,000 plus $6,500 to Ideal Stamp Company, New York. Same description as above. Offered in advertisement in *Stamps* February 4, 1984, by Atlas Stamp Company, New York (an Ideal Stamp Company affiliate) for $90,000. Described as having "small thin that does not detract from its beautiful appearance."

90. SE at right, perfs close at left. Sold as part of a vertical pair with position 100 October 15, 1945, in Green Sale XXIII, by Hugh C. Barr for $1,800. Stamps had been offered as singles or a pair, depending on the higher bid. Position 90 described as having "tiny speck in paper in figure '4' of left '24' . . . mint." Later separated from position 100. Sold at auction November 20, 1956, by Sylvester Colby for $2,100. Sold at auction June 30, 1964, by John A. Fox to a Pennsylvania collector for $8,000. Described as "full OG NH." Position 90 has PFC 22871 which describes mark in figure "4" as "small black spot."

91. See 81.

92. See 81.

93. Centered slightly to left. Has three tiny red dots inside curved border around right "24." Originally had bottom sheet selvage which was removed some time before October 26, 1939, when stamp was sold at auction by F.W. Kessler as part of airmail collection of Dr. Philip G. Cole, Tarrytown, New York, for $2,100. Described as having "slight crease which is, however, completely invisible from front or back . . . OG." Sold at auction May 22, 1956, by Harmer, Rooke for $1,650. Described as having "ironed-out crease and repair. Regummed." Sold at auction May 10, 1961, by Harmer, Rooke with collection of Dr. Robert Fisher, Sharon, Pennsylvania to a New York dealer for $7,250. Was misidentified in catalog as position 32. Described as having "diagonal crease (not noticeable on face)" that had been "slightly strengthened. Large part OG" and with "COLE" identification mark on back. Given to Coe College, Cedar Rapids, Iowa, in 1967 by Ellen Douglas Williamson as part of her collection of airmail stamps of the

world. Sold at auction January 7, 1977, by Robert A. Siegel for the college for $21,000. Described as having "small filled thin & strengthened crease under regumming, negligible soiling . . . Sanabria and Cole handstamp guarantees." Sold at auction February 10, 1979, by John W. Kaufmann for $70,000. Described as "OG redistributed over reinforced crease." Offered at auction November 26, 1983, by Maryland Stamp Auctions, Bethesda, Maryland. Offered in private treaty sale June 22-23, 1984, by Kaufmann. Described as having 1979 Friedl certificate stating " 'genuine with small filled thin and strengthened crease . . . regummed.' We believe it is disturbed OG redistributed over the above faults . . . Price on request." Sold January 17, 1985, by Steve Ivy to a Midwest collector for $52,000 plus $5,200. Described as "regummed over small faults."

94. Centered slightly to left. Has bottom selvage attached. Sold at auction December 16, 1960, by Harmer, Rooke as part of collection of the late Major T. Charlton Henry, Chestnut Hill, Pennsylvania, (died 1936), to Erwin N. Griswold, Belmont, Massachusetts, dean of the Harvard Law School and later solicitor general of the United States, for $9,200. Described as having "one or two fibers disturbed on face above 'S' of 'CENTS.' " Sold at auction October 16, 1979, by Harmers of New York for Griswold to James Torelli, Pelham, New York, for $90,000 plus $9,000. Described as "OG . . . Evidently the stamp has been struck by a small blunt object causing two dimples, one resembling a thin and the other a surface flaw above the 'S' in 'CENTS,' both of little significance." Sold by Torelli to Andrew Levitt for $120,000.

95. See 85. With position 96 comprised bottom arrow pair sold at auction October 30, 1951, by H.R. Harmer as part of Y. Souren stock for $3,300. Pair described as "somewhat creased and left hand stamp (position 95) thinnings near left margin." Pair sold at auction September 20, 1955, by H.R. Harmer as part of collection of Lieutenant Colonel Donald L. Harvey, Mobile, Alabama, to Jack Molesworth, Boston dealer, for $6,100. Molesworth broke pair into singles and removed bottom selvage with half arrow from position 95. As a single, position 95 is centered to left. Traces of vertical red guideline visible on right perfs. Offered at auction July 12, 1966, by Corinphila, Zurich, Switzerland. Sold at auction November 21, 1971, by Jacques Schiff Jr. for $18,000. Described as having "few tiny stains, crease and tiny thin, disturbed OG (&/or possible regum)." Sold at auction March 11, 1973, by Schiff for $19,000. Description similar to above. Has "a few stains, a diagonal crease and regummed covering thinning at left" (per PFC 36662).

96. See 85, 95. As single, has near-perfect centering. Selvage with

half-arrow is attached at bottom. Sold at auction June 14, 1961, by Robert A. Siegel as part of the "Brothers Collection" to Richard Engel, a West Coast collector, for $9,750. Described as having "the usual gum wrinkles." Offered at auction May 29, 1975, by Corinphila. Described as OG with "light gum crease." Withdrawn by owner and sold to Superior Stamp and Coin Company. Sold September 3, 1975, by Superior to a Western buyer. Sold by Western buyer to Raymond H. Weill. Sold at auction April 5, 1980, by Siegel for $125,000 plus $12,500. Described as having "small light thin." Has PFC 14500.

97. See 85, 87.

98. See 85, 87.

99. No record.

100. See 90. The lower right corner stamp, with SE at right and sheet selvage at bottom. Perfs close at left. Owned by Rafael Oriol, Havana, Cuba, and taken with him from Cuba in 1959. Sold at auction April 4, 1961, by F.W. Kessler, for owner of collection described as originally formed by Oriol, for $6,800. Described as "OG . . . with small diagonal crease in the lower left corner." Sold at auction November 20, 1982, by Robert A. Siegel as part of collection of Martin L. Butzel to Irwin Weinberg for $62,500 plus $6,250. Described as having "barest trace of hinging, small minor natural bend," with signatures on back of Sanabria, Kessler, Oriol. Offered in private treaty list dated December 9, 1982, by Weinberg for $86,500. Described as "full OG, very lightly hinged. Barest trace of hinging." Sold in March 1983 by Weinberg to Kenneth Wenger for $50,000 and a stamp collection. Offered in May 1986 at AMERIPEX by Wenger.

# Acknowledgements

I am indebted to, and must thank, the scores of people who made this book possible through the generous gift of their time, help and resources.

They include Herbert A. Trenchard, who repeatedly delved into his magnificent collection of philatelic literature on my behalf; Daniel M. Bagby and Clifford C. Cole Jr., scholars who have spent years tracking the travels of each individual Jenny invert; Raymond H. and Roger G. Weill, who call the Jenny one of their favorite stamps and have bought, owned and sold more copies than any other stamp dealer, and their assistant, Carol C. Davini; Peter Robertson, curator of the Philatelic Foundation; James H. Bruns, curator of the National Philatelic Collection at the Smithsonian Institution, and Bernard Harmer, son Keith and daughter Alison, who have auctioned many copies of the invert over the years.

Also, the team at the American Philatelic Society and its superb Research Library: Col. James T. DeVoss, Keith A. Wagner, William L. Welch Jr., Virginia L. Horn, Kathleen Wolsiffer, Barbara Boal and Joanne Mast, and James H. Beal, chairman of the APS Stamp Theft Committee, who worked tirelessly and traveled far to help track down and recover the stolen McCoy inverts and the stamps taken from the New York Public Library.

Also, Werner Elias, librarian at the Collectors Club of New York, where I spent many productive hours; Stanley M. Bierman M.D., whose Bierman Philatelic Library is another splendid resource; Jeanne O'Neill and William Halstead of the U.S. Postal Service; Edward R. Felver, Betty L. Russell, and Leah Akbar and Linda Coleman of the Bureau of Engraving and Printing, and Aloha P. South and Richard Cox of the National Archives, an under-utilized treasure house for the philatelic researcher. The staffs of the New Jersey State Library, the Free Public Library of Trenton, Temple University's Paley Library and the Free Public Library of Philadelphia were most helpful.

A number of outstanding philatelic students and writers gave assistance, among them Ernest A. Kehr, Herman Herst Jr., Philip Silver, George W. Brett, Barbara Mueller, John S. Meek and Fred Boughner. Stamp dealers who shared their records and recollections were John A. Fox, Irwin R. Weinberg, Robert A. Siegel, Kenneth R. Wenger, Scott Trepel, Stanley J. Richmond, Michael Orrenstein, Susan Kono, Jack E. Molesworth, Bruce G. Daniels, Charles Shreve, Ezra D. Cole, Robson Lowe, Julio Asseo, Lyle Clark, Louis K. Robbins, Andrew Levitt, Greg Manning, Steve Markoff and Gordon Harmer.

Others helping in a wide variety of ways were Leonard Sherman, a discoverer of the Hammarskjold inverts; Larry Wilson and Paul Garber of the National Air and Space Museum; H. Paul Schiller, attorney for Ethel McCoy's estate; Peggy A. Haile of the Norfolk Public Library; Maurice G. Lauzon, librarian at The Standard-Times of New Bedford; Kathryn Ray of the District of Columbia Public Library; Dr. William Close at Charles County, Maryland, Community College; Alexander Hunter, assistant to the Marquess of Bute; Dorothy Nash of H.E. Harris and Company; George Eager of the Princeton University News Bureau; Jack Laugen of Coe College, and Philip H. Ward III, David L. Ganz, James T. Herron Jr., Willis F. Cheney, Robert S. Fisher, Edith Dodd Culver, Erwin N. Griswold, Richard Milian, Dr. Roberto M. Rosende, W.H. Schilling Jr., Louis Grunin, William Talbot, Hermann Schnabel, Hubert Skinner, Thomas Lamar, Nelson Wood and Joseph E. Schirmer. And, of course, the owner of the spectacular "locket copy" of the invert, who wishes to remain anonymous.

Finally, my thanks to Louise Robey Birch and her husband Merritt for sharing memories, pictures and mementos of her father, William T. Robey, the man who started it all.

# Notes

## Chapter One. The Purchase

Robey's three versions of his May 14, 1918, adventures were: Letter to Malcolm H. Ganser, dated May 15, 1918, quoted by Ganser in "Finding the Inverted Airplanes," A.C. *Roessler's Stamp News,* September 1918; article by Robey, "The Finding of the Aeroplane Invert," dated May 26, 1918, in the *Collectors' Journal,* June 1918; article by Robey, "The Story of the Discovery of the 24-Cent Inverted Center Airmail Stamps," in *Weekly Philatelic Gossip,* February 19, 1938. I have specified in the text, where appropriate, which version is being cited.

### Page

1 "If he took a chance": Caroline Scott Robey, answer to written questions submitted by Gerald H. Strauss, Bloomsburg (Pennsylvania) State College, in 1962.

2 Wartime conditions at the Bureau: Thomas F. Morris, "The History of the Bureau of Engraving and Printing," *Stamp Specialist (Gray Book),* 1943, H.L. Lindquist, New York.

2 "It might interest you to know": Letter, Robey to Ganser, dated May 10, 1918, quoted in *Roessler's.*

2 "I have a very strange feeling": Interview, author with Louise Robey Birch, February 8, 1982.

2 "Of course hosts of other collectors": Ganser, in *Roessler's.*

5 The erroneous Post Office Department news release was dated August 12, 1954.

5 Ben Lipsner's duties are described by Otto Praeger, second assistant postmaster general, in three documents filed in the National Archives: letters to W.F. Parish of the U.S. Army Signal Corps, May 11, 1918, and to the adjutant general July 8, 1918, and a lengthy memorandum to Postmaster General Albert Burleson June 20, 1918. Lipsner's own, manifestly inflated account of his role and actions ("When I organized and conducted the first military flights both ways between Washington, D.C. and New

York . . . I had to worry about proving that planes were capable of flying the mail") is found in his autobiography, as told to Leonard Finley Hilts, *The Airmail: Jennies to Jets*, 1951, Chicago, Wilcox and Follett Company and in "August 12, 1918, A Day to Remember," *Airpost Journal*, August 1960.

**Chapter Two. The Experiment**

An excellent review of the Post Office Department's efforts to initiate airmail service, with particular emphasis on the role of the National Advisory Committee for Aeronautics, is contained in Paul T. David, *The Economics of Air Mail Transportation*, Washington, The Brookings Institution, 1934.

The Curtiss Jenny has its own fine biography in Jack R. Lincke's *Jenny Was No Lady: The Story of the JN-4D*, New York, W.W. Norton and Company Inc., 1970. Other useful information came from O.G. Thetford and E.J. Riding, *Aircraft of the 1914-1918 War*, London, C. Harbrough Publishing Company Ltd., 1954, and Arch Whitehouse, *The Military Airplane*, New York, Doubleday, 1971.

**Page**

9 Praeger is described in Lipsner, *Jennies to Jets.*

9 Edison interview: *New York Times*, August 1, 1909.

9 "Love letters will be carried": *New York Telegraph*, June 19, 1910.

10 Ovington's flight described: Albert S. Burleson, "The United States Aeromail," *Munsey's Magazine*, June 1918.

11 "Visionary, utopian": *Congressional Record*, May 8, 1918.

11 "We are at the height of a war": Lipsner, *Jennies to Jets.*

11 The visit of the Army officers to Praeger is decribed in Praeger's June 20, 1918, memo to Burleson, and in a letter, Burleson to Senator Kenneth McKellar, *Congressional Record*, January 6, 1920.

11 Postponement of announced first flight: *New York Times*, March 13, 1918.

11 The March 1 directive to the Equipment Division and the April 30 letter, Fleet to Praeger, are in the National Archives. The Jones memo to Fleet is quoted by Fred Boughner in his "Airmail Antics" column, *Linn's Stamp News*, March 8, 1976. Fleet's account of his meeting with Burleson is in a speech he delivered to the Air Mail Pioneers Convention, Reno, October 15, 1966, published in *Air Mail Pioneers News*, Oct.-Nov.-Dec. 1966.

13 Vernon Castle's death: *New York Times*, February 16, 1918; Irene Castle, *Castles in the Air*, New York, Doubleday, 1958.

14 Selection of Edgerton and Boyle: Fleet's speech at Reno.

14 Fleet's intention to fly the first Washington-Philadelphia leg, "if I can find the time to do so," is stated in a letter to Otto Praeger May 9, 1918, in the National Archives. The *New York Times*

on flight day — May 15, 1918 — reported that Fleet would be the pilot.

**Chapter Three. The Rush**

**Page**

15 Fleet and 24¢ rate: Fleet, speech to Air Mail Pioneers.

15 "If we are to establish": Senate action, *Congressional Record,* May 6, 1918; House action, *Record,* May 7, 1918; date of President's signature, *Record,* May 13, 1918.

16 "It has been impossible": Tumulty letter, illustrated in Philip Silver, "Someone Wrote to the President," *American Philatelist,* April 1978.

16 "Just see that they have": Lipsner, *Jennies to Jets.*

16 Estimate of quantities needed: J.A. Edgerton, Post Office purchasing agent, letter to the secretary of the Treasury, May 11, 1918, National Archives.

16 Information on Clair A. Huston: Obituary, by Hugh M. Southgate, *Bureau Specialist,* April 1938.

17 Information on Marcus Baldwin: Thomas F. Morris, "Marcus Wickliffe Baldwin, Bank Note Engraver," *Essay-Proof Journal,* July 1955.

18 Dates and other information on die preparation for the 24¢ airmail stamps are from Stamp History Information Form No. 384, undated, Engraving Division, Bureau of Engraving and Printing.

18 Wilmeth-Dockery correspondence is in the files of the National Philatelic Collection, Smithsonian Institution.

19 Baldwin diary: Illustrated in Philip Silver, "United States: Engravers of the First Air Mail Stamp," *Aero Philatelist Annals,* July 1969.

19 Post Office announcements of May 9 and May 11, 1918, quoted in Henry M. Goodkind, "United States . . . The 24¢ Inverted Center of 1918," *Collectors Club Philatelist,* Vol. XXXV, No. II (1956).

20 Cost of printing stamps: James L. Wilmeth, letter to secretary of the Treasury, May 17, 1918, National Archives.

20 Prophetic number: A thorough exploration of this intriguing feature of the stamp design is in Fred Boughner's "Airmail Antics" column in *Linn's Weekly Stamp News,* January 19 and March 8, 1976. Numbers used on planes during the early flights are listed on the Pilot's Daily Reports in the National Archives.

22 5¢ red error: R. McP. Cabeen, "The Five Cent U.S. Error," *Mekeel's Weekly Stamp News,* May 18 and May 25, 1917; Max G. Johl, *United States Postage Stamps 1902-1935,* Quarterman Publications Inc., 1935, 1976.

24 Description of airmail stamp plates and printing process: J.B. Leavy, "New Issue Notes and Chronicle," *Philatelic Gazette*, June 1918. The author has examined the certified plate proofs of plates 8492 and 8493 at the National Philatelic Collection. John S. Meek's theory about the extra registration marks on plate 8493 is discussed in a letter to the author, May 23, 1986.

27 The grounded plane variety is described in Philip Silver, "The 24-cent U.S. Air Mail Stamp of 1918," *American Philatelist*, March 1980, and Joseph R. Kirker Jr., "Proof Exists of Third 'Grounded Plane' Sheet," *Linn's Stamp News*, April 21, 1986.

28 Dates when plates went to press: James Wilmeth, letter to Harry E. Huber, Pittsburgh, Pa., August 13, 1918, National Archives.

28 First sale of airmail stamps: Leavy, *Philatelic Gazette* article.

28 The first day covers are described and illustrated in Henry M. Goodkind, "Scarcest U.S. First Day Cover? The First Air Mail Stamp," *Stamps*, July 11, 1959; Goodkind, "Only Three First Day Covers of C3," *Scott's Monthly Stamp Journal*, March 1961; Goodkind, article in *Aero Philatelist Annals*, January 1969; Philatelic Foundation certificate 22620; H.R. Harmer, catalog of Goodkind collection auction, May 6, 1971.

**Chapter Four. The Mistake**

**Page**

32 "The inverts could have occurred": J.B. Leavy, *Philatelic Gazette* article.

32 The point that the inverted-sheet theory would require that two separate rotations of the sheet have occurred is made by a supporter of that theory, John S. Meek, in "The Air Mail Stamps of 1918," *United States Specialist*, March 1980.

32 Post Office inconsistency: letters in the files of the National Philatelic Collection, signed by the third assistant postmaster general, December 8, 1938, and August 12, 1946.

33 Plate number block theory: Goodkind, *Collectors Club Philatelist* article.

33 May 15 date for the second printing: James L. Wilmeth, letter to Philip H. Ward Jr., January 22, 1919, National Archives.

34 Stern to Ward: Philip H. Ward Jr., in *Mekeel's Weekly Stamp News*, November 27, 1920.

35 Eight other sheets found: Philip H. Ward Jr., letter to James L. Wilmeth, January 4, 1919; J. Barry, chief of Stamp Perforating Division, memo to Wilmeth, January 17, 1919; Wilmeth, letter to Ward, January 22, 1919, all in National Archives. A retyped copy of Wilmeth's letter to Ward is also in the Bureau of Engraving and Printing.

35 Dates of last printings: James Wilmeth, letter to Huber.
36 "Has never been confirmed": Goodkind, *Collectors Club Philatelist* article.
36 "At the time I knew nothing": Lipsner, *Jennies to Jets.*
36 "The National Museum is desirous": W. deC. Ravenel, letter to third assistant postmaster general, June 12, 1918, National Philatelic Collection.
37 Quantities of stamps printed: Bureau of Engraving and Printing, undated document, "Data Concerning Certain Air Mail Postage Stamp Plates." Quantities of stamps delivered: letter from Bureau's superintendent of orders to a Mr. Deviny, July 16, 1926, Bureau of Engraving and Printing.

**Chapter Five. The Pursuit**
**Page**
39 Robey's early years: Interview with Louise Robey Birch.
39 Robey ad: *Collectors' Journal,* May 1918.
40 Robey-Perry correspondence: Philip Silver, "Elliott Perry, William T. Robey and the 24-cent Air Mail Invert," *Collectors Club Philatelist,* September-October 1983.
40 Robey's May 14 activities: Robey, in *Weekly Philatelic Gossip,* February 19, 1938.
41 "One of the few to hold": clipping found in Caroline Robey's scrapbook; item in *Mekeel's,* May 25, 1918.
43 Telegrams to Ganser, Perry: Ganser, in *Roessler's Stamp News,* September 1918; Perry, letter illustrated in Silver, *Collectors Club Philatelist* article.
43 Caroline Robey's account: Caroline Robey, "I Remember . . . The Upside Down Airmail Stamps," *Baltimore Sun,* Sunday magazine, June 8, 1958; quoted in Ben Pearse, "Tales of the Stamp Collectors," *Saturday Evening Post,* May 28, 1960.

**Chapter Six. The Takeoff**
In addition to the sources listed, I have drawn on contemporary accounts of the events of May 15 and subsequent days in the *New York Times, New York Herald, New York World, Washington Post, Philadelphia Bulletin, Philadelphia Inquirer* and *Philadelphia Public Ledger.*
**Page**
45 The account of the assembling of the mail planes and the flight to Philadelphia is from Fleet, speech to Air Mail Pioneers; Fleet, report on inauguration of airmail service to Colonel H.H. "Hap" Arnold, chief of the Air Service Division, May 18, 1918, in the

National Archives, and James C. Edgerton, "The Pilot's Story of the May 15, 1918, Air Mail Flights," speech to the Collectors Club of Washington, reprinted in *Western Stamp Collector* May 13, 1935, re-reprinted in the *Airpost Journal*, May 1962. Culver's flight to Bustleton Field in the dark in Fleet's repaired plane is described in Edith Dodd Culver, *The Day the Air-Mail Began*, Cub Flyers Enterprises Inc., Kansas City, Missouri.

46 No oil at Bustleton: Fleet, report to Arnold.

47 Hamilton watch ad: *Washington Post*, May 16, 1918.

47 May 15 at the Polo Grounds: Lipsner, *Jennies to Jets*. Lipsner incorrectly gives the scheduled takeoff time as 10:30 a.m. instead of 11:30.

48 Tree-cutting incident: Fleet, speech to Air Mail Pioneers.

48 Wilson's autographed cover: A full account is in Silver, "Someone Wrote to the President." The files of the National Philatelic Collection contain a memorandum from A.M. Dockery to the superintendent, Division of Stamps, dated May 7, 1918, saying: "This office has just received information that the Postmaster General desires to purchase the first stamp of the new series for aeroplane mail service to be sold, the money therefor to be furnished by the Second Assistant Postmaster General. It is understood that this stamp will be taken to the White House to be initialed by the President and then used to prepay postage on a communication addressed to the postmaster at New York. Please take the necessary action to have the stamp taken from the Bureau of Engraving and Printing to the post office at Washington and there sold in accordance with the arrangement contemplated as stated above."

50 The Great Gasoline Fiasco is described in Lipsner, *Jennies to Jets*. Fleet's version is in his report to Arnold and his speech to the Air Mail Pioneers. Lipsner's personally annotated copy of Fleet's speech is in the National Philatelic Collection.

51 Boyle takeoff: Lipsner, *Jennies to Jets*.

52 Webb takeoff: *Newark News*, May 15, 1918; *Scientific American*, May 25, 1918.

53 Boyle's pilot's daily report for May 15, 1918, is in the National Archives. Fleet's comment on the episode is in his report to Arnold.

54 Local press description of Boyle's landing: *The Times-Crescent*, Charles County, Maryland, May 17, 1918.

54 Burleson explanation: Albert S. Burleson, "The Story of Our Air Mail," *The Independent*, April 3, 1920. The railroad-track account is found, among other places, in the *American Air Mail*

*Catalogue*, Fourth Edition (1966), published by the American Air Mail Society.

56 The May 15 and 16 handstamped cancellations are illustrated in Johl, *United States Postage Stamps 1902-1935*. Edgerton's account of carrying the May 15 mail on May 16 is in Edgerton, "The Pilot's Story."

56 Boyle's second flight is described in Fleet's May 18 report to Arnold and in Edgerton's pilot's daily report for May 17. The chief of Air Service's memo to Personnel is dated May 20, 1918. All are in the National Archives. A photo of Boyle's plane, crashed on its second flight, with the numbers 62 visible on the fuselage, was published in the *Christian Herald* June 12, 1918.

58 Sketchy information on Boyle's later life is in Margaret McChord Boyle's obituary, *Washington Star*, August 16, 1960. He is listed as an attorney in editions of *Polk's Washington City Directory*, 1919 through 1924.

58 "Pilots of this early day": Fleet's speech to the Air Mail Pioneers.

58 Edgerton promotion: *Washington Times*, December 10, 1918.

59 "It would not be a pink tea": Praeger's June 20 memorandum to Burleson, National Archives. Lipsner's brief career as superintendent is discussed in his *Jennies to Jets*.

59 First-year record of airmail service: *Report on Aeroplane Mail Service, Washington-Philadelphia-New York Route, for Year of May 15, 1918, to May 15, 1919*, Post Office Department.

59 First anniversary: *New York Times*, May 16, 1919.

## Chapter Seven. The Sale

The Robey-Perry, Perry-Lindquist, Perry-Jefferys and Perry-McCoy correspondence, and Caroline Robey's telegram to Perry, are quoted and/or illustrated in Silver, *Collectors Club Philatelist* article. The account of Robey's trip to New York is in Robey, *Weekly Philatelic Gossip* article.

**Page**

61 Postal inspector visit: Ganser, in *Roessler's Stamp News* article.

67 Robey trip to Philadelphia: Caroline Robey, *Baltimore Sun* article; interview, author with Louise Robey Birch.

68 Briefcase anecdote: in Goodkind, *Collectors Club Philatelist* article.

69 16¢ Jenny cover: A picture of the cover, postmarked Washington, D.C., July 13, 1918, two days before the new rate went into effect, was furnished by the owner, the Raymond H. Weill Company.

## Chapter Eight. The Resale

**Page**

71 Information on Klein: *Philadelphia Stamp News*, October 25, 1913; obituaries, *Philadelphia Record* and *Philadelphia Inquirer*, May 1, 1944.

71 Klein interview: Charles J. Phillips, in "Reminiscences of the Veterans," *Philatelic Classics*, November 1930, as reprinted in *Mekeel's* August 10, 1931.

71 Steinmetz-Travers case: The case is covered in the *Philadelphia Inquirer*, April 4, 1911; the *Philadelphia Bulletin*, April 6 and 7, 1911, and November 3, 1912; the *Washington Star*, April 4, 1911, and October 29, 1912; *Mekeel's Weekly Stamp News*, April 4, 1911 and November 9, 1912. Steinmetz's World War I activities are described in his obituaries, in the *Philadelphia Bulletin*, July 11, 1928, and the *New York Times*, July 12, 1928.

74 "$20,000 by Col. Green": *New York Times*, May 21, 1918.

75 "Only by chance": Ernest A. Kehr, *The Romance of Stamp Collecting*, New York, Thomas A. Crowell Co., 1947, 1956.

75 Green's misunderstanding: Philip H. Ward Jr., in *Mekeel's Weekly Stamp News*, October 26, 1942.

75 Robey on Green: Robey, *Weekly Philatelic Gossip* article.

76 Klein "probably did not buy": Goodkind, *Collectors Club Philatelist* article.

77 "It came sooner": *Mekeel's Weekly Stamp News*, June 1, 1918.

77 Humorous responses: Column, "Heard and Seen," on clipping found in Caroline Robey's scrapbook; *Mekeel's Weekly Stamp News*, June 22, 1918.

77 Leavy-Townsend search for inverts: Capt. A.C. Townsend, "The 24¢ Invert — Aftermath of the Find," *Weekly Philatelic Gossip*, March 5, 1938.

77 "Even for a set": *New York Times*, May 22, 1918.

78 "The Bureau . . . has recently become famous": *Albemarle Stamp Collector*, June 1918.

78 "As far as Colonel Green is concerned": *Albemarle Stamp Collector*, July 1918.

79 Klein letter to Schlesinger: furnished by James T. Herron Jr. Schlesinger's letter to *New York Times* appeared December 13, 1928.

80 Red Cross sale: Lot 125, George R. Tuttle auction catalog, June 29, 1918, in Herbert A. Trenchard collection.

**Chapter Nine. The Eccentric.**

A basic source of information on Edward H.R. Green and his mother Hetty is Arthur H. Lewis's fascinating book about the family fortune, *The Day They Shook the Plum Tree*, 1963, Harcourt, Brace & World Inc., New York. Some of the details on Green's introduction to stamp collecting and on specific purchases of collections are from Charles J. Phillips, "Colonel Edward H.R. Green," *Stamps*, June 27, 1936.

**Page**

82 "Before the year ended": Lewis, *Plum Tree.*

83 "I have never achieved my ambition": letter to author from Robson Lowe, January 10, 1986.

83 "The colonel gave me an envelope": Robson Lowe letter.

84 Green's waning interest in stamps: U.S. Supreme Court opinion, State of Texas vs. State of Florida *et al* (Green domicile case), (306 U.S. 398-435).

84 "Don't remember": Kehr, *Romance of Stamp Collecting.*

84 "I would place Colonel Green": Walter S. Scott, in *Mekeel's Weekly Stamp News*, August 3, 1942.

84 Leavy collection story: Phillips, *Stamps* article.

85 "(After Klein had been)": Phillips, Klein interview, *Mekeel's* article.

85 Planted news story: Lewis, *Plum Tree.*

87 *New York World* account of sinking: reprinted in *Mekeel's*, November 29, 1919.

87 Other reports of sinking: *A.C. Roessler's Stamp News*, November 1919; *Albemarle Stamp Collector*, quoted in *Mekeel's*, December 27, 1919.

87 Account of yacht's purchase, use and sinking: Lewis, *Plum Tree*; articles in *New Bedford Standard-Times*, August 29, 1917; January 26, 1920; March 29, 1923; June 20, 1923.

87 "No truth whatever": Charles J. Phillips, brief item in *Stamps*, July 11, 1936.

87 "Walter Scott told me": letter, Elliott Perry to Harry L. Jefferys, February 25, 1944, quoted in Silver, *Collectors Club Philatelist* article.

88 "How many air mail fans": Phillips, *Stamps* article of June 27, 1936. Among those repeating the Mabel Green anecdote as fact were Johl, in *U.S. Postage Stamps.*

89 Appraisal of locket: George Sloane in *Stamps*, July 7, 1956.

## Chapter Ten. The Dispersal

Much of the information on specific sales of Jenny inverts is taken from auction catalogs and reports of prices realized.

**Page**

91 An excellent description of the characteristics by which individual stamps can be identified is in Clifford C. Cole Jr., "Plating the U.S. 24-cent 1918 Air Mail Invert: A Scientific Reconstruction," *American Philatelist*, February 1982. The pictorial reconstruction of the original sheet of inverts, shown on page 91, was created by Cole as part of his research. He made it by photographing one invert, making 100 prints, cutting out the centers and

adjusting them within the frames to show the downward "drift" of the planes on the sheet, then carefully drawing in the perforations and marginal markings.

93 "A recent auction": Philip Ward Jr., in *Mekeel's*, May 15, 1920.

93 Eagle sale: *New York Times*, April 1, May 8, 1923.

94 Klein ad: in *Mekeel's*, January 28, 1924.

94 "I got in early": attributed to Miller by *Milwaukee Journal*, quoted in *Mekeel's*, February 23, 1925.

94 1928-1929 sales summarized in *New York Times*, April 28, 1929.

94 Klein sale to Klemann: *New York Times*, January 25, 1931. Klemann prediction, Ward comment: *Ward's Philatelic News*, March 1931. Frelinghuysen sale: *New York Times*, December 18, 1932, May 28, 1933; Adolph D. Fennel, in *American Philatelist*, February 1933.

96 Klein block anecdote: Herman Herst Jr., "Philadelphia Story: Philatelic Feuds and Feuders," *American Philatelist*, October 1982.

96 Hind block sale: *New York Times*, November 23, 1933.

97 Palmer gift: confirmed by Richard Ludwig, associate director, Firestone Library, Princeton University, June 30, 1986.

97 Ward sale to Bruechig: *New York Times*, February 16, 1933; *Philadelphia Evening Bulletin*, February 16, 1933.

98 Logan purchase: in F.B. Warren, *The Pageant of Civilization*, The Century Company, New York and London, 1926.

98 Wood block: *Ward's Philatelic News*, November 1930, November 1932.

98 Aspinwall purchase: *New York Times*, July 10, 1931; *Mekeel's*, August 3, 1931.

98 Ackerman block offered: *Ward's Philatelic News*, April 1933; *New York Times*, May 28, 1933.

98 Costales recollection: quoted by Calvet T. Hahn, in copyrighted article in *Stamp Collector*, January 31, 1983.

98 Sale of block to Ethel Stewart: Ethel Stewart McCoy, quoted by Robert C. Smith in *Norfolk Virginian-Pilot*, September 24, 1955.

99 Anderson purchase, Sanabria comment: *New York Times*, February 27, 1937.

99 Steffan sale: *New York Times*, October 31, 1937.

99 Brown sale: *New York Times*, November 1, 4, 12, 1939.

99 Ward list: Henry M. Goodkind reproduced the list in his *Collectors Club Philatelist* article, saying it was lent to him by Ethel McCoy. The author has been unable to find a copy of the original Ward list.

**Chapter Eleven. The Forty-One**

The basic information in this chapter is from the catalogs of the 28 Green auctions and from Herbert A. Trenchard, "The Colonel Green

Collection," *Philatelic Literature Review*, Vol. 18 (1969), an excellent summing-up of the sales.

**Page**

103 The planning of the Green auctions is described in the *New York Times*, November 26, 1939; May 24, June 14 and September 20, 1942.

104 Total money realized: *New York Times*, November 3, 1946.

104 Green Sale I: *New York Times*, September 27, October 4, 1942.

105 Y. Souren: Transatlantic telephone bid, *New York Times*, November 25, 1938; obituary, *New York Times*, October 7, 1949. A good description of his personality and career is in Herman Herst Jr., *Nassau Street*, Duell Sloan and Pearce, 1960.

108 Auction catalog sale: *Stamps*, January 12, 1985.

## Chapter Twelve. The Memories

Most of the detailed information on William Robey's life and career in this chapter is from the author's interview with Louise Robey Birch, February 8, 1982.

**Page**

110 Robey's picture of the New York Avenue Station was in *Ward's Philatelic News*, March 1931.

110 Robey's first day cover of the 16¢ Jenny stamp, formerly in the Goodkind collection, was sold by Robert A. Siegel January 9, 1973, for $3,500. It is illustrated in the catalog for that sale.

110 Goodkind's anecdotes about Robey are in his *Collectors Club Philatelist* article. Robey's statement that "while it is true I was called before my local board, my status was not changed" is in *Mekeel's*, November 2, 1918.

112 "Billy said if he could get a car": Quoted in Ben Pearse, *Saturday Evening Post* article.

114 Robey's report on the freak perforations is in *Mekeel's*, April 26, 1919.

## Chapter Thirteen. The Climb

Information on specific sales described in this chapter is taken from the auction catalogs and prices-realized reports for those sales.

**Page**

118 The Weills are profiled in David Snell, "The Weills Deal in the World's Rarest of Stamps," *Smithsonian*, January 1973, and Bill Huey, "The Case of the Fraternal Philatelists," *Louisiana Life*, July/August 1985.

118 Smithsonian stamp: *New York Times*, June 15, 1958; letter to author from James H. Bruns, curator, National Philatelic Collection, October 2, 1985.

118 Mauritius cover purchase: *New York Times*, October 22, 1968.

119 Weinberg's stamp business and his ownership of the British Guiana 1¢: Weinberg, interview with author, February 3, 1981; letter to author, January 10, 1986. Sale of British Guiana stamp to Weinberg: *New York Times,* March 25, 1970. Sale of stamp by Weinberg: *New York Times,* April 6, 1980; *Washington Post,* April 7, 1980.

121 Douglas stamp: *New York Times,* July 31, August 9, 1959; John A. Fox, interviews with author, September 13, October 25, 1985.

121 Stevens stamp, Henry stamp: *New York Times,* November 13, December 17, 1960; Erwin N. Griswold, letter to author, December 9, 1985.

121 "Brothers" stamp: *Stamps,* July 1, 1961; *New York Times,* June 25, 1961.

122 "Mr. B": Raymond Weill, letter to author, July 18, 1985; interview with author, August 1, 1985.

122 Arrow block: Weill interview, August 1, 1985; "The Provenance of a Block," Raymond H. Weill Company advertisement, *Collectors Club Philatelist,* May-June 1984, and other publications.

123 Center line block: Weill interview, August 1, 1985; *New York Times,* February 28, 1964.

123 Close block: *New York Times,* June 26, June 29, 1952.

123 Lilly's dealings with the Weills: *Smithsonian* and *Louisiana Life* articles. Lilly collection sales; Stanley M. Bierman, *The World's Greatest Stamp Collectors,* Frederick Fell Inc., New York.

124 Eno block: *New York Times,* May 19, 1954; Hubert Skinner, New Orleans, associate of Eno, interview with author, October 1, 1985; Weill interview, August 1, 1985.

125 Harvey pair: *New York Times,* November 4, 1951; October 2, 1955; Jack Molesworth, letter to author, July 15, 1985.

125 Klein-Hertz block: Fox interview, September 13, 1985; Weill interview, August 1, 1985.

126 Weill-Bruechig block and Jennies at AMERIPEX: George Amick, "Jenny Goes to AMERIPEX," *American Philatelist,* May 1986.

## Chapter 14. The Peak

As in Chapter 13, information on specific sales is taken from the auction catalogs and prices-realized reports.

### Page

127 *Linn's* U.S. Stamp Market Index: *Linn's Stamp News,* June 3, 1985 *et seq.*

127 $100,000 copy: *New York Times,* November 22, 1978.

128 $180,000 copy: *New York Times,* April 25, 1982.

128 "Investment quackery and flackery": *Wall Street Journal,* December 28, 1981.

128 United States Trust Company recommendation, Salomon Brothers report: *U.S. News & World Report*, August 13, 1979.
129 "There is some degree of risk": *Nation's Business*, May 1978.
129 "Rare stamps have performed admirably": Myron Kaller & Associates Inc. press release, July 25, 1979.
130 "The only block we hadn't owned": Raymond H. Weill, interview with author, July 14, 1984.
131 "First million dollar single philatelic property": Kaller press release.
132 Manter comments: George E. Manter, interview with author, 1979.
132 Decline in collectibles market: *Business Week*, June 15, 1981; *New York Times*, June 28, 1981; *Time*, July 20, 1981.
133 Princeton block sale announcement: Harmers of New York, advertisement, *Linn's Stamp News*, November 29, 1982.
133 Details on the Manter loan are disclosed in papers filed in George Manter, Susan Manter, Philatelic G.E.M. Associates, plaintiffs, against Harmers of New York, Gulfstream National Bank, John Doe and Richard Roe, defendants: order to show cause, complaint, memorandum of law, and attachments, Supreme Court of the State of New York, February 11, 1983 *et seq.*
134 Details of sales agreement with Harmers: Bernard Harmer, interview with author, November 14, 1984; Keith Harmer, interview with author, August 19, 1985.
134 Siegel offer: Robert Siegel, letter to Lindsay Andrews, Summit Bank, June 29, 1981; copy is in court papers.
134 "Being a collector"; *Linn's Stamp News*, November 22, 1982.
134 "That's your problem": Quoted by John F. Dunn in *Linn's*, January 10, 1983. Description of auction, Manter's comments: Michael Laurence, in *Linn's*, December 27, 1982; Dunn article. Wenger comments: *Newsday*, December 14, 1982.
137 "The bank had asked about reserves": Keith Harmer interview.
137 Plaintiffs' contentions: in court papers.
138 Wenger's ownership of block: Kenneth Wenger, news release, February 7, 1984; interview with author, November 1985.
138 Lawsuit inactive: David L. Ganz, attorney at law, letter to author, November 26, 1985.

## Chapter Fifteen. The McCoy Heist

Biographical information on Ethel McCoy is from her obituary in the *American Philatelist*, October 1980; from the legal papers of her estate, and from personal recollections of a friend who wishes to be anonymous, in a letter to the author, December 5, 1985.

**Page**

144 Robey's reunion with his stamps: Robey, *Weekly Philatelic Gossip* article; interview with Louise Robey Birch.

144 Theft of McCoy block: *Norfolk Ledger-Dispatch*, September 23, 24, 1955; *Norfolk Virginian-Pilot*, September 24, 1955.

146 Insurance paid: Opinion, January 30, 1981, by Robert W. Sweet, U.S. District Judge, in United States of America vs. American Philatelic Research Library *et al*, complaint in interpleader, U.S. District Court, Southern District of New York.

146 Offer of McCoy stamp to Weills: *New Orleans States and Item*, October 27, 1958; *Norfolk Virginian-Pilot*, November 2, 1958; *Linn's Stamp News*, November 17, 1958; *Stamps*, November 22, 1958; *New York Times*, December 12, 1958.

147 Stamp offered at auction: Simmy's Stamp Company, catalog and prices realized, auction of October 16-17, 1970. Simmy's, letter to author, November 1985.

147 Castelli offer to Faiman, Philatelic Foundation examination of stamp: Opinion, U.S. vs. APRL *et al.*

148 McCoy assignment to APRL: Copy with McCoy estate papers, dated January 12, 1979; James DeVoss, letter to author, February 9, 1983.

148 Castelli assignment: November 24, 1980, with U.S. vs. APRL *et al.*

149 Judge Sweet's award to APRL; Opinion, U.S. vs. APRL *et al.*

149 Kaufmann sale: John W. Kaufmann, catalog and prices realized, auction of September 25-26, 1981.

150 Recovery of second McCoy stamp: Basic details are from James DeVoss, "Affidavit re Stamp of McCoy Block, Position No. 65," notarized in Centre County, Pennsylvania, November 30, 1982, and James Beal, interview with author, November 23, 1985. News coverage of the FBI's announcement of the stamp's recovery included an Associated Press story December 9, 1982, and *Linn's Weekly Stamp News*, December 20, 1982. Additional information is in Stephen Esrati, "Tell It To The FBI," *Stamp World*, May 1983.

152 The DeVoss findings are in a report dated November 24, 1982, and a supplemental report dated December 2, 1982.

154 "Their current possessor": James H. Beal, in *American Philatelist*, April 1985.

**Chapter Sixteen. The Miller Heist**

**Page**

155 Description of burglary and investigation: *New York Times*, May 10, June 19, 1977.

156 Stolen items: List provided by Manuscripts and Archives Division, New York Public Library.

157 Miller-Library agreement: *Linn's Stamp News*, December 3, 1984.

158 Miller biography, gift to Library: *Mekeel's*, February 9, 1925; February 23, 1925; April 2, 1928.
158 Elliott Perry's hiring, 1934 theft: Charles J. Phillips, writing in *Stamps*, February 16, 1935.
158 "Unwanted stepchild": George B. Sloane, in *Stamps*, March 30, 1946.
159 "This is a hell of a way": Ernest A. Kehr, interview with author, 1981.
159 Appearance of stolen Jenny on stamp market: Clifford C. Cole Jr., *American Philatelist* article; Cole, letter, March 19, 1982; *Linn's Stamp News*, January 24, 1983; Calvet M. Hahn, *Stamp Collector* article; article, Springfield, Mass., *Morning Union*, February 1, 1983; article, Associated Press, printed in Springfield, Massachusetts, *Daily News*, February 1, 1983; Peter Robertson, interview with author, January 11, 1985; John Kaufmann, interview with author, February 4, 1985; Daniel M. Bagby, written recollection, August 3, 1985.
162 Philip Wall's discovery: *Linn's*, January 3, 1983; September 10, 1984.
162 Gerber advertisements: James H. Beal, "C3A and Lambert W. Gerber," unpublished manuscript.
164 The Gerber letter, dated November 25, 1960, has as its salutation "Dear Ez": probably the recipient was dealer Ezra Cole. It and the auction catalog referred to are in the literature collection of Herbert A. Trenchard.
164 Discovery of usable photostats: James H. Beal, interview with author, March 14, 1986.
165 Grand jury empaneled: *Linn's*, January 3, 1983.
165 William Grimm's discovery: *Linn's*, September 10, 1984.
165 FBI discusses stamp recovery: *Linn's*, October 29, 1984; May 26, 1986.
166 Justice Department civil action: United States of America vs. New York Public Library *et al*, complaint in interpleader, U.S. District Court, Southern District of New York, filed June 8, 1984.
166 Insurance compensation of $237,500: *Linn's*, September 10, 1984.
167 Kaufmann-Bustillo claim: *Linn's*, December 10, 1984.
167 Judgment in U.S.A. vs. N.Y.P.L. *et al*, signed by Judge Whitman Knapp June 10, 1986, filed June 13, 1986.
167 Library's plans: Donald Anderle, head of special collections, New York Public Library, interview with author, June 19, 1986.

**Chapter Seventeen. The Proofs**

**Page**

169 The preparation of two Jenny invert die proofs, their numbers and

disposition is recorded in a cover letter from A.W. Hill to W. Irving Glover, May 31, 1922, in the National Philatelic Collection.

170 Klein-Glover correspondence: quoted in *Mekeel's Weekly Stamp News*, October 21, 1922.

170 Three die proofs in the 1930s: George Sloane, *Stamps*, July 3, 1937.

170 Three later die proofs: Letters and print orders from files, Bureau of Engraving and Printing.

171 Die proofs currently accounted for: Author's inspection of U.S. Postal Service proof collection, February 10, 1986.

171 Die proof in Frisbie's possession: Associated Press story, quoted in *Western Stamp Collector*, October 1, 1957; George Sloane, *Stamps*, September 21, October 26, 1957. Frisbie's employment record: Bureau of Engraving and Printing, Resignations and Changes of Employees, National Archives, cited by John Meek in the *United States Specialist*, October 1985.

171 Bruns-Walter and Bruns-Holtzclaw correspondence: National Philatelic Collection. Return of proofs to Bureau: Edward Felver, chief, Office of Engraving, Bureau of Engraving and Printing, interviews with author, January 17, February 11, 1986.

## Chapter Eighteen. The Next Invert

Much of the detail concerning Leonard Sherman's experience with the Hammarskjold inverts is from Sherman's interviews with the author December 8, 1980, and subsequently.

**Page**

174 Giori press operation: Belmont Faries, in *Scott's Monthly Stamp Journal*, January 1963; Betty Russell, external affairs staff, Bureau of Engraving and Printing, interview with author, December 1980.

175 Clark's discovery: *Linn's Weekly Stamp News*, November 19, 1962.

177 Post Office reprint plans: Post Office Department, Philatelic Release 90, November 13, 1962; *New York Times*, November 14, 1962.

177 "The Post Office isn't running . . ." J. Edward Day, quoted in *Time*, November 23, 1962. Greensburg collector's letter to Kelleher and Kelleher's reply: National Philatelic Collection.

178 Press reaction: *Newark News*, November 15, 1962; *Nation*, November 24, 1962; *Newsweek*, November 26, 1962.

178 Kelleher background: Anonymous associate, interview with author, December 1980.

178 Show-cause order issued, Post Office sale of reprints: *New York Times*, November 16, November 17, 1962. "It was a petulant act": Richard L. Amster, interview with author, December 1980.

179 Sherman-Kelleher confrontation: *New York Times*, November 19, 1962; Leo August, interview with author, December 1980.

179 Suit withdrawn: *New York Times*, November 20, 1962; all plate combinations reprinted: Post Office Department, Philatelic Release 94, November 27, 1962; *New York Times*, December 2, 1962.

180 Authentication of Sherman's sheet: Ernest A. Kehr, in *New York Herald Tribune*, November 18, 1962.

180 George Grant's inverts: *Linn's Weekly Stamp News*, May 25, 1964. Carlo Stabile's first day covers: *Linn's*, June 1, 1964.

180 Gerald Clark's stamps: Interview with author, January 1981.

182 $1 "Americana" invert: *Linn's Stamp News*, April 28, 1986; *Scott Stamp Monthly*, June 1986.

183 Governor Fleming's announcement: United Press International story in *New York Times*, November 15, 1962.

183 Harris arguments: Henry E. Harris vs. Robert J. Fleming *et al*, U.S. District Court for the District of Columbia, memorandum of points and authorities in support of plaintiff's motion for preliminary injunction, November 23, 1962. Judge Hart's ruling and terms of consent agreement: *American Philatelist*, May 1965; Belmont Faries, in *Western Stamp Collector*, October 9, 1965.

**Chapter Nineteen. Jenny Miscellany**

**Page**

185 Those "Other Sheets": Goodkind, *Collectors Club Philatelist* article; Philip H. Ward Jr., in *Mekeel's*, December 22, 1941; Larkspur-Madeira *News*, quoted by Harry Weiss in *Weekly Philatelic Gossip*, September 21, 1946.

186 The Other Heist: Seamus Brady, *Doctor of Millions*, Dublin, Anvil Books Ltd., 1965; *Catalog of Postage Stamps Stolen from Shanahans Stamp Auctions Ltd. of Dublin*, published on behalf of the official liquidator, G.W. O'Brien, by Robson Lowe Ltd., London; *New York Times*, May 10, May 14, May 31, June 2, 1959; January 24, October 23, 1961; January 25, 1962.

189 Caught in the Blitz: Bute obituary, *New York Times*, April 26, 1947; Paul Johnson, *National Trust Book of British Castles*, New York, G.P. Putnam's Sons, 1978; Alexander Hunter, for the Marquess of Bute, letter to author, September 24, 1985.

190 High and Dry: Irwin Weinberg, interview with author, February 3, 1981; Weinberg, letter to author, January 10, 1986.

191 The Cuban Connection: J.L. Guerra Aguiar, director, Cuban Postal Museum, letter to Stamp Theft Committee, October 22, 1982; Dr. Roberto M. Rosende, Cuban Philatelic Society of America, letter to author, February 25, 1986; Julio Asseo, letter to author, March

20, 1986; Richard Milian, letter to author, April 8, 1986; John Fox, interview with author, March 26, 1986.

192 Institutional Jennies: Smithsonian copy: Philip H. Ward Jr., letter to Franklin R. Bruns, November 11, 1957, in National Philatelic Collection; James H. Bruns, curator, National Philatelic Collection, letter to author, October 2, 1985. Franklin Institute copy: Donald M. Steele, "The Franklin Institute's Jefferys Collection," *American Philatelic Society 1952 Convention and Exhibition, National Philatelic Museum* (journal), Vol. IV, No. 2; Coe College copy: Jack Laugen, Coe senior gift officer, interview with author, August 22, 1985.

193 Jenny on Other Stamps: *Scott Standard Postage Stamp Catalogue, Scott Specialized Catalogue of United States Stamps.* Torrey Webb interview: *New York Times*, May 13, 1968.

195 Jenny on Souvenir Cards; *Scott Specialized Catalogue of United States Stamps.*

199 The Counterfeits: California arrest: *Western Stamp Collector*, August 22, 1950. New York counterfeit: *Stamps*, March 30, 1940. Goodkind's anecdote: in his *Collectors Club Philatelist* article.

## PICTURE CREDITS

| Page | |
|---|---|
| Cover | Jenny invert position 78, Christie's/Robson Lowe. |
| 3 | Washingtoniana Division, D.C. Public Library. |
| 6, 26, 47, 48, 49, 50, 53 | National Philatelic Collection, Smithsonian Institution. |
| 12, 177 | U.S. Postal Service. |
| 17, 18 | Bureau of Engraving and Printing. |
| 19 | *Aero Philatelist Annals.* |
| 33, 34 | John A. Fox. |
| 52, 55 | National Air and Space Museum, Smithsonian Institution. |
| 54, 57 | National Archives. |
| 57 | *The Christian Herald*, June 12, 1918. |
| 62, 63, 66 | *Collector's Club Philatelist.* |
| 68, 111 | Louise Robey Birch. |
| 72, 100, 141, 143 | American Philatelic Research Library. |
| 73 | *Bulletin* Library, Photojournalism Collection, Temple University Libraries. |
| 81 | Thomas Lamar. |
| 86 | Nelson Wood. |
| 91 | Clifford C. Cole Jr. |
| 97, 105, 106, 107, 117, 124 | Raymond H. Weill Co. |

| Page | |
|---|---|
| 131 | Flip Schulke/Black Star. |
| 135 | *Newsday*/Ozier Muhammad. |
| 142 | James H. Beal. |
| 145 | Mays/*Norfolk Virginian-Pilot*/Norfolk Public Library. |
| 152 | Col. James DeVoss. |
| 161 | Herbert Trenchard. |
| 163 | *Stamps*, Oct. 15, 1960. |
| 176, 180, 181 | *Linn's Stamp News*. |

# Index


## — A —

*A.C. Roessler's Stamp News* . . . . . . . . . . .86
Ackerman, Representative Ernest R. . .69, 94, 98, 124
Aisenstadt, Colonel E. Albert . . . . . . . .215
*Albemarle Stamp Collector* . . . . . . . . .78, 86
Allen, Frank B. . . . . . . . . . . . . . . . . . . . .207
*American Air Mail Catalogue* . . . . . . . . .199
American Philatelic Research Library . . . . 148-153, 181, 216-217
American Philatelic Society . . . . .144, 149, 159, 163-164, 192, 216-217
*American Philatelist* . . . . . . . . . . . . . .95, 143
AMERIPEX '86 . . . . . . .126, 138-139, 182, 203, 206-207, 209-212, 214-215, 217-218, 220, 222
Amster, Richard . . . . . . . . . . . . . . . . . . .179
Anderson, Spencer . . . . . . . . .98, 143, 205, 207, 216
Apfelbaum, Earl P.L. . . . . . . . . . . . . . . .204
Aspinwall, John . . . . . . . . . . . . . . . . . . . .98
Asseo, Julio . . . . . . . . . . . . . . . . . . . . . . .191
Atlas Stamp Company . . . . . . . . . . . . . .220
August, Leo . . . . . . . . . . . . . . . . . . . . . . .179

## — B —

"B, Mr." . . . . . . . . . . . . . . . . . . .122-123, 125
Bagby, Daniel M. . . . . . . . . . . . . . . . .161-162
Baker, Reid S. . . . . . . . . . . . . . . . . . . . . . .94
Baldwin, Marcus Wickliffe . . . . . . . . . . .17, 18fn., 19, 107
Barr, Hugh C. . . . . . . . . . . . . .103-104, 202, 207-208, 211, 220
Barrett, Sidney . . . . . . . . . . . . . . . . . . . . .83
Beal, James H. . . . . . . . . .150-151, 154, 164
Bergstresser, Charles . . . . . . . . . . . . . . .142
Bilden, William O. . . . . . . . . . . . . . . . . .219
Birch, Louise Robey . . . . . . . . . .43, 67, 69, 109, 112-115
Birch, Merritt . . . . . . . . . . . . . . . . . .113-115
Blair, J. Insley . . . . . . . . . . . . . . . . . . .80, 204
Bonsal, Lieutenant Stephen . . . . . . .14, 58
Boyle, Lieutenant George Leroy . . . . . .14, 46-59, 184
"Brothers Collection" . . . . . . . . . . . . . . .222
Brown, Stephen D. . . . . . . . . .99, 104, 120, 210
Bruechig, Emil . . . . . . . . . .97, 99, 126, 210, 212
Bruns, Franklin R. Jr. . . . . . . . .118, 171-172
Burdsall, Ellwood R. . . . . . . . . . . . . . . . .204
Burleson, Albert S. . . . . . . . . .9, 11-12, 14, 48-49, 55, 61
Burns, Al . . . . . . . . . . . . . . . . . . . . . . . . .109
Bustillo, Lawrence A. . . .162, 164-167, 206
Bute, Marquess of . . . . . . . . . . . . . .189, 215
Butterfield and Butterfield . . . . . . . . . . .215
Butzel, Martin L. . . . . . . . . . . . . . . . . . . .222

## — C —

Castelli, Louis John Jr. . . . . . .146-148, 217
Century Stamp Company . . . . . . . . . . .203
Chandler's . . . . . . . . . . . . . . . . . . . . . . . .206
Christie's/Robson Lowe . . . .138, 206, 218
Clapp, John H. . . . . . . . . . . . . . . . . .101, 205
Clark, Gerald P. . . . . . . . . . . . .175, 180-181
Close, Henry B. . . . . . . .121, 123, 211, 218
Coe College . . . . . . . . . . . . . . . . . . . .193, 220
Colby, Sylvester . . . . . . . . . . .203, 216, 220
Cole, Clifford C. Jr. . . . . .160-161, 206, 209
Cole, Ezra . . . .122-123, 147, 210, 216, 218
Cole, Dr. Philip G. . . . . . . .120, 193, 220
*Collectors Club Philatelist* . . . . . . . . . . . . .143
*Collectors' Journal* . . . . . . . . . . . . .4, 35, 109
Colman, Hamilton F. . . . . . . . . .40, 61, 67, 70, 77
Colson, Warren . . . . . . . . . . . . . . . . . . . .213
Corinphila . . . . . . . . . . . . . . . . . .214, 221-222
Cosmos Stamp Company . . . . . . . . . . .204
Costales, Eugene . . . . . . .98, 104, 123, 207, 210, 218

Cromwell, Caroline . . . . . . . . . . . . . . . . . 208
Curtiss, Glenn H. . . . . . . . . . . . . . . . . . . . 13
Curtiss JN-4H: see Jenny
Culver, Lieutenant Howard Paul . . . . . . 14, 45-46, 55


— D —


Daniels, Bruce G. . . . . . . . . . . . . . . 205, 219
Day, J. Edward . . . . . . . . . . . . . 173, 176-177
DeBinder, Samuel . . . . . . . . . . . . . . . . 25, 106
DeVoss, Col. James T. . . . . . . 148-153, 216
Deyo, Mrs. William . . . . . . . . . . . . 120, 209
Dick, Jack . . . . . . . . . . . . . . . . . . . . . . . . . 219
Doane, Percy G. . . . . . . . . . . . . . . . . . 64, 103
Dockery, A.M. . . . . . . . . . . . . . . . . 18-20, 49
Douglas, Frederick H. . . . . . . . . . . 121, 217


— E —


Eagle, Clarence H. . . . . . . . . . . . . . . . . . . 93
Economist Stamp Company . . . . . . 83, 97, 99, 104, 130, 210, 213-214
Edgerton, J.A. . . . . . . . . . . . . . . . . . . . 14, 20
Edgerton, Lieutenant James Clark . . . . 14, 45, 55-58
Emerson, Walter . . . . . . . . . . . . . . . . . . 208
Engel, Richard . . . . . . . . . . . . . . . . . 121, 222
Eno, Amos . . . . . . . . . . . . . . . 106, 124, 219
Everard, Sir Lindsay . . . . . . . . . . . . 101, 206
Ewing, George R.M. . . . . . . . . . . . . 120, 208


— F —


Faiman, Robert L. . . . . . . . . . . 147-149, 209
Farrell, Leo . . . . . . . . . . . . . . . . . . . . 164-165
Federal Bureau of Investigation . . . . . . 147, 150-154, 164-165, 206, 216-217
Feldman, David . . . . . . . . . . . . . . . . . . . . 207
Ferguson, Russell . . . . . . . . . . . . . . . . . . 175
Fifield, Edson J. . . . . . . . . . . . 104, 202, 213
Fisher, Dr. Robert . . . . . . . . . . . . . . . . . 220
Fisher, Robert S. . . . . . . . . . . . . . . . . . . . 218
Fitts, William . . . . . . . . . . . . . . . . . . . . . . 220
Fleet, Major Reuben H. . . . . . . . . . . . 11-12, 14-15, 45-48, 51fn., 54, 57-58
Fleming, Governor Robert J. . . . . . . . . . 183
Forster, Bernhard . . . . . . . . . . . . . . . . . . 206
Fox, John A. . . . . . . . . . 121, 125, 191, 212, 217-218, 220
Framen, Justice Arnold . . . . . . . . . . . . . 138
Franklin Institute . . . . . . . . . . . . . . 192, 202
Frelinghuysen, Adaline Havemeyer . . . . 95, 217
Frelinghuysen, Senator Joseph . . . . . . . . 94
Frisbie, Edward R. . . . . . . . . . . . . . . 171-172
Frudakis, Sam . . . . . . . . . . . . . . . . . . . . . 214


— G —


Gallinger, Senator Jacob H. . . . . . . . . . . 15
Ganser, Malcolm H. . . . . . . . 2-3, 5, 42, 61
Gerber, Grace . . . . . . . . . . . . . . 163-164, 166
Gerber, Lambert W. . . . 159, 162-164, 166, 202-203, 206
Gianakos, Paolo . . . . . . . . . . . . . . . 135, 137
Gilbert, Lee . . . . . . . . . . . . . . . . . . . . . . . . 104
Glover, W. Irving . . . . . . . . . . . . . . . 169-170
Goodkind, Henry M. . . . . 18fn., 29fn., 33, 36, 39, 68, 75-77, 100-101, 110-111, 185, 200, 216
Grant, George . . . . . . . . . . . . . . . . . . . . . 180
Green, Col. Edward Howland Robinson . 65, 71, 74-91, 93, 95-97, 101, 103-108, 117, 122, 124, 127, 160, 202-205, 207-208, 210-213, 216, 218-220
Green, Hetty . . . . . . . . . . . . . . . . . . . . . 81-82
Green, Mabel Harlow . . . . . . . . . 82, 87-89, 107, 204
Green, Sylvia: see Wilks, Sylvia Green
Gregorian, Dr. Vartan . . . . . . . . . . . . . . 164
Grimm, William R. . . . . . . . . . . . . . 165-166
Griswold, Erwin N. . . . . . . . . . . . . 121, 221
Gronouski, John A. . . . . . . . . . . . . . . . . 183
Grunin, Louis . . . . . . . . . . . . . . . . . . . . . . 209
Guest, J.E. . . . . . . . . . . . . . . . . . . . . . . . . . 109
Gulfstream National Bank . . . . . . . . . . 134, 137-138, 214


— H —


Hagendorf, Harry . . . . . . . . . . . . . . 128, 213
Hahn, Calvet M. . . . . . . . . . . . . . . . . . . . 161
Harmer, Bernard . . . . . . . 118, 120, 135-137
Harmer, Gordon . . . . . . . . . . . . . . . . . . . 191
Harmer, H.R. and Company (Harmers of New York) . . . . . . . . 118, 130-131, 133-138, 204-205, 207, 210, 214-216, 219-221
Harmer, H.R. and Company (London) 95, 206, 209
Harmer, Keith A. . . . . . . . . . . 134, 136-138
Harmer, Rooke and Company . . . . . . . . 99, 103, 105-107, 118-119, 121, 124, 191, 202-203, 205-211, 218-221
Harris, H.E. and Company . . . . . . . . . 183
Harris, Milton J. . . . . . . . . . . . . . . . 204, 208
Hart, Judge George L. . . . . . . . . . . . . . 183
Harvey, Lieutenant Colonel Donald L. . . 125, 221
Haydon, Mrs. . . . . . . . . . . . . . . . . . . . . . . 215

Heathcote, Mrs. Metta .........100, 205
Heiman, Irwin ........103, 106, 202-205, 208, 211-212, 218
Heitman, Milton ....................219
Henry, Mrs. Mattie..................185
Henry, T. Charlton ............121, 221
Herst, Herman Jr................200, 218
Hertz, Dolores Klein (Mrs. Jay) .......68, 96, 110, 122, 125, 212
Hessel, Sidney A.....................210
Hewitt, James O......................207
Hind, Arthur ................96, 99, 215
Hoffman, Mrs. Louise F. ............205
Hoffmann, Joseph ....................98
Holtz, Andrew ......................206
Holtzclaw, Henry J..................172
Hoover, Mr. ........................213
Hudson, Mr..........................202
Huston, Clair Aubrey.......16-18, 18fn., 21, 36

## — I —

Ideal Stamp Company ..............220
INTERPHIL '76................208, 220
"Isleham Collection"................204
Ivy, Steve, Philatelic Auctions .......138, 202-203, 207-208, 211, 213, 221

## — J —

Jefferys, Harry L. ........70, 87, 192, 202
Jenny aircraft (Curtiss JN-4H) ........11, 13-14, 59fn., 193-197
Jenny invert: purchased, 4; "other customer" story, 5; nine error sheets printed, 32-33; eight sheets intercepted, 35-36; reprints requested, 36; Robey sells sheet, 61-70; Klein resells sheet, 74-78; Klein breaks sheet, 78-80; "waste basket" story, 85; yacht story, 86-87; locket copy, 88-89; individual stamp variations, 91-93; prices increase, 93-99; Ward's inventory, 99-101; in Green auctions, 103-107; Robey on later sales, 112; Robey grandchildren see invert, 115; prices resume increase, 121-122, 127-128; blocks change hands, 122-126; Princeton block sold, 129-132; sold by Manter, 133-137; McCoy block stolen, 144-146; McCoy singles appear, 146-154; library single stolen, 155-156; single identified, recovered, 159-162, 164-168; proofs made, 169-172; stories of other sheets, 185-186; Shanahans single stolen, 186-189; singles caught in Blitz, 189; singles escape flood, 190-191; singles owned by Cubans, 191-192; singles in institutional hands, 192-193; pictured on stamps, souvenir cards, 193-197; listed in catalogs, 197-199; counterfeits, 199-200.
Jenny stamp (24¢): planned, designed, engraved, 15-19; airplane number mystery, 20-21; sheet markings, 24-26; printing, 26-28; first-day covers, 28fn.; sheet markings changed, 34
Jenny stamps (6¢, 16¢) ........36-37, 110
Johl, Max G. ........................85
Jones, Bob..........................180

## — K —

Kaller, Myron .............122, 129-132, 134-135, 214, 219
Karlsson, Hordur....................193
Kaufmann, John W. ...........138, 149, 159-162, 164, 166-167, 202, 206, 213, 215, 217, 221
Kaufmann, Urs Peter ................209
Kehr, Ernest A. ............84, 159, 200
Kelleher, Daniel F. Company .......103, 202-203, 205, 210-211, 213, 215, 219
Kenedi, Peter ......................206
Kennett, William C. .................215
Kessler, Fred W. ..........192, 204, 208, 214, 218, 220, 222
Kimball, Reverend Thatcher R. .......205
King, Senator William H. ...........9, 11
King-Wainwright, F. .................209
Kistner, E.E.........................208
Klein, Eugene ..........61, 66-71, 74-80, 85, 91, 93-94, 96, 98, 101, 106-107, 109-110, 121-122, 125, 169-170, 204, 206, 212, 215
Klemann, John J..........65, 79, 94, 121
Knapp, Judge Whitman.....165, 167, 206

## — L —

Laurence and Stryker ......103, 203, 208
Laurence, Michael...................134
Leavy, Joseph .......26, 32, 34-35, 41-42, 77, 84
Lehman, Robert ...............189, 207
Levitt, Andrew ............209, 217, 221
Lichtenstein, Oscar R. ..............210
Lieb, Dr. Charles C..................218
Lilly, Josiah K. Jr. ..........123-124, 218
Lindquist, Harry L....................70
*Linn's Stamp News* ..127, 164-165, 202-203
Lipsner, Captain Benjamin B. .......5-7, 11, 16-17, 36, 47, 50-51, 51fn., 56, 59
Logan, Allen .......................98

Lowe, Earl........................216
Lowe, Robson................83-84, 95
Lundgren, Ray....................214
Lutwak, Marcel...........150-152, 216

## — M —

Madden, Representative Martin B. ....11
Mann, Percy McGraw.........43, 64-66, 71, 80
Manning, Catherine L.........40-41, 169
Manning, Greg, Company......202, 214
Manter, George E.............127, 129, 131-138, 214
Manter, Susan................133, 135
Marcus, Barry.................128-129
Markoff, Steve....................203
Maryland Stamp Auctions...........221
Matthews, Thomas A. ....35fn., 121, 219
Matthies, Katharine...............203
McChord, "Judge" Charles C. .........14
McCleverty, Mrs. Anson............207
McCoy, Ethel B. Stewart.........70, 99, 141-146, 148-149, 216
McCoy, Walter R...................143
Meek, John S. ......................25
Meilstrup, Dr. Drew B. .............205
*Mekeel's Weekly Stamp News*......34, 43, 64, 73, 75-77, 86, 113
Milian, Richard.................191-192
Miller, Benjamin Kurtz...........91, 94, 156, 158, 206
Miller, Lt. Walter...................14
Mohrmann, Edgar, and Company....218
Molesworth, Jack.............125, 221
Morales del Castillo, Dr. Andres Domingo...........191
Morgenthau, J.C. and Company......40, 50fn., 93, 103, 203, 209, 216

## — N —

National Philatelic Collection: see Smithsonian Institution
*New Worldwide Postage Stamp Catalogue*.......................198
New York Public Library............94, 155-160, 164-168, 193, 206
*New York Times*.................74, 77
*Norfolk Virginian-Pilot*...............146

## — O —

Ovington, Earle L. ...............10, 12
Oriol, Rafael.................192, 222

## — P —

"P, Mr." ......................123, 211
Palmer, Edgar..........97, 126, 129, 214
Paramount Philatelics...............208
Pelander, Carl E...................207
Perez, Alberto.............120, 192, 208
Perry, Elliott..............40, 43, 61-65, 66-67, 69-70, 87, 110-111, 158
*Philadelphia Bulletin*..........57, 97, 212
Philatelic Foundation.........28fn., 147, 159-160, 199
*Philatelic Gazette*..............26, 32, 34
Philipp, Philip B. ..................209
Phillips, Charles J. .........71, 71fn., 85, 87-88, 215
Pollock, W.E. ......................214
Pollitz and Paige...................205
Posner, Gary.......................203
Power, Eustace B. ...................65
Praeger, Otto...........9, 11, 49, 54, 59
Princeton University............97, 129, 129fn., 193, 214

## — R —

Richmond, Stanley.............127, 134
Robertson, Peter...................147
Robey, Caroline............1, 39, 43-45, 65, 67, 69, 111-115
Robey, Louise: see Birch, Louise Robey
Robey, William Thomas.........1-5, 31, 33, 39-45, 61-71, 74-75, 81, 109-115, 144, 158, 173, 175-177, 184-185
Robson Lowe International Ltd......189, 207-209, 215
Robinette, H.A. ............94, 209, 217
Roosevelt, Franklin D. ...............48
Rubel, Charles....................209

## — S —

Sanabria, Nicholas............96, 98-99, 199, 202, 205, 209-211
Salomon Brothers..............128, 132
Schafer, Charles A..................205
Schiff, Jacques Jr. ......204, 208-210, 221
Schilling, Wilber H. Jr. and Wilber H. III.................219
Schlesinger, Baldwin.................79
Schnabel, Herman.............208, 218
Scott Auction Galleries.............205
Scott Stamp and Coin Company.....65, 83, 96, 98, 203, 216
Scott, Walter S...............81, 84, 94, 103-104

*Scott's Standard Postage Stamp Catalogue* . . . 197
Seymour, W.T. . . . 214
Shanahan, Desmond and Jerome . . . 187-188
Shanahans Stamp Auctions . . . 186-189, 206
Sheppard, Representative/Senator Morris . . . 9, 28fn., 48
Sherman, Leonard . . . 173-184
Sherman, Roslyn . . . 177, 184
Siegel, Robert A. . . . 118-119, 121-123, 125, 127-128, 134, 138, 149, 193, 202-205, 208-222
Silver, Philip . . . 27fn., 29fn.
Simmy's Stamp Company . . . 147, 205, 214, 217
Simon, Max L. . . . 211
Sine, Richard . . . 151
Singer, Paul and Irma . . . 186-189
Sinkler, Wharton . . . 98, 101
Sloane, George B. . . . 88-89, 158-159, 217
Smith, Carlton . . . 208
Smithsonian Institution . . . 36, 50fn., 115, 169, 171-172, 183, 192, 217
Sotheby Parke Bernet . . . 127, 208, 210-211
Souren, Y. . . . 105-106, 122-125, 211-212, 218-219, 221
Southgate, Hugh M. . . . 217
"Speigel" . . . 219
Spilotro, Victor . . . 148
Stabile, Carlo . . . 180
Stamps: British Guiana 1¢ (1856), 96, 119, 191; Canal Zone "missing bridge," 182-183; Honduras "red" airmail, 99; Honduras "black" airmail, 126; India 4-anna invert, 31, 71fn.; U.S. pictorial inverts (1869), 31, 128, 156, 193; U.S. Pan-American Exposition inverts (1901), 31, 36, 75, 80, 93, 107, 124-125, 156, 158, 169, 193; U.S. blue paper varieties (1909), 72, 107, 156, 166; U.S. 5¢ color error (1917), 22-24, 39, 42, 70, 107; U.S. Hammarskjold invert (1962), 173-184; U.S. $1 rush lamp invert (1979), 182.
*Stamps* (magazine) . . . 69, 88, 159, 162, 199, 202, 205, 207, 210, 212
*Stamps of Fame* . . . 209
STAMPSHOW '78 . . . 209; '86, 203
*Standard Catalogue of Air Post Stamps* . . . 198-199
Steffan, Roger . . . 99, 112, 210
Steinmetz, Joseph A. . . . 71-74, 80, 94, 107, 204
Stern, Edward . . . 34, 97
Stevens, Theodore A. . . . 121, 216
Stewart, Bert A. . . . 142-143
Stewart, Ethel B.: see McCoy, Ethel B. Stewart
Stilwell, John . . . 123, 212
Stolow, J.&H. . . . 202, 206, 215
Stone, Franklin H. . . . 167
Storrow, J.K. . . . 83, 104, 210
Summit Bank . . . 132-134, 210
Superior Stamp and Coin Company . . . 133, 203, 222
Sweet, Judge Robert W. . . . 149

## — T —

Taussig, Noah T. . . . 50, 50fn.
Throop, William . . . 175
Torelli, James . . . 221
Townsend, Capt. A.C. . . . 77
Travers, Arthur M. . . . 72-73
Tuttle, George R. . . . 80, 93

## — U —

"Uncommon Market" . . . 209
*United States* (yacht) . . . 86-87

## — W —

Wagner, Keith A. . . . 207
Wall, Philip T. . . . 162, 164
*Wall Street Journal* . . . 128
Walter, L. Rohe . . . 172
Ward, Philip H. . . . 34-35, 64, 86, 93-94, 96-101, 104, 110, 122, 126, 185, 207, 211, 216
*Washington Post* . . . 43
Webb, Lieutenant Torrey H. . . . 14, 47, 52, 194
*Weekly Philatelic Gossip* . . . 4, 70, 99, 109-110
Weeks, Edward M. . . . 17, 18fn.
Weill, Raymond H. . . . 101, 117-118, 121, 125-126, 129-131, 134
Weill, Raymond H. Company . . . 117-119, 122-126, 130-131, 134, 146-147, 172, 192, 205, 208, 210-214, 216-220, 222
Weill, Roger . . . 117-118, 121
Weinberg, Irwin . . . 117, 119, 128, 130, 134, 139, 190-191, 202, 211, 213-214, 216-217, 222
Wenger, Kenneth R. . . . 133, 135-138, 202, 209-210, 215, 222
West, William . . . 207

Whitbridge, Dr. .....................217
White, L.D. .......................211
White, Kirsh and Company .........210
Whitman, Gov. Charles S. ........ 52, 56
Wilks, Sylvia Green ......... 82, 89, 103
Williams, John C. .................. 94
Williamson, Ellen Douglas ......193, 220
Wilmeth, James L. ........ 15, 18-20, 35
Wilson, President Woodrow ... 6, 9, 15, 45, 48-51, 55, 62
Wise, Paul .........................204
Wolffers, Richard ..................215
Womer, James L. ...................195
Wood, Edward Randolph Jr. .......... 98

# Biography

George Amick is editorial page editor and former Washington correspondent of *The Times* of Trenton, New Jersey, and is a frequent writer for philatelic periodicals. He has collected U.S. and Canadian stamps since his boyhood in the 1940s. A graduate of Ohio Wesleyan and Ohio State Universities, he was a 1968-1969 Nieman Fellow in Journalism at Harvard University, where he studied urban problems. He is the author of *The American Way of Graft*, a study of political corruption, published in 1976 by The Center for Analysis of Public Issues, Princeton, New Jersey.